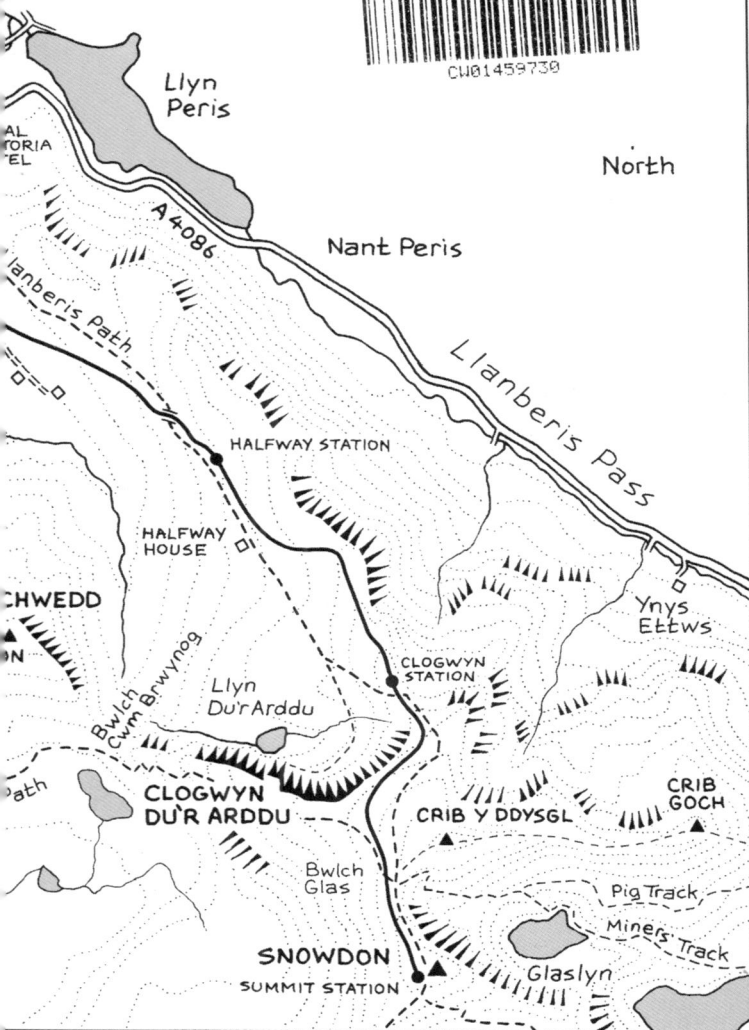

Llyn Padarn

CAR PARKS

Llyn Peris

AL
TORIA
EL

A 4086

North

Nant Peris

Llanberis Path

Llanberis Pass

HALFWAY STATION

HALFWAY
HOUSE

CHWEDD

ON

Bwlch Cwm Brwynog

Llyn
Du'r Arddu

CLOGWYN
DU'R ARDDU

ath

CLOGWYN
STATION

Ynys
Ettws

Bwlch
Glas

CRIB Y DDYSGL

CRIB
GOCH

Pig Track

Miners' Track

SNOWDON
SUMMIT STATION

Glaslyn

Climbers' Club Guides to Wales
Edited by John Willson

Clogwyn Du'r Arddu

by

Nick Dixon

Artwork

by

Don Sargeant

Published by The Climbers' Club

A Climber's Guide to Snowdon & the Beddgelert District (The Climbers' Club 1926)
by Herbert R C Carr

Clogwyn Du'r Arddu (The Climbers' Club Journal 1942)
by J M Edwards and J E Q Barford

Llanberis Pass (The Climbers' Club 1950)
by P R J Harding
(reprinted 1955, with a supplement of new climbs by R Moseley)

Clogwyn Du'r Arddu – First Edition (The Climbers' Club 1963)
by H I Banner and P Crew

Clogwyn Du'r Arddu – Second Edition (The Climbers' Club 1967)
by H I Banner and P Crew

Clogwyn Du'r Arddu – Third Edition (The Climbers' Club 1976)
by Alec Sharp

Clogwyn Du'r Arddu – Fourth Edition (The Climbers' Club 1989)
by Paul Williams

Clogwyn Du'r Arddu – Fifth Edition (The Climbers' Club 2004)
by Nick Dixon

© The Climbers' Club 2004

Dixon, Nick   Clogwyn Du'r Arddu   (Climbers' Club Guides)

British Library Cataloguing in Publication Data

A catalogue record for this book is available from the British Library

796.552

ISBN 0-901601-73-X

Front Cover: *Shrike* (E2) The Pinnacle
Climber: Ed February
Photo: Ray Wood

Rear Cover: *Red Slab* (VII) The West Buttress
Climber: Paul Braithwaite
Photo: Roger Baxter-Jones (Braithwaite col.)

Typeset and prepared for printing by the Editor
Slide scanning by Redheads Digital, Sheffield
Produced by The Ernest Press, Glasgow G44 6AQ
Distributed by Cordee, 3a de Montfort Street, Leicester LE1 7HD

Contents

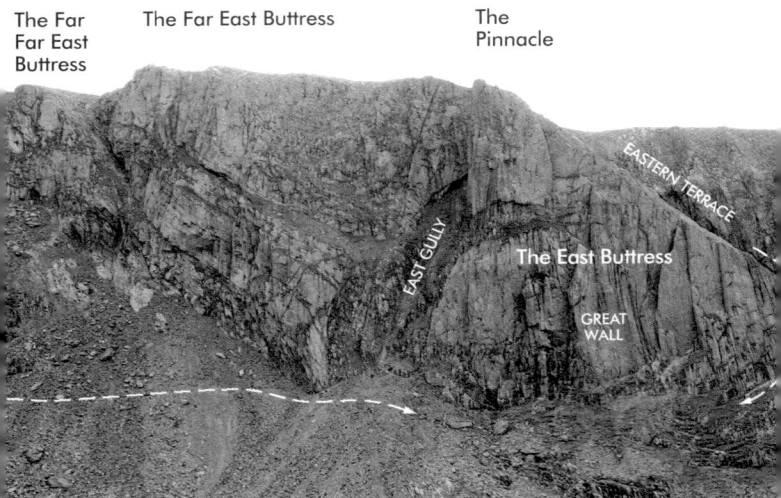

The Far Far East Buttress   The Far East Buttress   The Pinnacle

EASTERN TERRACE

EAST GULLY

The East Buttress

GREAT WALL

Maps and Diagrams

The West Buttress

The Far West Buttress

Bwlch Cwm Brwynog

WESTERN TERRACE

The Steep Band

FAR WESTERN TERRACE

The Boulder

The Middle Rock

Photo: Don Sargeant

Photos: [1]Ken Wilson
[2]Martin Whitaker
[3]Don Sargeant
All others: Nick Dixon

Climbers' Club Guides

The Climbers' Club

The publisher of this guidebook is The Climbers' Club, which was founded in 1898 from origins in Snowdonia and is now one of the foremost mountaineering clubs in Great Britain. Its objects are to encourage mountaineering and rock-climbing, and to promote the general interest of mountaineers and the mountain environment.

It is a truly national club with widespread membership, and currently owns huts in Cornwall, Pembrokeshire, Derbyshire, Snowdonia, and Argyll. Besides managing seven huts, The Climbers' Club produces an annual Journal and runs a full programme of climbing meets, dinners, and social events. Club members may also use the huts of other clubs through reciprocal arrangements. The club publishes climbing guidebooks (currently 20 in number) to cover most of Wales and Southern England. The club is a founder-member of, and is affiliated to, the British Mountaineering Council; it makes annual contributions to the Access and Conservation Trust, as well as to volunteer cliff and mountain rescue organizations. In 1999, the Climbers' Club Colin Kirkus Guidebook Fund was established as a means of distributing some of the profits earned from guidebooks to assist climbing-related projects that are in keeping with the aims of the club, though they need not be confined to the club's guidebook areas.

Currently, membership is around 1,300, and at present there are no limits on growth. Members of two years' standing may propose a competent candidate for membership and, provided that adequate support is obtained from other members, the Committee may elect him or her to full membership; there is no probationary period.

Climbing Style

The following policy statement on climbing style was agreed in principle at The Climbers' Club Annual General Meeting on 25th February 1990:

The Climbers' Club supports the tradition of using natural protection and is opposed to actions which are against the best interest of climbers and users of the crags. This applies particularly to irreversible acts which could affect the crags and their environs.

Such acts could include: the placing of bolts on mountain and natural crags; retrospective placing of bolts; chiselling, hammering, or altering the rock appearance or structure; excessive removal of vegetation and interference with trees, flowers, and fauna.

The Climbers' Club policy is that guidebooks are written to reflect the best style matched to the ethos and traditions of British climbing.

Helyg[1]   Photo: Ian Smith

Guidebook Disclaimer

This guide attempts to provide a definitive record of all existing climbs and is compiled from information from a variety of sources. The inclusion of any route does not imply that it remains in the condition described. Climbs can change unpredictably: rock can deteriorate and the existence and condition of *in-situ* protection can alter. All climbers must rely on their own ability and experience to gauge the difficulty and seriousness of any climb. Climbing is an inherently dangerous activity.

Neither The Climbers' Club nor the author and editor of this guidebook accept any liability whatsoever for any injury or damage caused to climbers, third parties, or property arising from the use of it. Whilst the content of the guide is believed to be accurate, no responsibility is accepted for any error, omission, or mis-statement. Users must rely on their own judgement and are recommended to insure against injury to person and property and third party risks.

The inclusion in this guidebook of a crag or routes upon it does not mean that any member of the public has a right of access to the crag or the right to climb upon it.

www.climbers-club.co.uk

[1]The Climbers' Club's first hut, and the base from which much of the inter-war years exploration of Clogwyn Du'r Arddu took place.

Acknowledgements

First, my thanks must go to my editor John Willson for his tireless work correcting my syntax and spelling and ordering my thoughts, this being a major undertaking for anyone. Second, Don Sargeant has also been an enthusiastic helper and has been responsible for the production of the photodiagrams, as well as the maps and diagrams, and preparation of the photographs.

A large team of friends and activists have helped with the route-checking, and I am indebted to all of them, particularly: Bill Birch, Paul Braithwaite, Joe Brown, Ian Carr, Norman Clacher (who has climbed more than a hundred routes at Cloggy), John Cousins, John Cox, Martin Crook, Johnny Dawes, Martin Doyle, Mick Fowler, Neil Gresham, Alan Hinkes, Dai Lampard, Mike Lawrence, Steve Long, Leigh McGinley, James McHaffie, Andy Newton, Andy Popp, John Redhead, Paul Stott, Dave Towse, Mike (Twid) Turner, Ken Wilson, and Dave Wrennall.

I must also thank Chris Naylor for his forbearance over the last few years checking routes for this guide, sometimes under less than safe circumstances when I'm sure he would have rather been bouldering in the Pass.

I am especially grateful to Neil Gresham for the contribution to this guide of his riveting but very personal account of his ascent of *The Indian Face*, which is printed as a Prologue.

It is widely acknowledged that a guidebook is built only on the hard work of previous guidebook authors; and I am particularly fortunate that Cloggy's roll of honour lists some of the most distinguished guidebook authors in our history.

And last, I'd like to thank my wife Sheila for being so tolerant of the considerable time I have spent both on this project and at the cliff.

ND   December 2003

Mainly in connection with The Anthology of Ascents, the following have very kindly provided information about, or permission to print previously published material: John Cleare, Robin Collomb, Peter Crew, Jack Soper, Tony Smythe, Ken Wilson.

We are grateful to all who have provided photographs: Paul Braithwaite, Martin Crook, Steve Crowe, Keith Davies, Johnny Dawes, Neil Dyer, Malcolm Eldridge, Chris Griffiths, Chris Naylor, John Redhead, Keith Robertson, Don Sargeant, Andy Sharp, Martin Whitaker, and Ray Wood. An especial debt is due to Ken Wilson for the use of a number of his crag photos for the diagrams.

Finally, sincere thanks to a dedicated team of proof-readers: Nigel Coe, John Cox, Bob Moulton, Ian Smith, and Mike Vetterlein.

ND & JW   January 2004

Prologue

Although I've done the hard routes on Cloggy, it's my early days that I remember most, when I did the E3s and E4s. Like in 1982 when I did Silhouette, Medi, Troach, and Great Wall in a day.   (Johnny Dawes, 2002)

Clogwyn Du'r Arddu; The Black Cliff; who can forget their first glimpse of this most majestic of mountain crags – The Temple; The Mecca; The Shrine of British climbing. The cliff is revealed in its full splendour as you crest the rise beyond the green tin shack that is Halfway House. The impact is absolute; there is no compromise; the sight is stunning; sweeping lines and a sombre appearance plus a high angle conspire to produce an impressive atmosphere, and often make the leads more difficult than might be expected. One's eye is immediately drawn to the centre of the East Buttress and a magnificent sheet of the roughest flinty rhyolite: Great Wall, which the cliff's devotees regard as 'almost hallowed ground' … The altar!   (Paul Williams, 1989)

Slaying the Beast
by Neil Gresham

Call it a spell, mystical and enchanting, or call it a curse, but the test here is the ability to say no, to walk away and put out the fire. So often with bolts I must force to continue, manufacture motivation, and finish the existing job when something else more tempting starts to call. The walk to Cloggy has now become a necessity to satisfy a drug-like urge. Each stony step increases the accumulating voltage by a tiny increment and the end product is a belly full of nerves by the time I reach the foot of Great Wall. But today is different, light relief from the usual anguish 'cos I know the top's wet. A practising day and, for once, a chance to relax and soak up the surroundings. Chatting away with Airlie, remembering old song lyrics, for the first time I don't even bother to look up. Dump my sack, quick drink, and turn round in my own time to realize in horror that it's bone dry.

Wires tripped, I'm thrown into a flurry of automated activity. The routine gear-racking and uncoiling of ropes is therapy in the escalating tension. Questioning the moment is futile. This crag is different, so rarely extending the privilege, and I know I must rise to the gesture. The usual four hours of psyching must now be squeezed into twenty minutes: no build-up and it's hit me like a steam train. This is the day, and in half an hour I will be free. I'm in deep so far now that all I want is an outcome. Deep breaths to clear my head and I'm insignificant compared to the beast which rears up behind me.

We scramble up to the base for the 'belayer's brief': 'Obviously I won't be falling off but...' I position Airlie at the top of the bale-out zone. Her face says it all and her timid chuckle as I stumble carelessly on some wet grass does little to diffuse the situation. I suppose they do say in this sport that you learn who your friends are. OK, boots now, this'll be fun, gripping enough before sport routes. Where has this petty concern for their lacing suddenly come from? I'm not tuning a bloody piano here, yet each tug seems to tighten the knots in my stomach. Rope next, lifeline, umbilical to mother earth – I ponder the irony as my fingers again perform our common task.

How long to sustain this ritual of procrastination? What can I do next? Chalk, that's it, more chalk. Forget it, go now, the groundwork is done. Stooping for one last check that my soles are clean feels like a bow of courtesy. For God's sake, stop this superstition. How can I possibly show any more respect? Eyes closed now, deep breath, touch rock. The beast stirs and the black gargoyle on the skyline laughs and cracks his whip as I step up into the arena. The game begins.

History has made me all too aware of the wall's trickery, so the comparative ease of this first section serves only to unnerve me further. I dither with the choice between two huge spikey jugs and try to ignore the extravagance of such a decision. The arch is a place for contemplation of the upper path, which it seems to guard, and I peer rightwards through its bows to Fowler's *Spreadeagle* meandering off to sanctuary, content merely with paying its respects. No time to waste and I'm moving up into line now, yellow brick road, red carpet, or just the shaft, soaring and tubing towards the skyline. I don't notice this next bit and I'm already at the stopper placement at forty feet. 'Stopper'. I love that word, and so too must have Redhead, cartwheeling and tumbling from the upper reaches. Best forgotten. Press on and it's actually starting to feel like climbing now, almost relaxing, technically absorbing. A tiny offset nut placement reminds me of Moffatt's escape right. Historic, brave, but eliminate; more a master of route-finding.

Kick in now, concentrate. The need to chalk my left hand twice for a tiny nubbin gives me a small reminder of what's to come. The holds are getting smaller now and I make the mistake of looking down to the stopper. Remind myself that I'm still in range and thank the Lord for sticky rubber as I smear up onto Redhead's tormented moves. I'm at the final gear placement now, and from here on the mechanics will be blissfully simple.

Calm down, take stock, and clip into the *RP*s. That network of insecurity. Tiny pieces of brass lodged in the surface veins of this creature's skin. They're gonna hold as far as I'm concerned now. There can be no room for any doubt up here. A dip and I hurriedly swing out right away from the gear before I allow the significance of the manœuvre to register. Tunnel vision for that rest-ledge below the crux. The gargoyle turns to the beast with a knowing sneer as I move past my previous high-point into the psychological unknown.

To my left, the scars of previous battles. Aroused and angered, the beast sheds its skin in the winter and now the flake is gone. A trivial blemish is left in its magnanimity, yet with dire consequences to any challenger. No longer that peg to go for, and as I undercut rightwards I see Dixon, manic eyes of fire. His words ring hollow in the back of my mind: 'There are no more islands of retreat, you'll just have to go.'

Macabre indeed to fall whilst moving onto the rest-ledge, but a sudden stab hits me as I realize in disgust that I can't lean back enough to see the crucial foot-pocket which is my password to temporary sanctuary. Who is doing this? Why does it all feel so different? Behold the transformation of my top-roping companion into a devilish stranger. Dawes spoke of the sparks, no rules to this game, just transient fields of energy. An infinite number of tempting solutions, yet an equally infinite number of dead-ends leading to disaster. Forced to bodge the foot placement I feel it creeping and just make it onto the ledge before it pops. I'm stood there now, clawing at crystals, torso pressed against the cold rock. My heartbeat pulsing like war-drums feels almost strong enough to tip me off backwards, and my attempts to slow it down so far have been futile.

This rest-ledge is perhaps the beast's greatest irony. Perched on the brink of its gaping jaws, I must now stop and 'rest'. Rest when I'm not even tired. Rest when I'm desperate not to break the continuity of the climbing. Rest and allow my fragile bubble of focus to be burst and the true horror of my position to come flooding in and sweep me away. That was Mike Tomkins's prediction anyway – one which caused him to think better of an attempt. Come on now, 'be positive' Smythe would say. You can't fall off a 7b+ that you've got worked. For God's sake, it's a formality. Isn't it? For Christ's sake, I just don't know any more.

A faint burning cramp in my calves, and I shuffle to try to get some weight on my heels. The rope falling off down to my left, pulling me awkwardly, is perhaps its breath, affecting my balance and stopping me trusting. Then the Wainwright words: 'A rope's just tricking you into being there – you'd be better off solo.' Yet the glimmer of hope it offers me is the only thing I've got to cling to. Somehow this, the second delaying ritual of the day, doesn't frustrate me so much. It's beckoning me now, but this time there'll be no going back. The chalked line of crystals above me is my one-way ticket to judgement. And the worst thing about this is that it's not even going to call me. I must make the decision to go myself. I consciously force my mind not to wander to the option of rescue for a second. I know from Johnny's experience that I'll only return, so it may as well be now. I'm fully aware that leaving this spot is utterly unjustifiable using any form of logic, but my immense urge to get this over with ought to be enough. I breathe in to announce to Airlie, far down below, that I'm going for it, but the thought of how the words will sound prevents me and no sound seems to come out. There is no logical time to do this. It's like spinning the barrel and asking when it's safe to pull the trigger. So, without thought, I simply use the obvious progression of the holds to lead me. This is it now; I'm stepping out.

As I teeter across the lip of the overlap, the foot change I dreaded passes with discerning ease. I carefully use my vision's depth-of-field facility to focus only on the intricacies of the smears and not the void below upon which they rest. For a foolish second, I kid myself it's going well. But now comes the move – there had to be one somewhere. My chalk-line out left marks the huge but hidden foot-pocket which I must step across to, and I'm palpably aware that the urge to perform this move in control will also be the very urge that will cause me to miss it and continue my downward arc. I grip tightly and my right leg starts to shake. Must loosen and allow myself to go; I shut my eyes and fall across kicking violently to seat my foot. I stop in balance but for a second my mind continues churning downwards and I feel nauseous.

A hundred and twenty feet and, with the last hard move to go, the *RP* is now too low to save me anyway. Can't take a hand off to dip. A brittle side-pull bites into my sweaty and unchalked finger-tips, causing them to slide. Stepping high onto a sloping boss, I drive upwards, the tension in my thigh causing me to shake further. Both legs shaking now and, as I extend with the key for Dawes's crucial three-finger crystal cluster for my right, I realize for the first time what this thing is doing to me. As if spreading like a cancer, this tremor is now in my forearms and hands too. I'm unable to arrange my fingers just so and I'm not sure whether I dare move from here. Facing the last and hardest move in the sequence, I'm staring head-on into the beast's eyes. How can this be happening, a full body shake beyond my control? Like a trivial fly it is trying to shed me. Moves I once knew intimately are now to be on-sighted by a strange vibrating body which is slowly being torn apart by its mind. Creeping hands on borrowed time, I race to move my feet. This precariously high step-up is at the limit of my flexibility at the best of times, but now, as I try to lift my rigor-mortised leg, I realize that I can't lean back enough to make room for it. I can't even see the foot spike and, now desperate, I realize that scraping my face against the rock is the only way to stay on. Stop breathing, heart burning, like raising my own guillotine, the more I lift my leg, the more it throws me off backwards; and yet I must lift it. As I drive up I feel myself melting into a timeless vacuum. For a split second of complete tranquillity, I actually don't mind giving in. I resign myself to defeat and prepare for the unimaginable.

But wait. My foot hits the spike and I sway, realizing that I'm still on. As if mocking me and with the last hard move still to go, the bastard's given me another chance. Almost laughing as I flail up desperately, left foot well seated now, I duck my head to one side and lash out for the undercut in front of my face. Balance. The tremor subsides like a banished curse. Finishing-jug looms and I hurriedly build my feet on smears, hand straining on the flake. Extending now, feet starting to creep, but no room now for any more adrenalin. Extending, like reaching out for the grail, knife poised for the kill. I stretch, plunging; fingers curl, sink, and lock. The beast roars, and the deep tremors within the mountain are not enough to shake me off now.

Sixty feet out from the forgotten *RP,* clipping the bomber nut which protects the easy upper groove and I'm sliding my sword back into its scabbard. The sun has come out to soak the rock above me like spilt blood and I am released. Darkness of the void beneath, the beast is dying, and I'm pulling out into the light.

Cwm Du'r Arddu is warm and still as I melt back into the grassy sanctuary of the belay ledge. Shimmering lake and strolling clouds. Senses unmasked, I realize for the first time that the creature I've slaughtered lived, not within these cathedral-like walls, but in the walls of my own skull. As I trudge off down the path, glowing all over, the scree makes a hollow echo beneath my feet, piercing the quietness. My floating mind wanders to the great unclimbed line on the wall high up left from the pinnacle, and suddenly I feel a strange, sickening stirring inside me. I turn round with a start to reassure myself that, of course, there is nothing there.

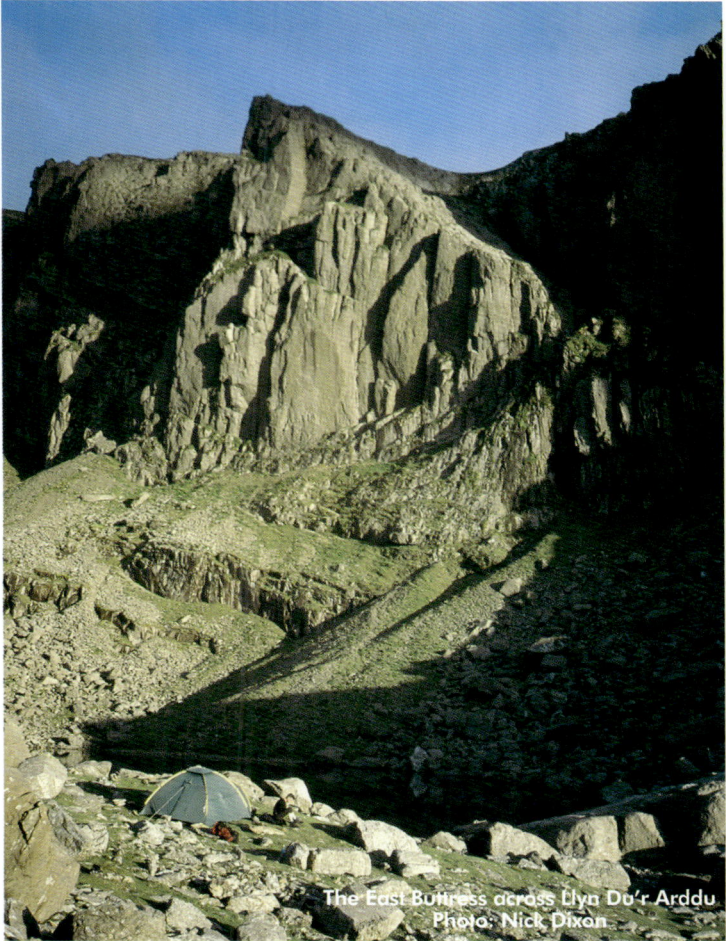

The East Buttress across Llyn Du'r Arddu
Photo: Nick Dixon

Introduction

Clogwyn Du'r Arddu: much maligned. A dark, damp place – not!

In the morning on The Far East or The Pinnacle, in the afternoon on The East or in the slanting folds of The West, then the evening on the Far West, or in the orange glow of sunset on The Great Wall, this place is the antithesis of the sentiment above. It is the cathedral of British Climbing, beautiful yet sombre, the great teeth of The Far East and The West curving into a huge syncline to frame the central rectangle of The Great Wall. This, then, is the scene of some of the finest climbing achievements of the twentieth century.

Fashions in climbing come and go; however, the climbing on Clogwyn Du'r Arddu has always maintained its reputation for quality and difficulty. It is true that Cloggy has not been as popular in the last ten years as in the previous fifteen (which may come to be regarded as a golden age), and also that Cloggy does not have a sufficiently steep environment or ethical broad-mindedness to encompass modern sport climbing; but its walls do give a difficulty of move and routes that are psychologically testing to measure against any.

It is fitting, then, that this guide should appear now, as it rides a crest of activity that has recently calmed. And it is as true now as it ever was that if you really want to understand British climbing, to know where we come from and who we are, then this cliff tells a crucial and integral part of the story.

The crag has had its devotees: Fred Pigott, Jack Longland, Maurice Linnell, Colin Kirkus, Menlove Edwards, Joe Brown, Hugh Banner, Peter Crew, Rowland Edwards, Alec Sharp, Pete Whillance, Ron Fawcett, John Redhead, and Johnny Dawes – they have all been intimate with this cliff and have made sure they were in the right place at the right time to make their 'killer ascents' and dance their dance upon the cliff.

In a departure from recent guidebooks, there is no historical essay at the start, and the guide is in just two major sections. The first is concerned with the factual relaying of information: about where routes go, how hard they are, and how good. The second is in the form of an extended anthology, where each route is presented in chronological order, with space being given below for the comments of the first ascensionists, then of other climbers of the day, and finally of a variety of subsequent ascensionists, especially those of our own generation; and these are linked by brief assessments of the routes' historical contexts from the author. Referring to the anthology may be found helpful when preparing for a climb, and for this reason the anthology page numbers are also provided in the index after the route-description entries.

I hope this will make the guide more coherent and inspirational. I am deeply indebted to the leading activists whom I have contacted in the preparation of the book, and I hope that this section of the guide allows them to tell their story.

Despite the image and reputation of the cliff, there are actually quality climbs in most grades on Cloggy, and raising the profile of some of the better of the easier routes has been an important objective.

Winter climbing on Clogwyn Du'r Arddu has always been a rare and magical pursuit, and no less so now with global warming keeping the cold spells short. However, it is the case that most winters will afford some days of snow and ice climbing on these high, north-facing Welsh cliffs, and so it has been decided to include all known winter routes. There are further notes on winter climbing below.

No single traditional cliff has played such a major part in every advance in the history of our sport. Every era and advancement has been represented, and even now the cliff has some of the hardest, as well as finest, of British rock-climbs on its walls. And so, on a fine, still, orange summer's evening, there is no grander place on earth to be than at Clogwyn Du'r Arddu. The guide needs no further introduction save, perhaps, the words of Peter Crew, one of the major activists of the 60s: 'Cloggy is the finest cliff in Wales, probably the whole of Britain, and in a special way its history epitomizes that of the sport of rock-climbing.'

Winter Climbing

All known winter routes on the cliff are included in this guide. Several have not been recorded elsewhere and were particularly significant ascents, the history of which was in danger of being lost. It is hoped that this will act as a catalyst and further information about the history of the winter climbing on Cloggy will be forthcoming. And with a trend towards the climbing of summer lines in full winter condition, it was felt that these routes now fit comfortably in a definitive guide.

All the climbs described were completed in very wintery condition, with deep snow, hoar frost, and verglas in evidence. However, the inclusion of these routes should not encourage 'winter' ascents in dry or marginal conditions; certainly, winter ascents of any routes on Cloggy should not scratch or otherwise damage the rock, and **no** additional pegs to those needed in summer should be placed.

Descriptions of the winter routes take their place alongside the summer ones in the main routes section, and are not duplicated where they follow the same line.

Special mention should be made here of the best descent in winter: this is to take the long way round towards the railway and avoid the crag altogether. Cornices, avalanches, and ice pitches can be found on the Eastern Terrace!

Upgrading of Routes

Several routes on Cloggy are considered to be of a higher grade than previously. Many of the old protection pegs are now unreliable at best, and

Great Wall (E4), The East Buttress
Climber: Patch Hammond   Photo: Ray Wood

often missing altogether; and some areas of the crag have tended to become dirty.

With the rise of bouldering and easy-access climbing, Cloggy can be an intimidating place to those without experience of large and remote crags, and the associated boldness required on some routes can make them *feel* relatively difficult to today's average climber.

Dry routes, wet routes

Cloggy unfairly suffers from the reputation of being a 'slow-to-dry' crag. In fact, away from the corners and cracks this is not so – the wall routes take little seepage and dry quickly. Of course, the real trick is to get on the right route at the right time.

A selection of routes that dry in one day of fine weather

Human Touch E4	Pinnacle Flake E2	The Orphan Flagellator E4
Little Krapper E3	The Spire E3	Silhouette E3
Feeding Shmae E4	The Troach E2	Scorpio E2
Authentic Desire E7	Curving Arête E4	Slab Climb
Fecundity Ridge E7	The Purr-Spire E5	Right-Hand HS

A selection of routes that dry in two or three days of fine weather

The Axe E4	Serth E2	Womb Bits E5
Shrike E2	The Sweeper E2	Face Mecca E9
Llithrig E1	Dinas in the Oven E7/8	The Boldest E4
Pistolero E5	A Midsummer… E6	Farfallino E2

A selection of routes that take some time to dry thoroughly

Woubits E2	The Indian Face E9	White Slab E2
Diglyph HVS	November E3	Great Slab VS
Great Wall E4	Curving Crack VS	Bloody Slab E3

A selection of routes that are rarely dry

Trapeze E5	Vember E1
Pigott's Climb VS	The Corner HVS
Chimney Route VS	The Black Cleft E2 (in fact never dry!)

Location and Altitude

The cliff is situated within grid squares 59 65 and 60 65, to be found on the 1:50,000 OS Landranger map 115 (Caernarfon) and the 1:25,000 Outdoor Leisure map 17 (Snowdon and Conwy Valley). These show also all walkers' routes on Snowdon and all crags included in the current *Llanberis*, *Lliwedd*, and *Cwm Silyn* guides.

The base of the cliff lies at 700 metres, while the top of the West Buttress rises to almost 900 metres.

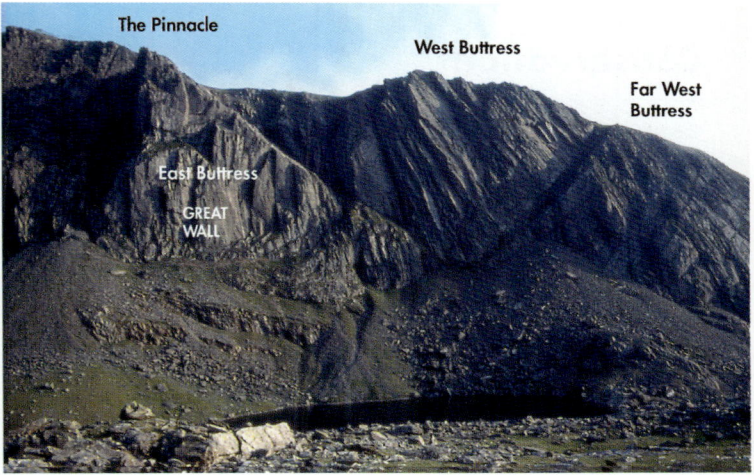

The Pinnacle
West Buttress
Far West Buttress
East Buttress
GREAT WALL

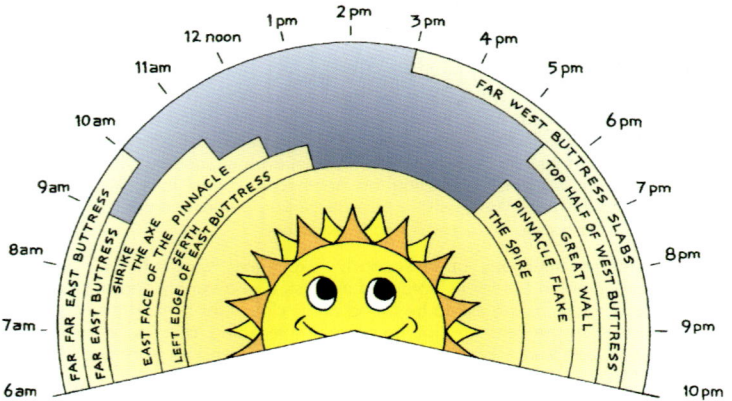

6am — 7am — 8am — 9am — 10am — 11am — 12 noon — 1pm — 2pm — 3pm — 4pm — 5pm — 6pm — 7pm — 8pm — 9pm — 10pm

FAR FAR EAST BUTTRESS
FAR EAST BUTTRESS
SHRIKE
THE AXE
EAST FACE OF THE PINNACLE
LEFT EDGE OF EAST BUTTRESS
FAR WEST BUTTRESS SLABS
TOP HALF OF WEST BUTTRESS
GREAT WALL
PINNACLE FLAKE
THE SPIRE

'When's the Route in the Sun?'

The chart above will help those unfamiliar with the crag to identify routes and areas of the crag that might be in the sun given a fine day in May, June, July, and August. Obviously, as one moves away from 21 June the proportion of time for each route in the sun diminishes.

Conservation

by Barbara Jones

Clogwyn Du'r Arddu has long been visited by local people living and hunting in the mountains of Snowdonia. As the early medicine they practised would have relied heavily on local plants, they would have needed a good knowledge of the location and habitats of different types of vegetation containing these plants. Certain localities in Snowdonia stood out for their diversity of plant life and would therefore have been well frequented by these early apothecaries. Clogwyn Du'r Arddu was one of such sites, the importance of which was further recognized once renowned apothecaries and plant-hunters from outside Wales also started to visit these mountains in the seventeenth century, prompted by the publication of a famous Welsh herbal treatise by the Revd William Salesbury in the sixteenth century. One of the earliest visits was from Thomas Johnson from London, who probably collected from Clogwyn Du'r Arddu in 1639, followed by Brewer in 1727 and Sir Joseph Banks in 1773 soon after his return from journeying round the world with Captain Cook in the *Endeavour*.

Prior to these visits, the mountains were generally considered to be unkempt wilderness and the abode of devils, and so the earliest explorers were treading what was then unknown territory. They were most often accompanied by local guides, utilizing their knowledge of the mountains and of the location of these interesting botanical sites to ease their passage. Even so, not all the trips were successful, with one explorer saying that his guide decided to turn back for fear of eagles! Probably the most famous botanical expedition to Clogwyn Du'r Arddu was in 1798 when the Revd W Bingley and his local guide the Revd P Williams from Llanberis decided to climb the cliff to search out more plants, an expedition which became the first recorded rock-climb on the cliff, probably a frightening experience at the time, even as modern climbs can be for different reasons! Collecting by apothecaries and later by botanists continued for many years, with some enterprising guides even selling roots of some rare plants to unsuccessful early explorers.

Despite the attentions of these early 'explorers', Clogwyn Du'r Arddu remains a noted site for its botanical interest, and a variety and number of rare plant species are still to be found on its cliffs – for similar reasons that appertain to the other major botanically interesting cliffs in Snowdonia, which include the rock type, aspect, altitude, and freedom from grazing.

The rocks outcropping on these cliffs are a mixture of rhyolites, tuffs, dolerite, and bedded pyroclastic formations. Fortunately, those providing the best material for plant growth are not generally the same as those which are most attractive to climbers. The effects of ice during the last glacial advance are also responsible somewhat for both the botanical and climbing wealth, producing steep, north-facing rocks that provide a suitable environment for arctic-alpine plants which need the cool conditions and freedom from competition from more aggressive grassland species. They also provide a refuge from the predations of sheep, which manage to graze vegetation in most places in the British uplands except steep rock faces and fenced exclosures. It is no accident that the best sites to botanize in the uplands are often on rock faces and very steep ground.

As mentioned above, there tends to be little conflict between climbing and botanical interest on Clogwyn Du'r Arddu. This isn't always the case, however, so particularly when climbing on some of the more 'esoteric' gems on the cliff care should be taken to cause the least amount of damage possible to the vegetation. There are some very rare plant species growing on and around this cliff, some of which are fully protected by law and regularly visited by botanists. They are not always readily seen, but if you have an interest and a keen eye, then in summer, tiny splashes of colour can be made out, or delicate ferns and mosses noted in some of the wet seepages and gullies.

In addition to the botanical interest, upland bird species nest in and around cliffs adjacent to the climbing areas. Delight in the swooping antics of chough and kestrel, the stately progress of the raven, and the chattering of ring-ouzel, but if you do note any significant bird species nesting on, or alongside, climbing routes, then please avoid the area if at all possible and send any records to the Countryside Council for Wales (CCW) in Bangor (see below).

Another interesting species you would be very lucky to come across is the Snowdon rainbow beetle. It is known from several areas on Snowdon, but is rare and very difficult to find and is fully protected. It is a beautiful beetle, however, so do keep your eyes open and if you are lucky enough to see one, leave it where you find it, but CCW would be very interested in the locations of any sightings.

Clogwyn Du'r Arddu is part of the Eryri SSSI and Special Area of Conservation, an international designation. It has a long history of human use, including copper mining. The copper occurs in veins cutting the dolerite, particularly on the broken crags of Clogwyn Coch to the east of the main cliff. Climbing, botanizing, and bird-watching are just the latest in a series of human activities here. Fortunately, the era of collecting has largely ended, but we cannot be complacent that all is well, as modern day pressures on the biological diversity in the mountains are far more pervasive than a few Victorians scrambling about the rocks and ridges searching for plant and animal specimens. Unfortunately, as we have lost so much of our natural biodiversity in the more 'accessible' parts of the uplands through activities such as agriculture, forestry, energy generation, and pollution, what is left on these less accessible and less impacted sites has an even greater value. Clogwyn Du'r Arddu is a very special site in this respect, with conservationists probably assigning it as much value, albeit for different reasons, as do climbers. Its interest lies in more than just lists of plants and animals, so they haven't been included in this short conservation account. Information on these and on its general diversity can be found in the many books and leaflets written about the uplands of Snowdonia. To obtain specific information on any particular conservation interest of the cliff, contact the CCW Area office on 01248 672500.

Approaches

On Foot

Unfortunately, it is no longer possible to park at Hafodty Newydd and walk up the railway; so the most common approach, and the fastest, is to use the Llanberis path that goes to the summit of Snowdon (Y Wyddfa). Park in Llanberis; then take the narrow road opposite the Royal Victoria Hotel, keeping left across a cattle grid, and ascend a very steep hill to a locked gate at Cader Ellyll (1 kilometre). From just beyond, go left along the Snowdon path for 2½ kilometres to the Halfway House. After one further kilometre, when the path steepens, bear right instead along the old miner's track, which contours round to the cliff past the old copper mines. This approach takes approximately one and a half hours.

Other routes are possible. The shortest in distance, but steeper, is from the Llanberis Pass, up Cwm Glas Mawr directly to Clogwyn Station, from where there is a short descent to the crag. A good approach from the west is to ascend via the excellent Snowdon Ranger Path from Llyn Cwellyn (on the A4085 Beddgelert to Caernarfon road). Pass through Bwlch Cwm Brwynog and contour rightwards to the cliff.

By Train

For those leg-weary and with a healthy bank balance it is, at the time of writing, possible to get the train one-way from Llanberis to Snowdon summit and then descend to the cliff. In summer 2003 the Snowdon train company introduced a booking-system that made commuting to the cliff far more appealing. Tickets are sold on a daily first-come first-served basis; or one can make a telephone booking the previous day using a credit card. On busy days, all tickets can be sold out by 10 a.m.; so it is advisable to get to the booking-office in Llanberis early, or, much better, book by phone the previous day.

It should be noted that the Snowdon railway does not consider itself to be the provider of a commuter service for rock-climbers and its systems are not designed to be climber-friendly (e.g. large rucksacks not allowed). Nevertheless, it can provide a useful service, and the author has always found the staff to be most helpful; it is often even possible to disembark at Clogwyn station.

The train takes approximately one hour to reach the summit, and in 2003 the fare was £13 single. The booking telephone number: 08704 580033. There are also seasonal restrictions.

As to the ethical validity of ascents after a rail approach, it can only be said that so far no difficult routes have thus been climbed, but to have one's legs fresh and bouncy would surely make standing on tiny edges for prolonged periods easier!

Silver Machine (VII)
The Far East Buttress
Climber: Mick Fowler
Photo: Chris Griffiths

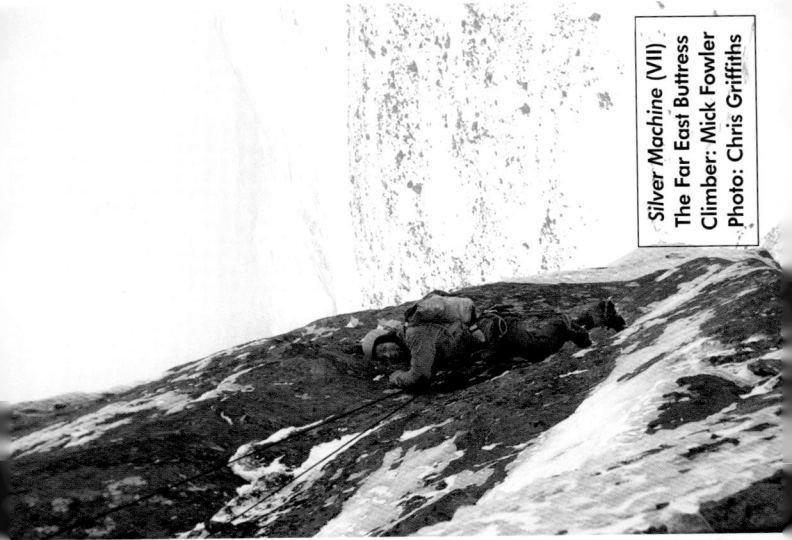

Jubilee Climb (V)
The Far East Buttress
Climber: Steve Long
Photo: Nick Dixon

The Far Far East Buttress

This is the small squat buttress sitting at the top left extremity of the cliff. A curving green slab on its lower left side runs up to meet enormous overhangs. To the right of this, across a steeper section of rock, lies a prominent corner/groove. A tricky descent can be made down the loose and slippery gully (*Boomerang Gully*) just left of the buttress.

Boomerang

Boomerang Gully   Winter II
The obvious snow gully to the left of this buttress.
Variation
★Boomerang Gully Direct   Winter IV
The icefalls on the left can be climbed before trending right across
snowfields to reach the gully proper.

★Boomerang Left-Hand   56 metres   E2   (1970s)
Better and slightly harder than *Boomerang*. Extreme care should be taken
on pitch 2 as rope-drag will result from sloppy rope management. Start as
for *Boomerang*.
1 28m. 5b. Climb precariously up the left edge of the slab – bold and
with little protection.
2 28m. 5b. Climb the rib up to the left of the overhang, whence an
exposed rightward traverse on a narrow ledge leads across the lip of the
overhang (one hard move) to a junction with the normal route in a short
corner. Continue direct to finish with an outrageous mantelshelf.

★Boomerang   56 metres   E1   (24.5.59)
The pleasant and enjoyable slab leads to an exposed finale up the wall on
the right. Some suspect rock. Scramble across to the foot of the curving
slab.
1 28m. 5b. Take the thin crack in the slab to the base of the groove on
the right. Climb this via a difficult move at about 3 metres; then go left at
the overhangs to a grassy ledge.
2 28m. 5a. Gain another grassy ledge, up to the right below the large
overhang. Climb past a creaky pinnacle to the arête and move around it
into a niche. Swing right, then back left again to ledges. Continue up,
trending slightly right to finish with a rightward traverse across a steep wall.

Soledad Brother   45 metres   E1   (17.8.71)
A good route (and politically correct), tackling the steep corner/groove 15
metres right from the foot of *Boomerang*. Start below and left of this at a
left-slanting 3-metre crack.
1 15m. 5a. Climb the crack and, after a few feet of broken ground,
traverse right to below a steep right-angled corner, which leads to a small
stance and peg belay.
2 30m. 5b. Ascend the right-hand side of the slab for a short way; then
traverse left to the obvious flake crack. Climb the crack and continue in the
same line to the top of the cliff.

Little Eastern   46 metres   Very Severe   (30.5.64)
Below and to the right of *Boomerang* is a steep smooth wall bounded on
the right by an obvious groove. Start below the groove.
1 24m. 4c. Climb a short slab to the foot of the groove and ascend it to
a grassy ledge. Take the crack above, and move right at the top, then back
left to a perched-block stance.
2 22m. 4a. Move right awkwardly into a flake chimney, which leads to a
large grassy ledge. Scramble off rightwards to the Far Eastern Terrace.

The Far East Buttress

The Far East is a massive, broken buttress, split half-way up by the large grassy terrace of *Jubilee Climb* into the Upper Far East and the Lower Far East sections. However, this terrace deteriorates to the left and only the climbs on the Far East Upper right-hand section (*Sceptre* Area) start from it. The best climbing is to be found on the exposed Upper Buttress on the left (*Woubits* Area) and, at the other extreme, bottom right by *Little Krapper*.

The Far East Upper Buttress (*Woubits* Area)

The best approach for routes on this buttress is down the Far Eastern Terrace, which lies just to its left. Great care should be exercised on this descent, which does not continue all the way to the ground.

Brwynog Chimney   48 metres   E1   (1933)
Classically loose and hard, and one of the UK's first Extremes (though traditionally graded only VS). Start directly below the chimney about half-way down the Far Eastern Terrace.
1 20m. 4c. Climb the chimney until it eases back into a slabby formation; then climb the slab to an overhang and chockstone belay on the left.
2 28m. 5b. Step back into the chimney and climb to the slight overhang. Pull over and step right into a crack. Continue up this and finish up the easy but loose chimney.

★Brwynog Chimney   Winter V   (3.2.79)
Climb the chimney, passing a huge icicle with difficulty.

The Arête Start   Winter IV   (3.2.79)
A direct start to *Brwynog Chimney* up the rib in the terraces below the parent route. This allows the route to be started from the approach path.

The Key   67 metres   E3   (3.4.65)
An exposed route, which starts up *Brwynog Chimney* before following the ribbed wall to its right.
1 20m. 4c. *Brwynog Chimney* pitch 1.
2 24m. 5c. Very dirty. Traverse right across the wall on dubious holds to a tape runner on a creaking spike. Move boldly right into the corner (crux); then climb it to a quartz glacis. Continue by ledges to a stance.
3 23m. 5b. Step right and climb the obvious groove to an exit left at the top.

Sinistra   81 metres   E3   (2.6.65)
A loose, dirty, and rarely climbed route taking the wall on the left of *Woubits*. Start almost at the foot of the terrace, below the twin grooves, as for *Woubits*.
1 15m. 5b. Follow *Woubits* to a stance and belay on a block in the groove which forms an overhang.

2 26m. 5a. A loose pitch. Go up for 3 metres and move left into a groove. Traverse left until it is possible to climb up into a grass-filled slot. Continue traversing left, round the rib; then descend to a good stance.
3 20m. 5b. Reach a large hold above the left-hand edge of the ledge with difficulty, and ascend to a flake runner; then traverse left to a small ledge and corner. Climb the right arête of this to a stance and belay.
4 20m. 4b. Climb the groove for 6 metres (as for *The Key*); then step left to a smaller groove and a pleasant finish.

Direct Finish   E1
4a 30m. 5a. Where *Sinistra* joins *The Key*, climb up rightwards to below a slim clean groove. Climb this to ledges at the top of *Woubits Left-Hand*.

★Woubits Left-Hand   71 metres   E3   (9.59)
A sustained and varied route, if a little dirty and awkward at times.
1 36m. 5b. *Woubits* pitch 1
2 20m. 5c. Traverse left; then climb leftwards up a series of cracks and chimneys under overhangs to a good stance and spike belay.
3 15m. 6a. Go up the corner to a thread at 6 metres. Bridge carefully up for the next few moves; then continue more easily via the slabby groove to finish.

★Archaeopteryx   40 metres   E5 6b   (1989)
A fine pitch up an impending line, boldly climbing the arête left of the top pitch of *Woubits*. Start from the stance at the top of pitch 1 of *Woubits*. Climb the crux of *Woubits*; then make a traverse left to the arête (peg). Move left round the arête and up the wall (hard) until easier ground on the upper section of the arête is reached.

★★Woubits   80 metres   E2   (30.8.55)
An excellent mountain route, the second pitch of which takes the huge central curving groove in the nose of the buttress – a truly splendid feature. Start near the foot of the terrace, just right of the band of overhangs, below short twin grooves leading to more broken ground below prominent upper grooves.
1 36m. 5b. Climb the overhang into the right-hand of the twin grooves (often damp and slippery) and a runner. Either continue directly up the groove, or descend a little and move round into the other groove – both ways are hard, but the former is harder. Continue up the now more broken groove to a thin crack. Traverse right from the top of this to a stance on the arête below the overhanging wall.
2 44m. 5b. Step left and climb the groove to a small overhang at 12 metres. Swing out left to a good flake and stand on this in an airy position. Either mantel onto the ledge above and shuffle rightwards into the groove, or move right immediately and layback up to the same spot. Follow the now easier groove to the top of a slab; then move left to wriggle up a chimney in the corner. Finish up a slabby groove to block belays. An atmospheric pitch.

The Far East Buttress

1	Brwynog Chimney	E1	
2	Sinistra	E3	
3	The Key	E3	
4	Sinistra Direct Finish	E1	

5	Woubits Left-Hand	E3
6	Archaeopterix	E5
7	Woubits	E2
8	Hazy Days	E4

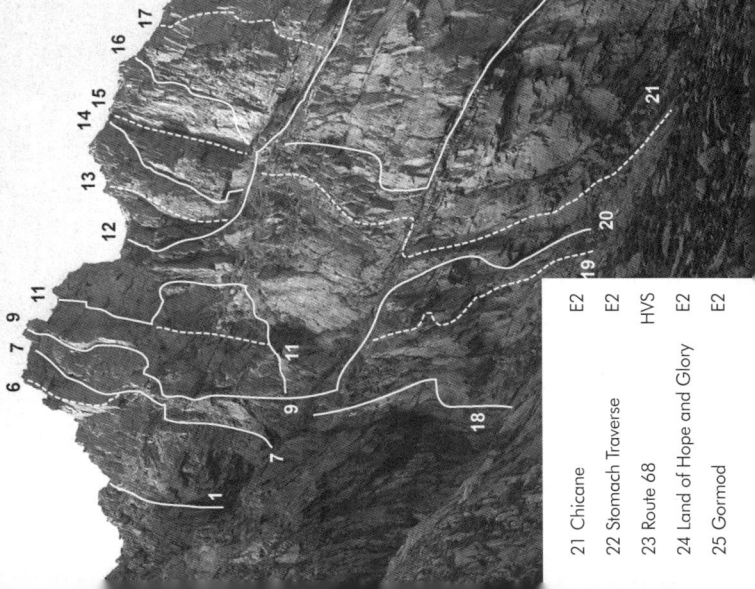

9 The Mostest	VS
10 Luaka	VS
11 Naddyn Ddu	HVS
12 Jubilee Climb	VIII
13 Coronation Finish	E2
14 The Sceptre	E3

15 The Orb	E2
16 Bauble	E4
17 Slurp	E2
18 Silver Machine	S
19 Rumpelstiltskin	S
20 Mostest Direct Start	E1

21 Chicane	E2
22 Stomach Traverse	E2
23 Route 68	HVS
24 Land of Hope and Glory	E2
25 Gormod	E2

★★**Hazy Days**   82 metres   E4   (6.7.77)
A bold, open climb taking the airy wall and rounded arête between
Woubits and *The Mostest*. The climbing is not too desperate, but spaced
protection, the isolated position out of sight of the second, and extreme
exposure all combine to yield a big experience for the leader.
1 36m. 5b. *Woubits* pitch 1.
2 46m feet. 6a. Move right to the arête and then climb diagonally up the
wall to a good flake. Make a long horizontal traverse back left to the arête
on good handholds . Swing round and climb precariously above the void
(it is possible to climb the right-hand side of the arête here, but much
harder). There is a gradual easing towards the top.

★★**The Mostest**   96 metres   E2   (9.4.57)
A well-protected route on sound rock, which traverses the steep wall below
Hazy Days to finish up the prominent bottomless groove on its right. The
situations are superb, whilst the difficulties are compressed into a couple of
very hard moves at the top of the third pitch. Start to the right of *Woubits*,
where the terrace fades into steeper rock.
1 36m. 4c. Go up the grassy groove on the right to climb a slab with
twin cracks. Continue up a short chimney to a grassy rake. Traverse left
into a chimney-groove and follow this to a cave stance.
2 28m. 5b. Climb the crack on the left to the top of a pinnacle. Step right
to a niche and surmount the bulge to reach the steep wall on the right. Go
up a short way to a spike, descend a little, and then follow a rising
traverse-line into the foot of the bottomless corner/groove.
3 19m. 5c. Climb the steep groove on good holds to the overhang; then
make a hard move out (often wet and particularly difficult) into another,
subsidiary groove on the left. Climb this and its left arête; then continue
more easily to a stance.
4 13m. Climb easily up the broken slab to finish.

★**Luaka**   37 metres   E4 6a   (10.9.91)
Essentially the right arête of *The Mostest*. Start as for pitch 3 of *The
Mostest*. From 3 metres up the groove of *The Mostest*, swing around
rightwards (poor peg and wire) to gain a ledge. Tackle the sharp arête with
hard moves past two pegs; then continue above the overlap to reach the
final airy section.

Naddyn Ddu   83 metres   E2   (2.6.62)
A poor route. After a scrappy rightwards start, it meanders back left to take the
groove/crack to the right of *The Mostest* and *Luaka*. Start as for *The Mostest*.
1 15m. 4a. Follow *The Mostest* to the first large grassy ledge. Spike belay.
2 18m. 4c. Step right and climb a short groove to more grass (the Direct
Alternative leaves here). Continue rightwards to an overhanging crack.
Belay to the right of this on a grass pedestal.
3 30m. 5c. Climb the overhanging crack for 12 metres to an easing (old
peg may be in place). Move down leftwards towards the main
groove/feature. Climb steeply up until it is possible to step left onto a

sloping ledge at the start of the crack in the groove (junction with Direct Alternative). Climb the groove to a grassy ledge.

4 20m. 4b. Finish up the crack and continuation chimney.

Direct Alternative   37 metres   E3

A more direct but equally loose and unsatisfactory climb, starting and finishing as for *Naddyn Ddu*.

2a 12m. 4b. Continue, as for *Naddyn Ddu*, up the groove to grass; then belay below a pinnacle at the foot of the wall.

3a 25m. 5c. Start in the vague groove on the left and climb up right to better holds. Continue straight up the wall past a very loose flake to a ledge where the normal route comes in from the right. Join this and climb up to the grass ledge.

The Far East Girdle   136 metres   E3 (1 pt aid)   (30.4.65)

An interesting expedition, crossing the buttress from left to right; never too hard and enjoying fine situations. A spare sling should be carried for the descent on pitch 3.

1 20m. 4c. *Brwynog Chimney* pitch 1 (page 26).

2 24m. 5c. *The Key* pitch 2.

3 30m. Traverse right along grassy ledges to a sling at foot-level. Using the rope, descend for 12 metres and traverse right to the *Woubits* stance.

4 14m. 5b. Move up and around the arête on the right. A descending rightward traverse leads to a junction with *The Mostest*. Follow this to belay at the foot of the steep corner/groove.

5 28m. 5b. Climb to the overhang, as for *The Mostest*. Move out right; then go up for 3 metres to a flake runner. Traverse right and descend a groove for 5 metres until it is possible to step right into the groove on *Naddyn Ddu*. Go up to the grassy ledge.

6 20m. 4b. *Naddyn Ddu* pitch 4.

The Far East Upper Buttress (*Sceptre* Area)

The next five climbs start from the terrace of *Jubilee Climb* and are best reached by climbing the first section of that route (page 33).

★The Sceptre   54 metres   E1   (3.56)

This is the left-hand of the three obvious breaks in the wall at the right of The Far East Upper Buttress. The 2-metre overhang does not yield without a struggle, but the crack above is easy.

1 30m. 5c. Climb the short groove to the overhang. Battle on, using your fists. Continue up the crack to shattered pinnacles.

2 24m. Amble up right to the easy chimney and grassy corner at the top of *The Orb*.

★The Orb   50 metres   Very Severe   (1.4.56)

A pleasant climb, taking the large central break above a short wall.

1 6m. 4b. Climb a thin crack in the wall to a ledge leading up into the corner.

2 30m. 4c. Layback and jam up the corner to an easing at 15 metres. Continue up over broken rock to shattered pinnacles on the left (junction with *The Sceptre*).
3 14m. Finish via the easy chimney and grassy corner above.

The Bauble   46 metres   Very Severe   (28.5.60)
This takes the break 10 metres right of *The Orb*. Loose and not recommended.
1 8m. Start as for *The Orb*, but go right up a slanting crack in the wall. Move right into the bottom of a groove.
2 38m. Climb the loose groove.

★**Slurp**   45 metres   Hard Very Severe   5a   (5.63)
A reasonable climb on the wall right of *The Bauble*. Good moves, though on friable rock. Climb more or less straight up the steep wall via a shallow weakness.

The Republican   118 metres   Hard Very Severe   (23.8.72)
This route takes a natural traverse-line across the face of the buttress from right to left. Not particularly worthwhile. To reach the start, go steeply up and left from the top of pitch 4 of *Jubilee Climb* to a peg belay a little below the overhanging band at the foot of the buttress, directly below a shallow grassy corner.
1 20m. 5a. Climb over the overhanging band of rock on the left; then take a steep wall rightwards to reach the right-hand end of a traverse-line leading left. Belay at the edge of a gully.
2 36m. 4c. Traverse left along the obvious slowly-rising central weakness. Peg belay in a very shallow bay.
3 18m. 4c. Continue along the same line, crossing *The Bauble*. Move up a little; then go horizontally left into the corner of *The Orb* and climb it for a little way to a stance.
4 44m. 4b. Continue up the corner for 5 metres; then trend leftwards over huge pinnacles and blocks to the left arête of the buttress, which leads easily up to finish.

The Far East Lower Buttress

The following routes climb the lower band of rock on The Far East Buttress, which improves in quality from left to right. The very fine huge orange shield of overhanging rock above *Stomach Traverse* is unbreached, and will provide great routes in the future for the totally keen and strong.

★★**Silver Machine**   Winter VIII   (24.2.79)
A long, difficult, and complicated route, though most of the difficulties lie on the first pitch. Sometimes an ice streak forms below the tip of the Far Eastern Terrace and just right of the large overhang. Climb the streak, accessing it from the left. Climb the groove above to join *Naddyn Ddu*, and swing right, avoiding the overhanging crack, to finish up icy grooves on the right. Finish in the same place as *Jubilee Climb*.

Rumpelstiltskin   45 metres   E2   (17.5.75)
Start as for *Mostest Direct Start*, on a small ridge below the foot of the Far
Eastern Terrace. Climb the left-slanting slaty slab to a ledge below the wall.
Go up the wall to the prominent overhang and swing leftwards round this to
a slab below a larger overhang. Bridge up under the overhang until it is
possible to swing out right and climb the wall to finish up the groove above.

Mostest Direct Start   62 metres   E3   (1957)
Loose, dangerous, and not recommended. Start on a small ridge directly
below the foot of the Far Eastern Terrace.
1 45m. 5c. Climb the ridge easily for a few metres. Traverse 3 metres right
to a vague groove and follow it for 5 metres until forced out right. Continue up
steeply to reach a grassy ledge below a corner. Ascend this to easy ground.
2 17m. Scramble carefully up to the start of *The Mostest*.

Mostest Direct Start   Winter VI   (18.2.79)
The first pitch of this climb gives a hard winter pitch.

Chicane   60 metres   E2   (29.5.66)
Very seldom climbed. Start 17 metres right of *Mostest Direct Start*, at the
foot of easy slabs below an obvious curving crack cutting the lower half of
the buttress.
1 45m. 5b. Climb the crack to an old peg in a short chimney at 24
metres. Go left and make difficult moves round the overhang (old peg) to
a good ledge. Move left under a sharp rib; then climb a short arête and
chimney to a stance and peg belay on the right.
2 15m. 4a. Step down right and follow the obvious cracked chimney to
easy ground.

Stomach Traverse   84 metres   E2 (3 pts aid)   (22.8.71)
A poor route taking the prominent diagonal break under the overhangs.
Start below a crack at the right-hand end of the overhangs.
1 24m. 4c. Climb either the crack or the rock on the right to a stance on
the edge of a 'field'.
2 36m. 5a. Go across the wall below the overhangs to the obvious slot,
which gives the first stomach traverse. Cross the undercut wall using three
pegs for aid. Follow the crack to finish along another stomach traverse.
Spike belay 3 metres left.
3 24m. 4c. Move back right along the traverse to a deep chimney. Climb
this and the continuation cracks to finish.

To the right, the large groove of *Jubilee Climb* is an obvious feature. The
corner on the left has been climbed, at a similar grade.

★★Jubilee Climb   213 metres   Severe   (5.5.35)
A long and vegetated route for those in need of a mountaineering fix. The
first section provides a useful means of access to the climbs near *The
Sceptre*. It starts up the obvious slanting groove to the right of the
overhangs taken by *Stomach Traverse*, and then traverses left across the

large grassy terrace to finish up broken rocks in the open gully left of *The Sceptre*. Start just left of the foot of the groove.

1 18m. Scramble across grassy ledges to the crack in the back of the groove.

2 18m. Climb the crack to a thread belay.

3 16m. Continue up to a belay where the groove steepens.

4 18m. Climb the steep crack to a small ledge on the left. The slight bulge above is hard; then the groove falls back. Go up easily to grass on the right.

5 18m. Scramble up grassy slabs until they steepen.

6 8m. Climb the slab on the left, moving to the left, and go along a narrow grassy ledge to a belay.

7 35m. Traverse across the large grassy terrace to its far end, and belay below a corner capped by a 2-metre overhang.

8 28m. Climb the slaty slab on the left and step round into the steep grassy gully. Ascend this to the base of an overhanging crack.

9 10m. Climb the crack and go easily up to a stance.

10 8m. Continue up past a chockstone.

11 36m. Finish up the loose gully.

Variations

5a Pointless, unless one happens to get lost. From the top of pitch 4, traverse out on a smaller terrace parallel to the upper one, which leads, in about 45 metres with some scrambling, to a bay on the left of the prominent twin ribs. Climb the steep wall on the right and go up the arête. Loose and exposed, and *very* Very Severe.

8a The Coronation Variant. Continue straight up the corner above pitch 7 at much the same technical standard, but on looser rock.

★★★**Jubilee Climb**   Winter V   (21.1.79)
A great winter mixed route, and often in condition. The bulge on pitch 4 is especially awkward in crampons.

Route 68   91 metres   Hard Very Severe   (14.6.68)
Start directly below the groove of *Jubilee Climb*.

1 28m. 4c. Traverse diagonally right into a leftward-leaning shallow groove and follow it to a grassy ledge; then move right onto a bulging nose which leads to a grassy pulpit and a belay on the left.

2 35m. 4c. Climb the shallow corner on the right until it is possible to step left into a corner with a crack in the back. Climb the corner and move left at the top to a grassy ledge. Possible peg belay.

3 28m. 4b. Go up the corner to the roof, move left, and continue up the groove to the top.

★**Land of Hope and Glory**   87 metres   E2   (22.8.71)
The fine central section of this climb goes up the obvious flake in the middle of the buttress. Start about 25 metres left of *Little Krapper*, directly below the flake.

1 32m. Go up, trending left; then move back right past the base of a short slab to the left of a groove. Climb the groove to a small niche at the top (thread). Exit right and move back left to a ledge. Large blunt spike belay.

2 15m. 4b. Continue with ease for a short way and then step awkwardly left onto a ledge. Traverse left along the ledge for 3 metres. Climb the steep wall and a shallow groove (tricky) to a ledge.

3 30m. 5c. Climb up right to the obvious flake crack and ascend it. Go up the clean groove (difficult) and move left at its top; then go back right to a cracked block and so up onto a short slab and belay ledge.

4 10m. 4c. Finish up the crack above.

Variation: The Original Line   50 metres   Hard Very Severe

2a 20m. Continue up the broken groove, and then trend slightly right to the foot of an open corner with a steep left wall.

3a 30m. Climb the corner for a few feet, and hand-traverse left across the wall to the arête and a small ledge (the top of the flake crack). Continue up the clean groove as for pitch 3 of the parent route.

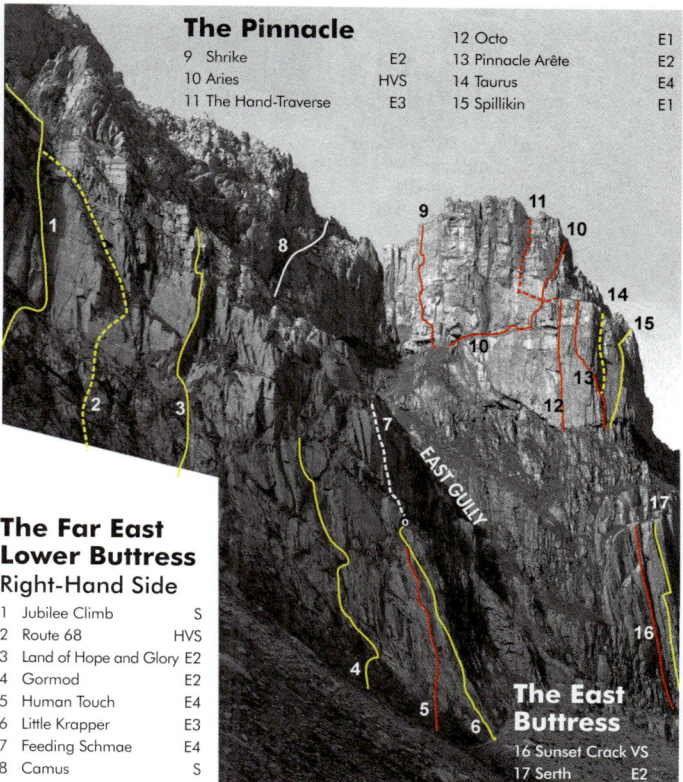

The Pinnacle			
9 Shrike	E2	12 Octo	E1
10 Aries	HVS	13 Pinnacle Arête	E2
11 The Hand-Traverse	E3	14 Taurus	E4
		15 Spillikin	E1

The Far East Lower Buttress
Right-Hand Side

1	Jubilee Climb	S
2	Route 68	HVS
3	Land of Hope and Glory	E2
4	Gormod	E2
5	Human Touch	E4
6	Little Krapper	E3
7	Feeding Schmae	E4
8	Camus	S

EAST GULLY

The East Buttress

16 Sunset Crack VS
17 Serth   E2

Feeding Shmae

Gormod

★Gormod

70 metres E2 (4 pts aid) (4.6.71)
A route that got 'lost' in recent guides. The first ascensionists had a bold approach and a futuristic eye and used four points of aid on pitch 2, all of which are now missing. An on-sight ascent of the route free will be *much* harder (more like E5). The English for Gormod is 'too much'! Start about 6 metres left of *Little Krapper*.
1 22m. 4b. Climb up and traverse left along a grassy gangway for 10 metres. Climb the right-hand shattered groove, rightwards round the overhang, and back to a good hidden ledge.
2 28m. 5b. Traverse left across smooth rock to reach a short groove. Climb out of the top of this onto the shattered, rightward-sloping band and up to the overhang (crux). Move left and up the overhanging groove.
3 20m. 4c. Move right, and climb grassy grooves to the top.

Feeding Schmae (E4)
The Far East Buttress
Climber: Nick Dixon
Photo: Chris Naylor

The Far East Buttress

1 Gormod   E2
2 Human Touch   E4
3 Little Krapper E3
4 Feeding Schmae E4

★**Human Touch**   60 metres   E4   (20.8.84)

A testing pitch, the substance of which consists of the open grooves just left of *Little Krapper's* crux; start 5 metres left of *Little Krapper*. Just as bold as that route, and considerably harder.

1 40m. 6a. Climb straight up to reach the first groove. Ascend this and its continuation (technical and run out) to finish at the left side of a long square-cut overhang. Scramble up the grassy ledges for 6 metres to the top wall.

2 20m. 5b. Finish up the fine open groove-line in the top wall.

★**Little Krapper**   60 metres   E3   (5.63)

A surprisingly good climb up the attractive grooved rib running down to meet the path at the bottom right-hand side of the Far East Buttress, a few metres left of the foot of East Gully. Protection is poor in its modern pegless state. A test of nerve, but fortunately not steep.

1 45m. 5c. Climb the rib to a bulge at 22 metres. Make a committing move up the groove (crux – poor spike and tiny wires), and continue first up, then across left and along a thin slanting crack onto a large sloping grass ledge.

2 15m. 5b. Climb a chossy crack right of the belay, and break out left.

★★**Feeding Shmae**   24 metres   E4 6a   (16.7.02)

Well protected, sustained, and really 'out there', this route climbs the obvious dog-leg crack above *Little Krapper*, starting from the grass ledge at the top of that route's first pitch.

Camus   110 metres   Severe   (5.6.55)

A poor route, loose and to be avoided. It takes the obvious curving chimney on the left of the upper part of East Gully and is reached by a 'scramble'. A direct line is taken to the top. For survivors, a descent exists via the Eastern Terrace.

★**Camus**   Winter V   (4.2.79)

The top chimney much improves when held together with ice! It can be started from *East Gully*.

East Gully   155 metres   Very Difficult   (5.12)

Some would say the date of first ascent is a better grade than 'Very Difficult'. The first 80 metres are just loose scrambling that leads to the final 30 metres, which consists of fairly easy but still very loose climbing. Definitely not recommended as a rock-climb.

★★**East Gully**   Winter IV

Things improve under good snow conditions when the gully can give a fine varied climb. The top pitch can be avoided by a long exposed traverse right under The Pinnacle and up into the Eastern Terrace above Great Wall (III).

The Pinnacle

Perched airily on top of the mighty walls of The East Buttress proper, The Pinnacle frowns down on the approach path as the latter contours round below The Far East. There are two distinct faces at right angles to each other: the impressive sidewall overlooking East Gully gets the morning sun, while the front Pinnacle Face above the left side of The East Buttress waits until evening.

The scramble up or down East Gully to reach the foot of The Pinnacle is very loose and unpleasant (some would say suicidal). The easiest approach is either by abseil or, for routes on The Pinnacle Face, via a route on The East Buttress.

To avoid falling or dislodging lethal debris onto climbers on or at the base of The East Buttress, great care should be taken while scrambling over the loose turfs and spikes that litter the hillside below The Pinnacle's base.

East Gully Wall Face

The sidewall of The Pinnacle is seamed with huge cracks and corners, and its rubble-like base is undercut. The rock in general is fairly good once above the chossy slopes and rubbly starts. This section is in the sun on summer mornings – until 1 p.m. in June and July.

Beanland's   48 metres   Hard Very Severe   (4.5.58)
Seldom climbed, this poor route takes the wall immediately right of East Gully. On the left side of the amphitheatre below *East Gully Wall* is an overhanging crack. Start below this.
1 20m. 5a. Make a difficult traverse left on the obvious line to a rib, and climb it to a stance on the right, virtually in East Gully.
2 6m. 4a. Move rightwards round the steep arête via a flake to a tiny ledge below Moseley's Crack.
3 22m. 4c. Climb the steep crack behind the stance until it is possible to step into the deep crack on the right. Continue up, passing the final chockstone on the left.

East Gully Wall   57 metres   E1   (7.6.53)
A pleasant enough route, steep and adequately protected. The first pitch is taken also by *Shrike* and *Death and the Maiden*, and has a couple of very hard moves. About 50 metres right of the steep part of East Gully a pinnacle leans against the overhangs. The route crosses the steep wall on the left of this and then disappears around the arête to finish up a corner.
1 20m. 5c. Climb the crack on the left side of the pinnacle for 3 metres. Traverse left for 5 metres to the foot of a thin crack, and climb it with difficulty past a good wire (crux) to a stance.
2 25m. 4c. Make a rising traverse to the arête on the left. Step down and move around the arête, avoiding a loose flake, into the groove. Climb the groove to a ledge and chockstone belay.
3 12m. 4c. Finish directly up the corner.

Variations
Direct Start   37 metres   E4 6a
A brutish horror which starts up the often wet, overhanging groove below
the finishing-corner of the parent route. Start 16 metres right of East Gully,
at a pinnacle under a large overhang. Climb the pinnacle and move
rightwards round the overhang into an overhanging groove (difficult).
Muscle up it to another overhang sporting a jammed block. Fight over and
continue, somewhat shattered, to join the normal route.

Moseley's Variation   39 metres   Hard Very Severe
An interesting way of finishing the original route.
2a 17m. 4c. From the top of pitch 1, make a leftward rising traverse to the
arête. Step down and across the corner to loose ledges on the left of the
groove. Cross the ledges to a large flake and climb it to a stance in the corner.
3a 22m. 5a. Finish straight up the crack in the corner above (Moseley's
Crack).

Norm's Finish   Hard Very Severe
3a 35m. 4c. Climb up the corner for 5 metres, then into the groove on
the left and to the top.

★**Death and the Maiden**   56 metres   E3   (10.4.82)
A surprisingly worthwhile eliminate giving a worrying and exposed trip.
1 20m. 5c. *East Gully Wall* pitch 1.
2 36m. 5c. Move left onto the arête (as for *East Gully Wall*) and up to a
niche. Ascend the wall above to the bulge. Trend rightwards across it and
continue boldly up the arête to a ledge just below the top. Finish direct.

★★★**Shrike**   58 metres   E2   (25.10.58)
One of the great Welsh mountain classics and worthy of three stars for
pitch 2 alone. A very steep climb on massive holds in a sensational
position. The *Shrike* wall catches the early morning sun, under which
conditions an ascent is a sheer delight.
1 20m. 5c. *East Gully Wall* pitch 1.
2 38m. 5b. Go up the groove to the overhang and arrange some
bombproof runners. Jam round this to good holds just left of a widening in
the crack. Go left for a metre or two to some ledges. Climb the crack for
about 3 metres to an obvious line of holds leading back right into the
main crack. Follow the crack past a couple of spike runners to a small
ledge, huge holds helping to neutralize the exposure. Go left to the arête,
which is taken for a few metres before moves rightwards gain a narrow
ledge. Finish awkwardly via the short wall above. A stunning pitch.

The Rumour   50 metres   E2   (20.5.78)
A good eliminate. The route starts up *East Gully Groove* before breaking
through overhangs onto the wall right of *Shrike*. Easier than it looks.
1 30m. 5b. Start as for *East Gully Groove* and climb to the top of the
pinnacle. Continue up to the roof which is attacked direct. Saunter up the
wall above on *Shrike*-like holds to a ledge.
2 20m. 4c. Move left to finish up a crack.

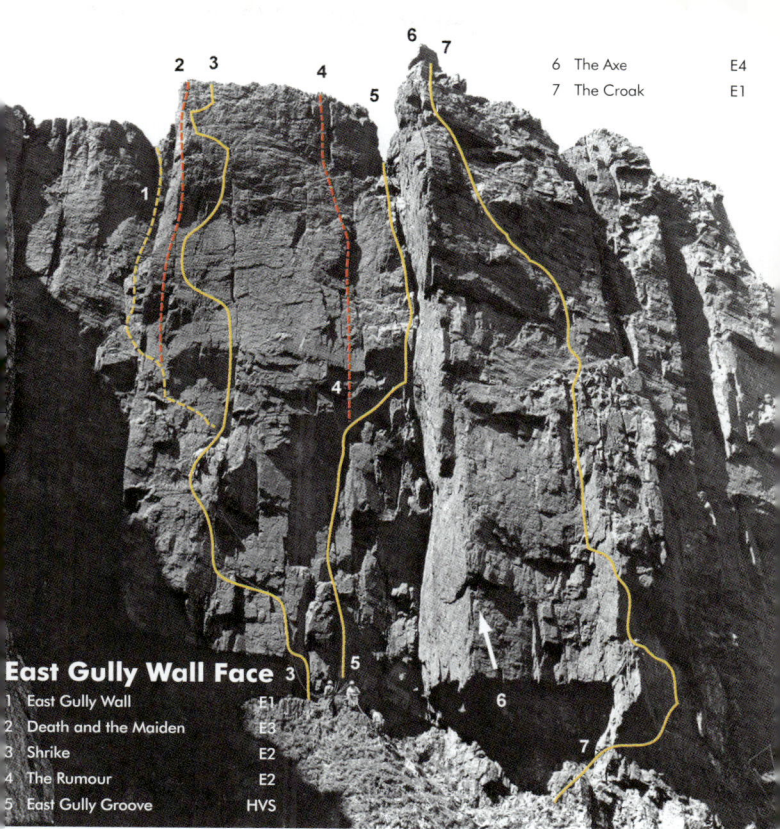

6   The Axe   E4
7   The Croak   E1

East Gully Wall Face

1 East Gully Wall   E1
2 Death and the Maiden   E3
3 Shrike   E2
4 The Rumour   E2
5 East Gully Groove   HVS

East Gully Groove   48 metres   Hard Very Severe   (14.6.53)
A popular route up the shattered groove. Start at the *Shrike* (*East Gully Wall*) pinnacle.
1 28m. 4c. Climb the right-hand side of the pinnacle to its tip; then take a shallow groove to the overhang. Swing rightwards round the edge on good holds and follow a sloping gangway into the main groove. Climb the groove, taking the overhang direct to a stance and belay. An exciting pitch.
2 20m. 4a. Continue easily up the groove to finish.

Direct Start   20 metres   E2
A strenuous and rather dirty pitch up the lower part of the groove. Often wet and hardly worth the effort.
1a 20m. 5b. Battle up the crack and over the overhang to join the parent route.

★★★The Axe   50 metres   E4 6a   (6.7.79)
A sensational and atmospheric route up the sheer, hanging arête immediately right of *East Gully Groove*. The climbing is extremely exposed but the rock is more accommodating than it appears from below: good holds come readily to hand just when needed. Start a few metres right of the arête, below the overhangs where a sort of flake crack/groove runs up to meet them. Climb the flake crack to the roof (some suspect rock). Make a fierce pull over on small holds (crux); then reach a juggy leftward traverse-line leading across to large hollow flakes. Climb a thin flake and the wall above to reach the true arête. Follow this until a spike is reached on the right. Make a move up the wall, and then regain the arête at a small overhang. Continue direct to a crevassed ledge about 5 metres below the top of the tower (belay possible). Finish in the same line.

Moonlight Shadow   46 metres   E4   (7.7.83)
A serious route following a scoop in the front of the tower taken by *The Axe*, with which it shares its start; a sort of direct on *The Croak*.
1 22m. 6a. Climb the crack/groove to the roof and make a difficult pull (crux) to get established in the base of the scoop/shallow groove above (*The Axe* traverses left here). Delicate and bold climbing up the shallow groove leads to a belay on a small grassy ledge.
2 24m. 5a. Take the centre of the wall behind to the girdle. Move slightly right, then back left to finish.

The Croak   64 metres   E1   (28.7.62)
Steep climbing at a technically reasonable standard; a 'Cook's Tour' of *The Axe* buttress. The second half follows *Pinnacle Girdle*. Start below overhangs, a few metres right of *East Gully Groove*.
1 12m. 4c. Traverse right for 8 metres (loose), as for *Gargoyle*, to the top of a pedestal. Climb steeply up the wall above to a stance in a niche. Thread belay.
2 22m. 5b. Traverse left to the arête and climb this with difficulty for a metre or two (crux); then traverse left again to enter a groove. Follow this to a narrowing after 8 metres. Move right on good handholds and continue up to belay on ledges.
3 20m. 5a. Climb the wall above to an obvious traverse-line and follow this to a peg. Go straight up the wall to reach a cave and peg belay.
4 10m. 4b. Move left and finish up the arête on large hollow holds.

★Easy Rider   58 metres   Hard Very Severe   (1970)
Easier than it looks and with a fantastic top pitch, though there is some dubious rock. The route short-circuits pitch 2 of *The Croak* before breaking out right to follow the narrow buttress left of *Gargoyle*'s finishing-chimney.
1 12m. 4c. *The Croak* pitch 1.
2 22m. 5a. Climb the overlap on the right, and then go directly up the overhanging groove and the arête above to the belay ledges at the top of pitch 2 of *The Croak*.
3 24m. 4c. Really 'out there' climbing. Take the easy chimney on the right until it is possible to move out right onto the narrow buttress. Ascend

the wall and the slab above until the buttress steepens at the top. Traverse right, and then climb the overhang to escape up a chimney.

Gargoyle 63 metres Hard Very Severe   (9.5.53)
The route starts below and just right of *East Gully Groove*. After a loose rightward traverse it takes the right-facing groove just beyond *The Axe* buttress, finishing up the right-hand of two chimneys.
1 12m. 4b. Make a slightly descending rightward traverse on shattered rock to a stance in the corner.
2 23m. 5a. Climb the crack; this proves rather trying for the first 12 metres and is best tackled facing left. Above, it falls back and broadens out into a wide chimney leading more easily to a stance. (It is possible, but pointless, to step left and escape up grassy ledges and the left-hand chimney.)
3 8m. Scramble up into the bottom of the narrowing chimney.
4 20m. 4b. Climb the chimney direct, and move right at the top over dubious rock.
Direct Start 37 metres E1 5b
A better way of doing the normal route. Below the second pitch of *Gargoyle* are two cracks a few feet apart. Start on the left from the foot of *Octo* at a large pinnacle belay. Climb a rib on the left (with the inevitable loose rock) to a grassy slope below a shallow cave. Make a difficult rightward traverse across improving rock to climb the left-hand crack, and so on to the stance at the end of pitch 1.

★Aries 50 metres Hard Very Severe   (4.7.65)
A fine, exposed high girdle of the *Margins of the Mind* wall. It takes the obvious line of weakness rightwards from the foot of the *Gargoyle* groove. The climbing is not particularly difficult, but the protection is only fair.
1 12m. 4b. *Gargoyle* pitch 1.
2 15m. 4c. Make an exhilarating rightward traverse across the wall, along a line of good holds to a belay by some large loose blocks at the foot of a crack – good value.
3 23m. 4b. Finish easily but airily up the crack and rock above.

★★★Margins of the Mind 44 metres E7/8 6c   (25.7.84)
Start about 12 metres left of the huge crack of *Octo*, at awkward nut belays below the overhang. Climb the overhang past a good large wire (and old bolt stud on the right). Make powerful moves up to a flake runner; then continue up to the rickety undercut flakes. Step left to a poor (sawn-off) peg runner, and climb the hard wall above (poor *RP2* if you can find it) leading to a step left and a good hold. Get onto the prow with a hard move and a long blind reach, and ascend the left side to a second peg. Move horizontally right for 3 metres and finish with relief onto the *Aries* stance.

★★It Will Be Alright in the Night 68 metres E7 6b   (1992)
The wall between *Margins of the Mind* and *Psycho Killer* with a direct finish into *The Hand-Traverse*.
1 44m. 6b. Belay as for *Psycho Killer*, move left, and pull over the overlap to a standing-position above. Move right and up towards the

The Pinnacle

East Gully Wall Face

1	East Gully	VD
2	Death and the Maiden	E3
3	Shrike	E2
4	The Rumour	E2
5	East Gully Groove	HVS
6	The Axe	E4
7	Moonlight Shadow	E4
8	The Croak	E1
9	Easy Rider	HVS
10	Gargoyle	HVS
11	The Hand-Traverse	E3
12	Aries	HVS
13	Margins of the Mind	E7/8
14	It Will Be Alright in the Night	E7

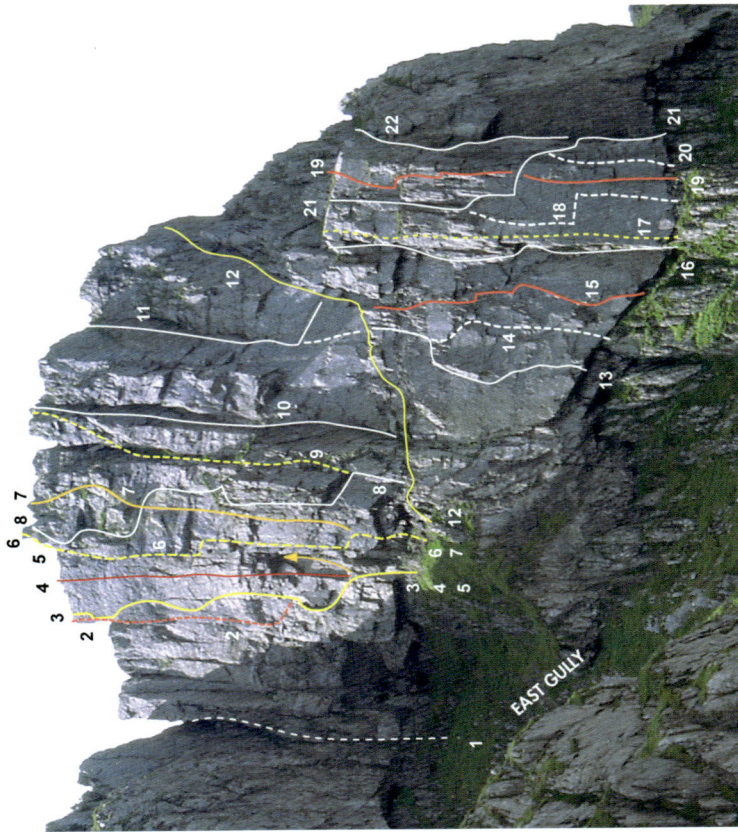

EAST GULLY

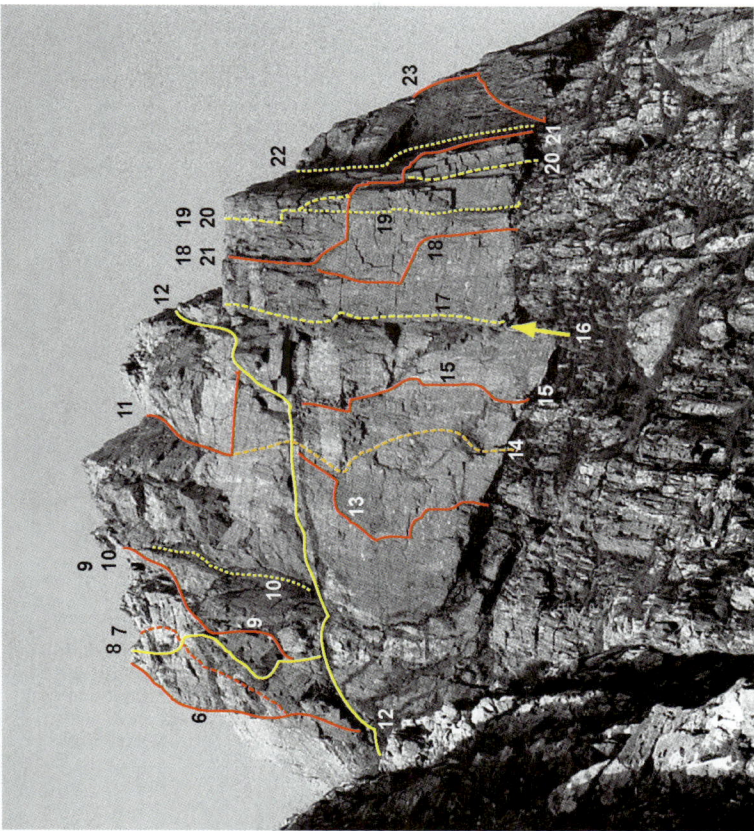

'Final Judgement' peg (see below). A hard move gains another peg. Traverse diagonally left on pockets with a reach down to a third peg, and then easier climbing leads to the *Aries* traverse and spike belay.
2 24m. 5c. Climb the wall above to the middle of *The Hand-Traverse*, and finish up this.

★★Psycho Killer   45 metres   E6 6b   (19.5.80)

A fine route with spaced protection and very old pegs. Start below the overlap about 8 metres left of the huge crack of *Octo*. Pull round the overlap on dubious rock and climb a shallow groove to an ancient poor peg, the original high point of 'The Final Judgement' (see page 171). Initiate an intense sequence on side-pulls past and above this peg (crux), and then trend awkwardly right, without much respite, to effect a precarious lodgement in a very shallow corner. Trend leftwards up this to reach a small overlap. Traverse left to gain an obvious crack, which quickly leads to the sanctuary of *Aries*. A continuously steep and surprising pitch.

★★Octo   51 metres   E1   (15.6.52)

The HVS that *is* an E1 (or even E2?)[1]. A powerful line and a powerful climb. The imposing corner/crack delineating the right edge of the 'Final Judgement' wall has an overhang at half height. Good protection and sound rock make this a popular outing. The base of the crack is reached either by an unpleasant and dangerous scramble out of East Gully, or from the foot of *Pinnacle Arête* (easier).
1 18m. 4b. Climb the crack (the right-hand one is easier and the usual choice) and take a stance in the chimney.
2 33m. 5b. Climb up to the overhang and struggle round, with another battle to enter the crack above. Fight the crack on massive jams until a merciful pull out to the right can be made. Easier climbing leads to a grassy platform on the right. An easy scramble then leads up to the top.

★★The Hand-Traverse   36 metres   E3   (7.5.60)

A fierce and intimidating pitch – very strenuous, exposed, and quite serious. The route traverses left above *Aries* across the smooth shield of rock on incut holds, before finishing up the bottomless corner right of *Gargoyle*. Start from the top of *Octo*.
1 30m. 5c. Step down and launch out across the void on a line of large, sharp-edged holds; then move left and pull up into the thin crack (crux). This soon leads up to a corner and straightforward climbing to a boulder-bridge near the top.
2 6m. 4a. Clamber easily up to finish.

To the right of *Octo*, three splendid, lonely routes breach the face of 'The Citadel'.

★★Authentic Desire   44 metres   E7 6b   (24.9.86)

A superbly bold and lonely lead following *Octo*'s right arête. Reported to be a very dangerous undertaking by the only known on-sight ascensionist. Start at two creaking jugs right of *Octo*. Follow the arête direct via a complex sequence of airy and intricate moves. Several 'snappy' flakes are utilized to assist upward aspirations.

1 'The HVS that thinks it's an E1.' (1989 guide)

Octo (E1) The Pinnacle
Climber: unknown
Photo: Ray Wood

★★★**Shaft of a Dead Man**   44 metres   E7 6b   (1991)
The wall right of *Authentic Desire*. Harder for the short. This also has been
climbed on sight. Start at the right-hand side of The Citadel, at a shallow
groove. Climb the shallow groove and the wall on the left until a
reasonable peg marks a difficult traverse left (crux) into the middle of the
wall and the lowest of a series of flakes. Climb these flakes with reducing
difficulty (for a fit climber). With luck and a fair wind, arrive at the groove
on *Pinnacle Arête*, and continue up it to a ledge.

★★**Fecundity Ridge**   44 metres   E7 6b   (1991)
Another fine route up the right edge of the impending tower.
Start as for *Shaft of a Dead Man* at the faint groove and overlap. Climb
the groove and arête above, passing a peg and keeping on the left side of
the arête (crux at 12 metres). On reaching the junction with *Pinnacle Arête*,
step left and climb straight to the top on more dubious rock.

Desperate Straights   40 metres   E4 6a   (26.8.78)
This takes the superbly-positioned groove tucked in the arête where the
side and front faces of The Pinnacle abut each other; a direct on *Pinnacle
Arête*. The route is bold and exposed, but the rock is very dirty at present.
Start below the groove. Climb over the roof and into the first groove. This
gives a worrying crux before a pull out to the right on better holds leads up
to a junction with *Pinnacle Arête* and good runners. Continue in the same
line with poor protection and unforgettable views to reach a horizontal
crack. Move left to an easier finish up ledges.

The Pinnacle Face

The front face of The Pinnacle is situated above the left end of The East
Buttress. It faces north-west and thus comes into the sun in the evening.

★★**Pinnacle Arête**   46 metres   E2   (17.6.62)
Another well-positioned route based on the arête between the two main
faces of The Pinnacle. Excellent climbing, mainly on huge holds and with
sound protection, makes this a classic of the cliff. Care is needed with the
belay at the start, rope-drag later, and loose stones above *Serth* etc. Start
below the groove of *Taurus*, just right of the arête.
1 40m. 5b. Climb the creaking groove of *Taurus* for 10 metres. Traverse
left, using flakes, to a ledge on the arête. Continue up to the arête proper;
then climb the difficult crack for 3 metres to an obvious leftward traverse.
Follow this for 5 metres to the foot of a groove and go up to a ledge.
2 6m. Finish direct.

Taurus   40 metres   E4 5c   (24.7.56)
A dangerous pitch, particularly at the start, though fortunately protection
improves for the strenuous upper sections. The climb takes a prominent
slanting groove capped by a triangular overhang on the left-hand side of
the front face of The Pinnacle. Scramble up over loose spikes to the foot of
the groove. Climb the groove on poor rock to a small ledge below the
overhang (virtually unprotected). Traverse across; then pull round the left

end of the overhang to enter a short groove. Sustained climbing leads to a smaller overhang: go over this to a ledge on the right. Climb the thin crack on the right of the next overhang to ledges and the top.

★Spillikin   40 metres   E1   (7.6.52)

A bold pitch up the exposed wall right of *Taurus*. The climbing is mainly in balance, but there is little protection on the initial wall. Start at the foot of *Taurus*.

1 28m. 5b. Pull awkwardly onto the wall and climb up, making for a ledge on the right arête at 15 metres. Continue directly up (steep) until a step right is made into a shallow groove, which leads to a stance.

2 12m. 4a. Traverse along the ledge on the right, then up more ledges to the large grassy ledge above and right of *Taurus* known as The Meadow. Finish easily above.

Vanishing Giraffes   42 metres   E4   (30.8.79)

A serious route up the obvious groove in the front face of The Pinnacle, right of *Spillikin*. Start below the groove about midway between the starts of *Taurus* and *Pinnacle Flake*, on the large grass ledge known as The Green Gallery.

1 22m. 5c. Climb easily up the loose groove to the overhang and a poor peg runner on the right. Pull awkwardly up into the groove above. Move up a metre; then go leftwards up a flake and into a scoop. Continue to a ledge and peg belay on the left (half-way up *Spillikin* pitch 1).

2 20m. 5b. Trend up to the right and gain a thin crack. Climb this and the wall above to the long grassy ledge on *Spillikin*. Finish via a thin crack in the short wall to reach The Meadow.

Guinevere   42 metres   E2   (26.6.60)

A serious route, which serves as a fine start to *The Pinnacle Girdle*. Starting from below the *Direct Finish to the East Buttress*, it traverses leftwards across the front face of The Pinnacle to finish up the left side of the Pinnacle Flake.

1 22m. 5b. As for *Pinnacle Flake*, pull onto the arête and climb awkwardly up to a sloping ledge. Then traverse left across to a point where it is necessary to step down before a difficult move is made into a short corner on the left, just short of the groove on *Vanishing Giraffes*. Ascend to a small stance and a chockstone belay.

2 20m. 4c. Climb the corner for 3 metres to a ledge. Move right across the steep wall to the base of the flake and go up the crack on its left side to grassy ledges. Scramble up to finish.

★★Pinnacle Flake   54 metres   E2   (6.6.52)

The once fearsome reputation of this fine and serious lead is re-emerging. Start as for *Guinevere*, at the foot of *Direct Finish to the East Buttress* – the corner right of The Pinnacle's front face.

1 26m. 5b. Pull onto the arête and climb awkwardly up to a sloping ledge. Move up and left to another ledge. Make the infamous and dangerous mantelshelf, and then move across left and climb the crack on the right of the flake to a belay on its top.

2 28m. 4c. Trend diagonally right to the arête and climb it direct on good holds to the top, or go up the face just to its left (not as good). The original (and much inferior) finish escaped up ledges on the left to The Meadow.

The Spire   62 metres   E3   (8.6.75)
The original route climbs up to include the crux of *Pinnacle Flake* before finishing up the fine arête on the right. Start below the obvious niche on the right-hand side, at the foot of the face.
1 23m. 5b. Climb into a niche up on the left (loose); then move out right into another niche. Go out left and move up to a junction with *Pinnacle Flake*, which is followed past its mantelshelf to a belay at the foot of the right-hand side of the crack up the flake (bold).
2 39m. 5b. Move right to the arête and climb a tricky shallow groove to reach better holds. Continue up until forced onto the right wall for 3 metres or so, after which a step back left is made to a ledge on the arête. The difficulties are now over and the remainder is a breeze.

★★**The Spire Direct**   50 metres   E4 5c   (1986)
This is the true right arête of the front face right of *Pinnacle Flake*. Start below and just right of the arête. Move left onto the arête and climb this boldly and directly to join the original route in its upper section.

Virgo   30 metres   E4 6a   (9.9.91)
Climb *Direct Finish to the East Buttress* for 12 metres; then move left at an obvious jug. Climb straight up to the top via a small niche.

★★**Direct Finish to the East Buttress**   50 metres Hard Severe 4b (26.6.32)
Generally useful for hand or foot. (Morley Wood)
A delightful pitch. (Paul Williams)
This is the obvious corner on the right of the front face of The Pinnacle and should be more popular. Scramble up across the rock platform to its foot or access the route from the upper slabs of the Eastern Terrace. Climb the corner, steep at first, past some awkward mantelshelves to a ledge at 12 metres. Continue easily in a fine position for another 25 metres or so to another stance. Keep in the crack for a short while before sidling out onto the left wall to avoid dubious rock.

★★★**The Pinnacle Girdle**   184 metres   E3   (31.8.61 to 2.9.61)
A superb expedition, enjoying some of the finest positions on the cliff. Difficulties are continuous rather than excessive on any one move, though the cruxes of several classic climbs are embraced as the route sidles crab-wise around The Pinnacle from right to left, prior to a frightening abseil down the steepest part of *The Axe*; *Shrike* gives a fitting finale to one of the finest routes in Wales. Although the abseil pitches have been down-climbed free, the route is traditionally, and best, done as described. Start as for *Guinevere* and *Pinnacle Flake* at the right-hand side of the front face.
1 24m. 5b. Pull onto the arête and make the awkward moves up to the sloping ledge of *Pinnacle Flake*. Traverse across leftwards to the point where a step down becomes necessary, just before the tricky move into the

short corner. Climb this to a peg runner at the top on the left. Climb down and across to a ledge on *Spillikin*.

2 18m. 5c. Go up the arête on the left, and traverse into *Taurus* below the large roof. Turn this on the left and climb the groove to a ledge on the right (as for *Taurus*).

3 28m. 5c. Climb the groove on the left for 3 metres; then move across with difficulty to a ledge. Step across to the arête, and continue round the edge at the same level on more broken rock to reach *Octo*. Climb a crack to the start of *The Hand-Traverse*.

4 16m. 5c. Traverse left along the incut holds of the *The Hand-Traverse* for 7 metres; then awkwardly start the thin crack and climb it to belay at the foot of the groove.

5 22m. 5b. Climb the groove until a traverse to the arête can be made. Step across the shallow groove; then descend slightly and continue left to the arête of *Gargoyle*. Climb up a short way; then step across to a stance.

6 16m. 4b. Climb (or, better, abseil) down *Gargoyle* for 10 metres, and then step left to grassy ledges. Go up these to the largest ledge, just below an easy chimney on the right.

7 20m. 5a. Climb the chimney for a short way to the obvious ascending traverse-line. Follow this leftwards for 6 metres to a small ledge. Climb the steep wall on the left to grass; then ascend to a cave and belay.

8 16m. Move left to a groove in the arête (*The Axe*). Make a difficult diagonal abseil into *East Gully Groove* via a thread runner on the end of a large flake.

9 24m. 5a. Step left and climb a thin crack for 5 metres. Make a slightly rising traverse left, and go across to the large spike on *Shrike*. Continue left to the arête. Go up a few feet; then move back right to finish up the short wall.

The East Buttress

At the centre of Cloggy's 'smile' and with its perfect rock, it is The East Buttress that compels most of us to walk again and again to Clogwyn Du'r Arddu. Slowly rearing up over the moraine ridge as we enter the cwm, the lines and faces become obvious as we complete the final stretch of our walk in.

Routes tend to follow vertical cracks or left-facing corners, or the bald faces of rock in between, and it is here that some of Britain's greatest climbing dramas and triumphs have been played out.

To aid indentifying the important features, this section has been sub-divided into three: Sunset Wall, The Great Wall and Upper Wall, and Pedestal Wall.

The sun reaches The East Buttress at approximately 7 p.m. throughout June and July and no finer place can one climb on a summer evening than above the cold, quiet waters of Llyn Du'r Arddu.

The East Buttress

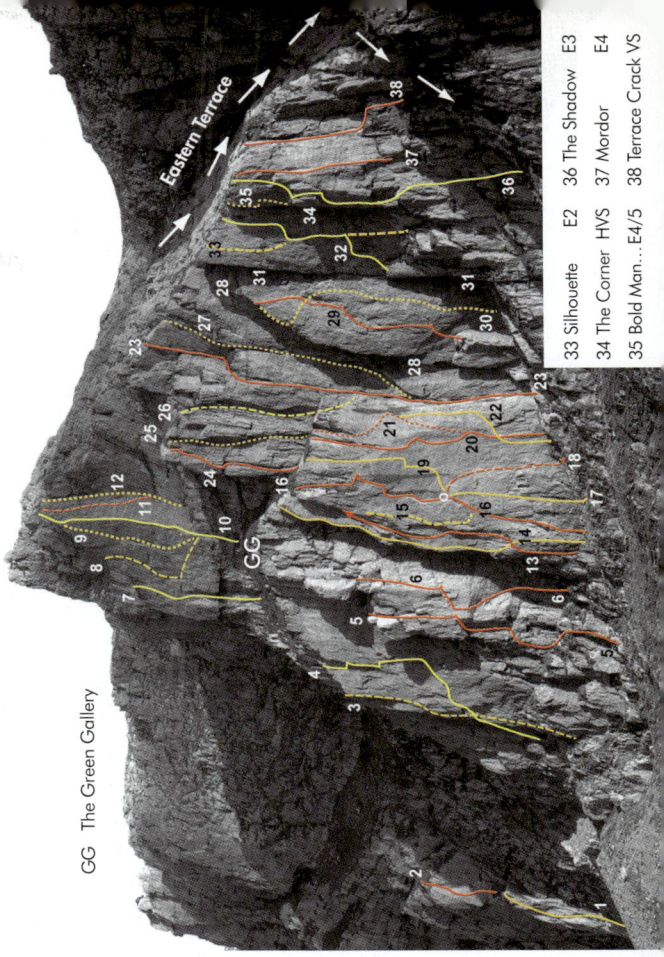

1 Little Kropper E3
2 Feeding Schmae E4
3 Serth E3
4 Lithrig E4

5 Wall Variations E2
6 Trapeze E5
7 Vanishing Giraffes E4

8 Guinevere E2
9 Pinnacle Flake E2
10 The Spire Direct E4

11 Virgo E4
12 Direct Finish HS
   to East Buttress

13 Daurigol E3
14 Dinas in the Oven E7/8
15 Cathedral Graffiti E7
16 Great Wall E4
17 Womb Bits E5
18 A Midsummer Night's...E6
19 Face Mecca E9
20 The Indian Face E9
21 Master's Wall E7
22 Spreadeagle E4
23 November E3
24 The Banyan Tree E6
25 Blancmange Sandwich E4
26 Jelly Roll E2
27 Vember E1
28 Curving Crack VS
29 The Troach E2
30 Purr-Spire Direct E6
31 Pedestal Crack HVS
32 Scorpio E2

33 Silhouette E2
34 The Corner HVS
35 Bold Man...E4/5
36 The Shadow E3
37 Mordor E4
38 Terrace Crack VS

GG The Green Gallery

The East Buttress
Left-Hand Side

1. LLithrig — E1
2. Sunset Crack — VS
3. Serth (with Dir. Finish) E2(E3)
4. Opening Bid — E5
5. Pigott's Climb — VS

Descents are best effected by climbing to the top of the cliff and then scrambling carefully down the Eastern Terrace. Do **not** descend East Gully.

Sunset Wall

The broken wall on the left of *Sunset Crack* gives a series of short pitches which could be done as variations to the main route. The best link is **Sunset Ramps** (68 metres Hard Very Severe 5a), which takes the stepped ramps from left to right.

★**Sunset Crack**   54 metres   Very Severe   (24.6.37)

A popular, steep route. It takes the first major feature of the East, a steep, left-facing chimney-crack which is no pushover, particularly at the start of pitch 2. Scramble up to the base of the crack.

1 32m. 4c. Go easily up to a grassy ledge. Move diagonally right into the crack and continue up with interest to belay, after 24 metres, on the left and below the overhang.

2 22m. 5a. Make a very awkward step up and squirm into the chimney on the lip of the overhang; or climb the left wall. The corner above leads much more easily to a rake. Finish up the short easy chimney to land on The Green Gallery (see page 49).

★★★**Llithrig**   75 metres   E1   5c   (14.6.52)

A superb route with some thin climbing. It can be done with an exciting traditional pendulum at HVS. Starting from *Sunset Crack*, the route traverses into the middle of the steep wall on the right, before finishing direct.

1 13m. 4a. Follow *Sunset Crack* to a stance and belay a short way up the crack proper.

2 22m. 5c. Traverse rightwards across the wall and climb a shallow groove for a few metres to a small ledge on the arête. Traverse right again below an overhang into the corner. Climb the overhang and follow the diagonal break on better holds to a good spike. Either climb down and finger right, or take a short swing (5a).

3 22m. 4c. Traverse right and climb the obvious break to a stance at the foot of a left-facing corner.

4 12m. 4c. Climb to a ledge 5 metres above. Traverse across the wall on the left, at either of two levels, to gain a crack. Climb the crack to better holds on the left wall leading up to a large grassy stance. Alternatively, take the corner direct.

5 6m. 4a. Climb the wall behind to The Green Gallery.

★★**Serth**   64 metres   E2   (7.10.61)

A surprisingly serth (Welsh for 'steep') and very worthwhile eliminate following the shallow grooves in the arête immediately right of *Sunset Crack*. In the sun until 11 a.m. in June and July. Start by scrambling up to the foot of *Sunset Crack*.

1 28m. 5c. Scramble up to the right to reach short twin grooves on the arête. Climb these awkwardly to a junction with *Llithrig*, which is followed

The East Buttress
Left-Hand Side

for 3 metres to the main arête; then traverse left into the bottom of a shallow slanting groove, almost on the arête of *Sunset Crack*. Climb the groove, which proves very stubborn near the top, to a sloping ledge. There is a better ledge and belay a metre or two higher.

2 24m. 5b. Descend to the sloping ledge and cross the steep wall on the right to a diagonal quartz break. Climb up into the obvious groove above and continue more easily to grassy ledges.

3 12m. 4a. Finish up the cracked wall and flake on the right.

★★Direct Finish   E3

A strenuous alternative, even sunnier!

2a 23m. 6a. Climb the obvious crack-system in the pillar behind the first belay: short and wide to start; then thin cracks lead to a bulge, which is turned on the right. Enter a slim airy groove in the arête and finish up this.

★★**The Leech**   83 metres   E4   (17.7.71)

This powerful eliminate, taking a direct line up to the final groove of *Serth*, gives fine climbing. The first pitch is very fierce, while pitches 2 and 3 are now bold *and* very fierce. Start by a spring issuing from the foot of the cliff, directly below *Serth*'s final groove.

1 23m. 5c. Climb the short buttress via a shallow scoop in its centre; this is gained from the left by a short diagonal crack, or reached direct, which is harder. Pull out to belay on a line of grassy ledges traversing the base of the wall.

2 20m. 5c. Climb the obvious groove (bold and fingery, especially if not chalked) to reach the small overhang on *Llithrig*. Pull over and follow *Llithrig* up the diagonal break to the pendulum spike. Move down slightly and rightwards to gain the stance.

3 40m. 5c. Regain the spike and traverse left to a blunt arête. Climb up and slightly left on small pockets to the quartz break below the final groove of *Serth*. Move up into the groove, which gives a fine finish.

Direct Finish   E3   (1975)

A fine, open pitch with a difficult start, although not as good as the original.

3a 37m. 6a. Move back left and climb directly up the obvious line above to reach the final crack of *Llithrig*. Finish up this.

The next four routes have complicated lower halves leading to superb, clean-cut upper pitches.

★**Opening Bid**   56 metres   E5   (20/21.6.88)

Steep and varied climbing taking a connection of 'hard bits' through *Llithrig*, finishing up the fine crack left of that route's finish. Start as for pitch 2 of *The Leech*, which can be reached by scrambling up from the left.

1 20m. 6b. Follow *The Leech* to good wires at the start of the steps in the stepped groove, traverse right onto the fang, and pull through the roof past a tiny, poor blade peg (crux) which helps define the line. Reach up to the right (good runner sideways in a pocket); then climb the shallow scoop and flakes to the stance on *Llithrig*.

2 36m. 6a. A fine, well-protected pitch, though somewhat dirty. Step back down and reverse the *Llithrig* pendulum. Climb up to a short blind groove and follow it, then the 'rattleflakes' above. Climb up trending slightly left to below the superb pencil-thin crack with a small, left-facing pod-shaped groove near the top. Finish delightfully up this past superb runner placements to a peg and nut belay.

★★★Pistolero   70 metres   E5   (30.5.78)
A big sustained lead, majestically taking a direct line up the blank-looking face left of *Capricorn*. Start from the right-hand end of the narrow grassy terrace above pitch 1 of *The Leech*.
1 24m. 6a. Go directly up the wall for 5 metres to a short flake crack breaking out rightwards. Follow this for a short way; then climb directly up the wall to a ragged crack 5 metres higher. Take this crack to its top; then traverse 3 metres left to the stance on *Llithrig*.
2 46m. 6b. Magnificent. Follow *Llithrig* for 10 metres until it is possible to traverse right to large flakes below a thin crack, which forms the substance of this route. Climb the crack steeply for 8 metres to a hard move past the old peg. The crack above remains hard and rest-free, though reassuringly well protected.

★★Capricorn   108 metres   E2   (8.73)
The first three pitches are merely functional in gaining the upper wall with its dramatically positioned and athletic final crack.
1 22m. 4b. *Pigott's Climb* pitch 1.
2 30m. 5a. Climb a steep shallow groove above the stance, and trend rightwards along flakes until a horizontal traverse leads left to the *Llithrig* stance.
3 32m. 5a. Follow *Llithrig* for 9 metres; then traverse airily rightwards on large flakes, gradually descending to a stance in *Pigott's Climb*, below the corner.
4 24m. 5c. The well-protected thin crack in the headwall is as tricky as it is superb. This pitch is often climbed on its own, though anchors above are difficult to arrange.

★★Pigott's Climb   84 metres   Very Severe   (1.5.27)
The original way up The East Buttress – historic, varied, and interesting. The first part of the route is scrappy by modern standards; however, the final steep corner is a *must* for any corner-crack connoisseur. Ledges and stances are commodious, though they can be crowded on warm summer days. The break right of *Sunset Crack* slants rightwards and is composed of enormous blocks resting on the cliff. The route traverses across to them from the left before finishing up vertical corners. Start by a mossy spring at the foot of the cliff, several metres to the right of that of *The Leech*, below an ill-defined break curving up to the left.
1 22m. 4b. Follow the break leftwards up grassy ledges for 12 metres. Climb a steep groove to a good ledge and belays on the left.
2 12m. 5a. From the right-hand end of the ledge, climb a steep rib; then traverse right to the foot of a short steep corner – the infamous 3-metre

corner[1] – and a notorious sticking-point. Just above this lies a broad grassy ledge, The Conservatory.

3 22m. 4a. Climb easily but steeply up the corner to a ledge on the right at 16 metres. Take the chimney above to the top of a massive pillar, The Pinnacle (not to be confused with *The* Pinnacle above).

4 28m. 5a. Climb directly up consecutive corner cracks to the top – a cracking pitch.

Variations

4a 20m. 4b. Climb the corner to a sloping ledge. Step up to a higher ledge and climb a subsidiary crack to a good ledge; or traverse easily around the edge and climb a short nose.

4b 10m. 5b. Climb the thin crack in the wall on the right of the corner. A struggle.

4c 10m. 4c. Traverse round the edge on the right and go up the left-hand of two grooves.

Wall Variations   84 metres   E2

A poor route, grotty and vegetated. It takes the area of rock immediately right of *Pigott's Climb* and shares belays with that route on The Conservatory and The Pinnacle. Start fairly high up at the base of a pinnacle below The Conservatory, reached along grassy ledges from the right.

1 22m. 5b. Climb to the top of this pinnacle. Move right and follow a rib to a ledge below a steep crack, which proves a difficult problem before The Conservatory is reached.

2 24m. 5b. From the right edge of The Conservatory, traverse right under the roof on large holds and (sometimes) slimy jams to an obvious crack. The crack and its easier continuation lead to a stance by The Pinnacle.

3 18m. 4c. Traverse right under the nose. Ascend for another 3 metres before a short, slightly broken wall leads with difficulty to a stance.

4 20m. 4b. Traverse right to, then go along a good ledge to a junction with *The Crooked Finish* of *Chimney Route*. Finish up this.

Variation

1a 22m. 5c. The steep crack can be started direct. It is always wet and vegetated, and has some rotten rock in its lower section. Protection is only moderate – a perverse pitch.

★Trapeze   78 metres   E5   (20.8.65)

A route of contrasts: an exhausting roof, eminently protectable, right of *Wall Variations* leads to a delicate and poorly-protected wall. Start about 6 metres left of *Chimney Route*.

1 10m. 5a. Climb the green corner and step out right at the top to a ledge and flake belay.

2 24m. 6a. Hard for the grade. Move left to a slab and ascend to the roof. Surmount it via a difficult crack, which is often wet (and has been climbed as such). Continue over the lip to reach the horizontal break; then make a tricky step right to a belay.

1 Well known hitherto as 'the 10-foot corner'.

3 22m. 5c. A good but serious pitch. Traverse right for about 5 metres, around a sort of blunt arête onto *The Sweeper* face. Climb the crack/groove-line immediately on the right (left of *The Sweeper*). Start this with difficulty on the right; then step left into it and continue on small holds with indifferent protection to a horizontal break. Step left and climb to a triangular grassy ledge.

4 22m. 5b. Take the corner above and continue up the first groove to join the variation finish to *Pigott's Climb*.

★**The Sweeper**   80 metres   E2   (4.7.75)
A popular route, though it suffers from its lower part being a little too close to *Chimney Route*. The thin crack in the left wall of *Chimney Route* provides the main interest, especially at half height, where one encounters a perplexing move. Protection is spaced.

1 20m. 4a. *Chimney Route* pitch 1.

2 40m. 5c. Follow *Chimney Route* for about 2 metres; then move left to the thin crack (this may also be done at a slightly higher level – easier). Sustained climbing up the crack leads to a hard step right at the break into a tiny niche below small roofs. Pull round these, move left, and then ascend a steep slab to a good belay ledge. A big pitch.

3 20m. 5a. Take the groove behind the belay; then move right into another groove. Go up into a niche and break out leftwards to the top.

Variation

3a It is also possible to move left to the base of *Capricorn's* final pitch, which makes for a great (★★) combination.

★**Chimney Route**   112 metres   Very Severe   (6.7.31)
This fine classic is the product of the partnership of two giants in our climbing history: Kirkus and Edwards. The chimney sections, usually bridged and thus avoiding the worst of the slimy rock, give fine climbing. Owing to the dangerous state of the top overhang formed by the rattling *Rickety Innards*, the route is described with the *Diglyph* finish, a fine open section in marked contrast to the enclosed initial damp pitches. Start almost in the centre of The East Buttress, below the prominent chimney-line just left of the vast smooth central wall, The Great Wall. Scramble up to the foot of the chimney.

1 20m. 4a. Climb the chimney to a good stance; or climb the wall on the right – harder but drier.

2 16m. 4b. The chimney has narrowed and is easy for 10 metres until one is forced out right. The climbing is then on good holds until the chimney reappears.

3 20m. 4a. Continue up without difficulty for 14 metres until the right wall falls back into a slab. Climb this to a belay.

4 24m. 4c. Climb down right and step round the arête into a groove. Go up this to a large flake. Traverse right and climb the steep and exposed wall on excellent holds to reach The Green Gallery (page 49). It is now possible to escape leftwards by scrambling; but, better, take The Continuation Chimney:

5 32m. 4b. Climb the obvious chimney in the corner to finish.
Variations
4a The Rickety Innards 20m. HVS 4c. Climb up to the overhang
formed by unstable flakes which rattle and creak alarmingly when manhandled.
Float gingerly over these (almost impossible) and continue to the top.
4b The Crooked Finish 22m. HVS 4c. From just above the stance,
traverse left to a good ledge. Climb up to the ledge above. Traverse back
into the narrow chimney above the overhang to rejoin the original route.

★★**Diglyph**   80 metres   Hard Very Severe   (24.6.51)
A fine artefact of a climb taking the crack in the right wall of the second pitch
of *Chimney Route*. The crack is strenuous, and hard to start, though the main
difficulty is reserved for a technical bulge, higher up. The last pitch is VS and
it is in a superbly exposed position overlooking The Great Wall.
1 20m. 4a. *Chimney Route* pitch 1.
2 28m. 5b. Traverse 3 metres right and climb the thin crack via an
awkward section where it widens; then continue to a small ledge in a short
corner. Surmount the fierce little bulge above, and follow the crack on
good holds to belay at the far end of a ledge.
3 32m. 4c. Climb the short wall to enter the obvious groove. Follow this
pleasantly for about 25 metres to a steepening at a large flake. Traverse
right, and climb the steep wall on good holds to The Green Gallery. The
groove can be climbed direct, but it is harder and not as enjoyable.

The Great Wall and Upper Wall
To the right of *Diglyph* the great sweeps of The Great Wall take shape.

★★**Daurigol**   80 metres   E3   (28.4.62)
Superbly intricate in line, this sustained route finds a way up the grooves
on the left side of The Great Wall. Start below the grooves, just right of
Diglyph, at the bottom left corner of the wall.
1 24m. 5b. Climb diagonally left past a large pinnacle. Step back right
and ascend twin grooves to a horizontal quartz break by a small roof.
Swing out onto the rib and go directly up to a stance.
2 24m. 5c. Move right into the first groove and climb it until holds lead
left into the second groove, which is by far the hardest part of the route.
3 32m. 4c. *Diglyph* pitch 3.

★★**Dinas in the Oven**   80 metres   E7/8   (4.7.85)
A modern route following the logical left arêtes of The Great Wall, the
central of these being the striking left arête of the main pitch of *Daurigol*.
Start just right of *Daurigol*.
1 24m. 6a. Climb directly up to the main arête. Climb the ill-defined
knobbly rib for 12 metres to a horizontal break and protection. Continue
to a jug at the base of a shallow little groove; then go up and left to the
stance of *Daurigol*.

Womb Bits (E5), The East Buttress
Climber: unknown
Photo: Martin Whitaker

The Great Wall

The Great Wall

1 Pinnacle Flake   E2   3 Direct Finish to
                                           East Buttress   HS

2 The Spire   E3

2 24m. 6b. Move left to the foot of the fine arête, which is totally devoid
of protection save one very poor peg. This gives a gritstone-like problem
requiring 'slaps' and à cheval manœuvres in a dangerous spot.
3 32m. 6a. Climb up to the base of the obvious 'S' arête of *A
Midsummer Night's Dream*, which provides the finish.

★Cathedral Graffiti   45 metres   E7 6b   (19.6.88)
A big lead up the prominent white streak left of *Great Wall*, with superb
positions and moves, though escapable into *Daurigol* on two occasions.
Probably low in the grade. Follow *Great Wall* to its first crux, pull out left,
and hand-traverse the quartz break for 2 metres. Make tricky moves up,
using a small fang of rock to gain a ledge at the base of a shallow white
groove (no-hands rest and good *RP2*). Climb the groove (crux) to an
in-situ Rock 4. Go easily up the rib to a peg; then continue up the rib for a

9-metre runout on 6a ground to the grassy belay 3 metres left of the crux on pitch 2 of *Great Wall*.

★★★Great Wall 72 metres E4 (27.5.62)

One of the great 'Hard Extremes' of Welsh Rock, finding the most reasonable way up this truly splendid piece of rock. The first pitch is well protected and sustained; the second is bold and airy before a fingery final pull. Start just right of the thin crack running up the left side of the wall.

1 30m. 6a. Climb diagonally left to a small overhang at 6 metres. Go over and follow the crack to a shallow groove. Delicate bridging now leads up to a thin crack, which is rapidly followed to a tiny stance. Peg and nut belays.

2 42m. 6a. Continue up a shallow depression for 12 metres without much protection to reach a short, thin crack with good runners. Climb this to a small left-facing corner. Move right on a sharp side-pull and make a long crucial reach for a good hold and a ledge. Traverse right along the ledge; then go back left up easier ground to belay at the foot of The Continuation Chimney. Care should be taken to avoid dislodging loose stones with the rope whilst scrambling up over the final ledges.

★★Direct Finish E4
2a 40m. 6a. Follow pitch 2 to the wires and small left-facing corner; then climb straight up.

★★★**Face Mecca**   24 metres   E9 6c   (6.89)
Another truly fantastic piece of climbing up a faint scoop and overlap between the top pitch of *Great Wall* and *The Indian Face*. Like *The Indian Face*, it requires Zen-like control and has not as yet been climbed on-sight. Start at the *Great Wall* stance. Place a runner at the top of the stance, return to the level at which *A Midsummer Night's Dream* comes in from the right, and reverse the traverse of that route for 3 metres. Then climb up for 12 metres and make a horrific move to gain the flake in the centre of the upper wall (one poor *RURP* and one poor cut-down blade). Climb straight up, with 5 metres of 6a and 6b, to reach the easy ground directly above.

★★★**Womb Bits**   24 metres   E5 6b   (23.7.84)
Essentially, an alternative first pitch to *Great Wall*, more direct but with less line. From a point about 6 metres right of *Great Wall*, go up for 8 metres to gain the obvious thin vertical crackline. Continue with fiddly protection past the left of the shallow sickle overlap to join *A Midsummer Night's Dream* where it steps left into the stance of *Great Wall*.

★★★**A Midsummer Night's Dream**   75 metres   E6   (8.7.73)
Delicate and bold, the first pitch of this route has become one of the most loved pieces of climbing in Britain, and combined with the upper pitches it makes a long varied outing. Often only the first pitch is climbed (a magnificent E6 in its own right) and an easy descent can be made from the *Great Wall* stance. Start midway between the start of *Great Wall* and the Drainpipe Crack of *November*.
1 25m. 6a. Trend leftwards up to ledges and a peg runner. Climb up rightwards; then make sustained moves on tiny holds straight up to a wire loop on an old bolt. Go up and slightly left for 4 or 5 metres until a peg can be reached (hidden in a shallow flake corner on the left and better reached than visited). Move up and right, then back left until a hard smear enables you to attain a standing-position over a vague bulge. Follow a line of holds diagonally left to a point level with the *Great Wall* stance. Step down and traverse left to belay. A brilliant pitch.
2 22m. 6a. Follow the groove of *Great Wall* for about 12 metres; then move left to an obvious mini-ledge on the wall. Go steeply up on minute holds until moves left gain the stance on *Daurigol* (hard).
3 28m. 6a. Easy and vague climbing leftwards over grassy ledges leads to a good belay on the slab of *Chimney Route*, below the steep 'S' arête. Go up to the arête – at close quarters the start appears to overhang

Face Mecca (E9), The East Buttress
Climber: Nick Dixon   Photo: Dixon col.

A Midsummer Night's Dream (E6)
The East Buttress
Climbers: Johnny Dawes & Martin Crook
Photo: Crook col.

alarmingly. Make strenuous moves, with lateral small-wire protection around to the right, to get established on the easier-angled section above, and continue up to finish.

West Indian Face   47 metres   E8 6b/c   (21.5.88)
A line has been led from the peg on *A Midsummer Night's Dream* to the good foothold on *Rite of Spring* and then on to finish up *The Indian Face*. On the only ascent to date the leader considered a crucial runner on *The Indian Face* to have been enhanced and he later filled the placement. Thus the route has not been climbed without this runner, though of course *The Indian Face* has.

Spreadeagle   52 metres   E4   (31.8.79)
This rarely repeated route artificially skirts the right edge of The Great Wall before majestically cutting back left near the top, to finish up a groove in its centre. Start at the foot of the shallow groove just left of *The Indian Face*.
1 30m. 5c. Climb the groove; then trend right to the edge of The Drainpipe Crack. Climb up just to the left of this to a small stance and belay where the angle eases. Unfortunately, it is possible to escape right into the crack at several points.
2 22m. 5c. Move left and go up to a horizontal traverse-line. Follow this leftwards along a narrow ledge. Ascend to a short crack leading to a groove and belay above. A good pitch.

★★★The Indian Face   48 metres   E9 6b/c   (4.10.86)
Sustained 6b climbing for 32 metres with poor and very distant protection on one of the best lines in the world makes this one of the finest and most dangerous goals for any climber. As yet, climbed only with prior

preparation. Start 5 metres right of *A Midsummer Night's Dream*. Climb up to the overlap, pull over, and climb up the shallow scoop, passing several poor runners, to a rest just right of the overlap at 28 metres. Spend some time calming and preparing for the 12 metres to come. Launch left and up across the blank expanse to the huge jug at the base of the finishing-crack.

★**Master's Wall**   51 metres   E7 6b   (14.7.83)
Like *Spreadeagle*, an escape from the line of *The Indian Face*, which avoids the main issue, yet gives climbing that has left a deep impression on ascensionists. A bold route that lacks line in its midriff, where it escapes right to join *Spreadeagle*. Start as for *The Indian Face*. Climb *The Indian Face* (or slightly right of it) for 20 metres; then trend right to join *Spreadeagle*, which provides the finish. The route has now had several ascents, some on-sight, though the exact position at which climbers have moved right has varied. The higher, the harder – the first ascensionist moved up and right from a position just right of the old (*Tormented Ejaculation*) bolt stud, which is 3 metres below and just right of the overhang.

★★★**The Rite of Spring**   28 metres   E7/8 6b   (17.4.87)
This superb, delicate, and technical left-to-right girdle of The Great Wall is so enchantingly enticing. The exact line is vague, tenuous, and difficult to follow, though the change in the angle of the wall gives the main clue. The second ascent was done on-sight. Start from the stance on *Great Wall*. Climb *Great Wall* for 5 metres to good nut runners – this eliminates the threat of a ground fall should the leader slip near the end of this precarious pitch. From the stance, step down, and reverse *A Midsummer Night's Dream* for 5 metres (still above its crux). Move up, right, then down to a good foothold. Step right; then go up slightly and continue right (crux) to a point where it is possible to place an *RP1* and a poor stopper (should you find it). Banishing all thoughts of the potential cheese-grating pendulum, continue across into *The Indian Face*. Move down slightly, then rightwards up into *Spreadeagle* to finish.

The next routes climb the grooved, steeper Upper Wall. This is directly above The Great Wall and has a pillar-like structure. The climbs are best approached from the top of *Great Wall* or from The Green Gallery (see page 49).

★**The Arête Finish**   30 metres   E4 5c   (29.5.66)
The steep arête right of The Continuation Chimney gives a good but poorly protected pitch in an incredibly exposed position. Apparently not as hard as it looks! Yet amazingly graded HVS by the first ascensionists. Traverse right from The Continuation Chimney and climb up to an ancient peg. Continue steeply up to enter the easier finishing-crack.

★**The Banyan Tree**   30 metres   E6 6b   (7.89)
The shallow groove and notched roof 3 metres right of *The Arête Finish*. Poor tiny wires protect the bold groove, though the roof is safer, offering wild views, particularly between one's legs.

★**Blancmange Sandwich**   34 metres   E4 6a   (11.6.75)
This strenuous route of continuous bridging is not to be trifled with. It takes the left-hand of the two huge grooves above The Great Wall. The groove is a drainage line and often wet and dirty. Start 5 metres left of the corner, below a small groove. Climb the groove to good handholds. Traverse right into the corner and ascend to a sloping ledge. Climb diagonally left across the wall; then go back right on good handholds to enter the groove. Continue directly up this with some hard, dirty, and serious splits moves to the top.

★★★**Jelly Roll**   94 metres   E2   (17.9.71)
An excellent route, the main interest of which centres on the superbly-positioned top pitch, which can be accessed from The Green Gallery: a jug-pulling extravaganza up the right-hand of the two grooves above The Great Wall.
1 32m. 5a. *November* pitch 1
2 22m. 5a. Continue as for *November* until the crack closes. Go left at a hidden flake crack, which soon leads to the large ledge at the top of *Great Wall*.
3 40m. 5b. Climb the airy groove mainly by bridging, using hollow flakes and side-pulls, to a rest at half height. Continue up the groove for a few metres; then follow a crack across the left wall to turn the final overhang by a crack on its left – all very tiring. Move up to finish on good holds in the short chimney at the top.

★★★**November**   112 metres   E3   (3.5.57)
A classic crack climb and a very direct way up the cliff. The crux pitch is sustained and strenuous in a fine situation. Immediately right of The Great Wall is a prominent arching face crack which splits at half height. *November* follows the main crack in its entirety, while *Vember* takes the right-hand branch. Start at the wide crack, The Drainpipe Crack, just left of the *Curving Crack* pedestal.
1 32m. 5a. Climb the crack for 28 metres. Move out to a ramp on the right and follow this up to good belays.
2 44m. 5c. Reverse to the foot of the ramp; then continue up the chimney/crack to a ledge on the left, where the crack narrows. Climb the crack, which is continually awkward, to a very difficult section just below the point where it widens into a shallow chimney. From a grassy ledge just above the chimney, move up to a larger grassy ledge. Belay at the back.
3 36m. 5a. Take the awkward corner-crack to a large rock platform. Finish more easily up the continuation cracks to belay on the Eastern Terrace.

★**Vember**   92 metres   feet E1   (13.10.51)
Another classic climb, which can be popular when the Drainpipe is dry. It shares the first pitch with *November*, then takes a parallel crack to the right. The notorious shallow chimney on the second pitch is the crux.
1 32m. 5a. *November* pitch 1.
2 36m. 5b. Climb steeply up the short cracked corner onto a small ledge. Above is the shallow chimney; this dirty slot leading up to a small overhang seldom yields without a struggle. The chimney reappears on the

left, leading up via a short V-chimney and its continuation to a large grassy ledge. Belays at the back.
3 24m. 4b. Climb the right wall of the corner and finish up cracks to the Eastern Terrace.

Medi 45 metres E5 6a (29.8.75)
This rarely-climbed route has protection when needed and follows the thin crack in the top wall right of *Vember*. Unfortunately, dirty at the moment. Start from the first stance of *Vember*, beneath a crack just to the right. Climb the crack, which trends right to a peg at 10 metres. Move awkwardly rightwards across the wall to a long thin flake. Follow this into the steep crack, which proves rather strenuous until it is possible to gain a sort of 'cleaned depression' in the overhanging wall on the right. Good nut on the left. Move left to climb the faint crack and continue to the top.

Pedestal Wall
This is the area of pillars, grooves, and walls between *Curving Crack* and the Eastern Terrace.

★★★Curving Crack 66 metres Very Severe (19.6.32)
The best VS on the East, being an accessible and uncomplicated climb. To the right of The Great Wall is a deep crack curving to the right in its upper half; its right wall, a massive flake nearly 60 metres high, protrudes so far as almost to form a gully. At the foot of the crack is a 10-metre pillar: start at the right-hand side of this.
1 12m. 4c. Climb the thin crack by either layback or jamming.
2 20m. 4c. Swing left into the main chimney/crack on a good hold and follow it, surprisingly steep and awkward at the bulge, to belay at a ledge on the left wall.
3 34m. 4c. Move back into the main crack and continue up until the right wall falls back to form a slab. Move out onto the arête for an airy finish on good holds. Alternatively, stay in the crack all the way. Belay at the back of the grassy ledge above.

Direct Start 10 metres Very Severe 5a
Climb the crack on the left-hand side of the pillar – harder and much dirtier.

★Curving Arête 62 metres E4 (8.71)
The arête of the massive flake to the right of *Curving Crack* gives a bold and serious route up a splendid line at the lower end of the grade.
1 20m. 4c. Follow *Curving Crack* to a chockstone belay in the chimney/crack at a point where it is possible to move out right onto the arête.
2 42m. 5c. Go out onto the arête, which is very steep for about 10 metres and climbed mainly on its left side. Above, the angle eases substantially – amble airily up to finish.

★★★**The Troach**   66 metres   E2   (4.10.59)

An excellent route: one of the best of its standard on the cliff. It takes the steep wall right of *Curving Crack*. The climbing is both bold and open, though only the start of the main pitch is technically hard. Quick drying.

1 12m. 4c. *Curving Crack* pitch 1.

2 37m. 5b. Move right past a shallow corner; then make a hard and bold move to gain the quartz ledge above. Step up and slightly left to enter a shallow groove. Follow this for 12 metres; then step right and continue awkwardly to a small overlap. Step right again and make thin moves up to reach better holds and a short corner leading to a large flake belay.

3 17m. 5a. Follow a line of mantelshelves diagonally leftwards with a hard move to gain the arête. Finish easily up the arête.

★★★**Purr-Spire Direct**   60 metres   E6   6b   (1982)

The line of the original route should have been taken. Start 3 metres left of *Pedestal Crack*. Climb directly up to the faint spire, passing ugly 'tat'. Then follow *The Purr-Spire* until it moves left into *The Troach*. Here, move up and right to climb a vague groove to the right of the top part of pitch 2 of *The Troach* directly to the belay. Finish as for *The Purr-Spire*.

★★**The Purr-Spire**   60 metres   E5   (29.8.79)

An intimidating and direct line attacking the wall between *Pedestal Crack* and *The Troach*. Hard climbing between spaced protection. Start at the foot of *Pedestal Crack*.

1 44m. 6a. Climb *Pedestal Crack* for about 7 metres to a good runner. Traverse left across the lower of two vague ramped scoops to climb a faint spire (hard). Continue boldly up the centre of the wall, passing a peg, then up and left to join *The Troach* for its final moves to the belay.

2 16m. 5b. Go directly up the wall above the belay to finish.

★★**Pedestal Crack**   56 metres   Hard Very Severe   (30.8.31)

The obvious vertical crack splitting the buttress right of *Curving Crack* gives steep jamming with ample protection. Scramble across the glacis below *Curving Crack* to the foot of the main crack, which starts up the corner formed by an enormous rock pedestal.

1 15m. 5a. Take the crack direct, and exit right to belay on top of The Pedestal.

2 10m. 4c. Continue up via a stubborn little crack to a stance in the corner.

3 31m. 4b. The crack, still steep, now has better holds and eases further after 12 metres. Continue up to a large grassy bay at the top.

The Original Start reduces the grade to VS.

1a 19m. 4b. Climb the rib round to the right of the crack; much easier.

★**The Orphan Flagellator**   41 metres   E4   5c   (27.7.79)

Spaced out protection and brilliant climbing up the compellingly obvious and 'out there' arête right of *Pedestal Crack*. Start from the belay at the top of The Pedestal. Follow pitch 2 of *Pedestal Crack* to the stance in the corner (runners). Step right, and climb boldly and directly up the arête, resisting the temptation to find a way back left.

★★**Scorpio** 44 metres E2 5b (27.4.61)

The left-to-right diagonal, and another of the cliff's great middle-grade routes: sustained, varied, and usually dry. Protection is plentiful up to the finale – a sprint up a blind flake near the top. Start from the top of The Pedestal, gained by climbing pitch 1a of *Pedestal Crack*. From the right-hand end of the ledge, climb a shallow groove to the hand-traverse line (thread runner). Follow this right for 6 metres; then move up to a good ledge. Awkwardly climb the shallow blank groove to the small overhang. Ascend the thin crack on the left to a peg, and then traverse right to a blind flake crack. Power rapidly up this to a good hold (crux) and finish more easily via the short wall above to reach the Eastern Terrace.

★★★**Silhouette** 43 metres E2 (23.5.75)

A memorable trip, following the obvious thin, left-trending crack up the centre of the *Scorpio* wall, joining *Scorpio* for its middle section. The route is sustained, but the crack is extremely protectable, and dries only hours after rain. The route can be climbed in a single runout, though it is probably best done in two. Start just left of *The Corner*.

1 11m. 5c. Climb awkwardly up the thin crack to the short groove on *Scorpio*. Nut and flake belay.

2 32m. 5c. Go up the groove, move left, and continue to the peg – *Scorpio* sidles right at this point. Follow the crack to a small roof. A reach round gains a good hold. Finish more easily up the crack above.

★★★**The Corner** 53 metres Hard Very Severe (20.6.52)

An immaculate jamming, bridging, and laybacking pitch, E1 in all but the very driest years! On the right-hand side of The East Buttress is a very obvious right-angled corner facing left. Start directly below it.

1 21m. 4c. Scramble up grassy ledges to the foot of a clean corner-crack. Climb diagonally left to more grassy ledges and thence to a sloping rock platform at the foot of the corner

2 32m. 5b. Take a deep breath and climb the corner. A short excursion left at 8 metres and the use of the crack on the right later may help. The top arrives all too soon.

★**Bold Man, Big Willie** 17 metres E4 6a (15.7.85)

The top of the arête right of *The Corner* forms the line for this route. Start from the grassy ledge at the top of *The Shadow*'s second pitch, by a subsidiary arête at its left end (just right of the top of *The Corner*). Climb the right wall of the arête via a system of shallow grooves and undercuts. (Peg at 5 metres, then poor wire placements to a pinch grip 5 metres higher, near the arête.) Finish directly up the wall.

★**The Shadow** 60 metres E3 (27.4.62)

A bold, quality climb, although the real technical difficulties are compressed into one fierce section in the middle pitch. The rounded arête right of *The Corner* has two prominent overhangs and a large ledge; start directly below it.

1 23m. 4c. Climb a shallow groove and twin cracks until able to move right across the base of the arête to a stance below the first overhang.

2 22m. 5c. Climb a shallow groove on the left for 6 metres. Move right across the steep, suspect wall; then continue up to the second overhang. Turn this on its right-hand side and climb the groove above to the large grassy ledge. Small flake belays. A superb pitch.

3 15m. 4c. Move right for several metres, and reach a sloping ramp to finish.

★★**Mordor**   47 metres   E4 6a   (1969)

A superb, sustained, and difficult route with some worrying moments up the clean thin crack splitting the wall right of *The Shadow*. Belay at the foot of the crack. Climb the thin crack and then the slight groove above to give a surprisingly bold outing; difficulties are continuous, and protection is spaced.

Terrace Crack   48 metres   Very Severe   (1931)

Worthwhile. At the extreme right-hand end of The East Buttress, where the cliff tapers off (just right of *Mordor*) are prominent twin cracks a few feet apart. Start in a corner just above the path and below the cracks.

1 24m. 4b. Climb the crack above the little starting-corner and ledges on the right to the foot of a groove (belay possible). Go directly up the groove to a stance and belay below the left-hand crack.

2 24m. 4c. Climb the crack for 11 metres and, after a short diversion on the left, re-enter the crack where it widens into a chimney. Either continue up the chimney or, better, take the left edge to a short slab leading to the Eastern Terrace.

The East Buttress Girdle

                      255 metres   Hard Very Severe   (3 pts aid) (10.5.53)

A rather outdated expedition, which crosses the buttress from left to right. The difficulty is not sustained, and some bush-whacking and abseiling is needed. An adventure nevertheless. Start as for *Sunset Crack* (page 55).

1 13m. 4a. *Llithrig* pitch 1.

2 22m. 5a. *Llithrig* pitch 2 (with the pendulum).

3 22m. 4c. Traverse right for 6 metres, descend slightly, and then follow the obvious rising line across into *Pigott's Climb*. Climb the chimney to The Pinnacle.

4 24m. 4c. Traverse right under the nose and climb the wall on the right to a long ledge. Go along this and reverse *The Crooked Finish* into *Chimney Route*.

5 22m. 4b. Make a descending traverse to the right; then go round the arête and climb the groove of *Diglyph* to a large flake. Traverse right, and go down to a grassy corner.

6 22m. 5a. Go down the crack on the right and make a long descending traverse to the right by reverse mantelshelves. Ascend a system of grooves and ledges on the right to belay on the large grassy ledge below *Jelly Roll*.

7 30m. From a large flake on the right, abseil down to the ramp on *Vember*. Amble up this to a belay by *Curving Crack*.

8 20m. 4b. Step into *Curving Crack* and climb it to a stance on the slab on the right.

9 6m. Step up and traverse around into *Pedestal Crack*.
10 30m. Abseil to the top of The Pedestal.
11 40m. 5a. Descend a little and make an ascending traverse into *The Corner*, which is climbed to finish. This pitch can be made easier by scrambling across ledges to the foot of *The Corner* – not as much fun.

★Rupert Road 158 metres E6 (28.4.87)

A tremendous expedition, which girdles the buttress from right to left, tracing a difficult-to-follow line across the upper walls. The first ascent was made on sight. Difficulties are maintained throughout the route and the views are superb. Both members of the party should be competent and brave, and swinging leads (or leaders) is advised. All pegs were ancient at the time; most have now gone! Start to the right of *Mordor*.

1 32m. 6b. Follow quartz breaks to join *Mordor*. Move diagonally down to a foot-traverse going across to the arête (rest; peg). Then make a downward traverse across into the corner. Spike belay.
2 30m. 6b. Move across and climb *Silhouette* to just below the peg. Traverse the compact wall to its left, linking a prominent foothold and an angular side-pull with a high crescent hold (out of view from *Silhouette*). Move down to *The Troach* belay.
3 10m. 5a. Continue across a break to belay in *Curving Crack*.
4 36m. 6a. Start up *Medi* to gain spiky flakes on the left. Move down to a peg, and so into *Vember*. Follow the faint weakness down and across into *November*; climb this for 5 metres, and make an undercut traverse left into *Jelly Roll*.
5 30m. 6b. Climb to a bulge, undercut left, and layback down and round into *Blancmange Sandwich* (crux), a trifle gripping. Follow a ramp out leftwards and go up to a crack. Traverse wildly left to a 'White Wand' type finish. Belay on nuts, 3 metres above a peg.
6 30m. 5b. Finish up the arête – light relief after the horrors that have gone before.

★★Eastern Terrace Moderate 140 metres (1798)

A way can be forged up the Eastern Terrace, most difficulties being passed early on. This was the UK's first recorded rock-climb, the first ascensionists having a botanical bent. A great, scrambly outing needing sure-footedness when carrying a sack, and care should always be taken not to dislodge rocks onto climbers below. Now the recommended descent route.

★Eastern Terrace Winter I/II

Follow the summer line.

Direct Start Winter IV

Climb up the ice smear at the right-hand side of The Middle Rock, below The Black Cleft.

The Middle Rock

Below the bottom section of the Eastern Terrace, and under The Boulder, is a subsidiary buttress some 60 metres high and triangular in shape, with a wet cave at its left-hand end. It is deceptively steep, ribbed with vertical grooves, and capped by a gentle grassy shoulder rising up to the foot of The Boulder. Unfortunately, this part of the cliff is usually damp or seeping. There are three major grooves, all much harder than they look.

Moonshine   65 metres   Hard Very Severe   (30.3.57)
This follows the left-hand of the three obvious grooves with a deviation at half height when the going gets tough. Start directly below the groove.
1 12m. Go leftwards up over ledges to a stance about 6 metres below the corner proper.
2 30m. 5a. Climb up into the corner, and follow it to the overhang at 22 metres. Traverse left to a grassy ledge, then further left to another grassy ledge.
3 23m. 4b. Climb the shattered chimney and its overhang. Traverse right, back into the main corner, and continue up it to a rightward exit at the top.

★Direct Finish   45 metres   E1 5c
Much the best way of doing the route; the hard section is very short. Follow pitch 2 up to the overhang at 22 metres. An insecure struggle round this (the peg has long since turned to dust) and then an awkward pull gain the easier continuation above.

Birthday Crack   56 metres   Hard Very Severe   (19.6.32)
The middle groove gives a pleasant climb; by far the most amenable of the three. Start below the right-hand arête of the groove.
1 32m. 4b. Climb up on good holds, trending left, and avoiding difficulties by moving left. A tricky move up leads to a constricted stance in the bottom of the groove.
2 24m. 5a. Climb the groove above (much steeper than it looks). Bridge up until it is possible to step right onto a good hold. Finish up grass and rock on the right.

Bridge Groove   40 metres   E1 5a   (25.10.31)
The entry to the right-hand groove is steep and poorly protected. Start directly below the groove. Boldly climb the initial wall, past the remnants of a peg, to enter the groove; the angle now eases. The back of the groove is filthy, but mercifully short, soon leading to a rightward exit onto grass.
Variation
Arête Alternative   40 metres   E1 5b
A more pleasant way, avoiding the slimy groove. Climb boldly up to enter the groove. Continue up a crack in the left wall, and finish just right of the arête.

The shallow groove on the right has also been climbed at around HVS.

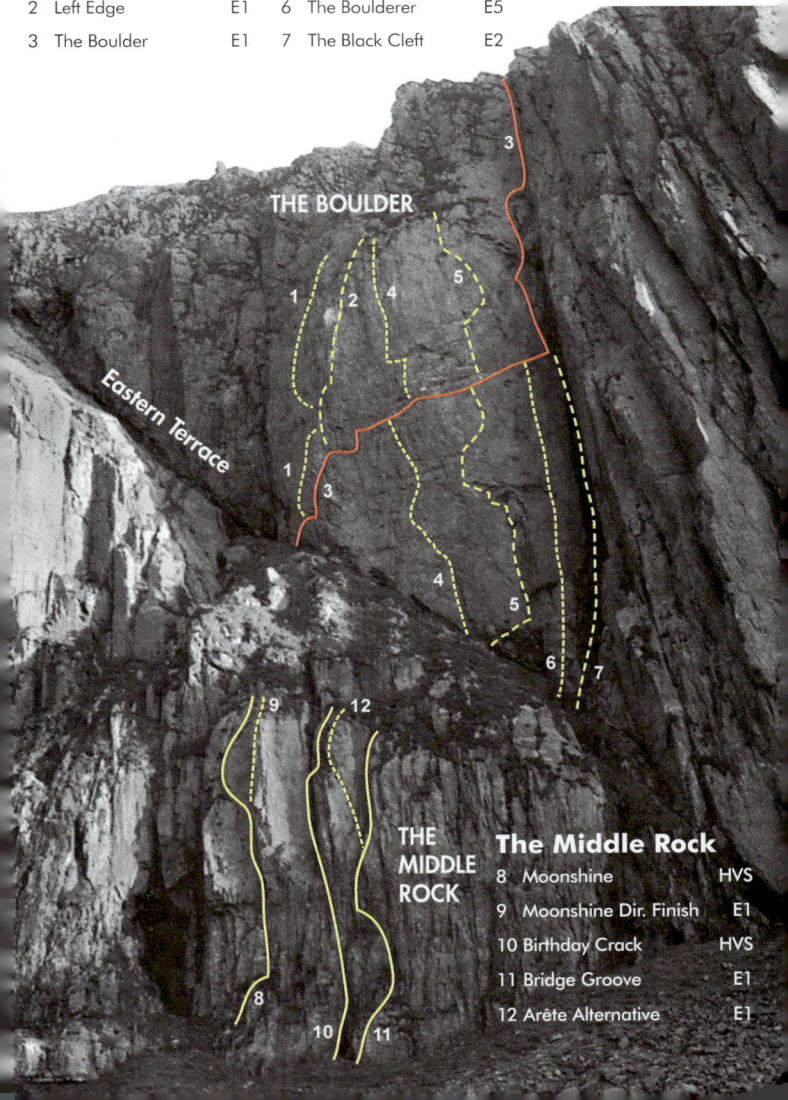

The Boulder

THE BOULDER

Eastern Terrace

THE MIDDLE ROCK

The Middle Rock

The West Buttress

The huge leaning triangle of rock that sits centre-right of Clogwyn Du'r Arddu, to the right of the Eastern Terrace, is The West Buttress. With a height approaching 160 metres the left-slanting slabs of The West Buttress give long, left-trending routes that can easily fill a whole day.

The base of the buttress is guarded by enormous overhangs, which make most climbs difficult of entry. A separate facet of the buttress, on the left directly above The Middle Rock, is called The Boulder, a sea of overlapping slabs separated from the West proper by a very obvious straight, black, wet groove – *The Black Cleft*.

The rock in general is good and not as slaty as it appears from a distance. Flinty rhyolite, in the main the base, is amazingly bedded on broken, fossiliferous limestone and thus eroded into the bounding overhangs. The routes, therefore, are good, often superb, particularly when the rock is unbroken by grassy platforms and kept clean by traffic.

The Eastern Terrace provides the easiest, recommended, and usual descent. The Western Terrace *can* also be descended, but it is much more dangerous than its Eastern counterpart – especially since the huge rockfall in 1986 (see page 144).

The Boulder

Prominus   40 metres   E1   (7.7.73)
A poor and serious route which follows the obvious hanging slab, up the Eastern Terrace from The Boulder; unbalanced, in that the poorly-protected start is much harder than anything encountered during the subsequent meander through turf and rock above.
1 20m. 5a. Make nerve-racking moves via a large hold to gain the overhanging prow at the foot of the slab. Move up to a block, and step right along the lip of the overhang to reach easier-angled rock. Climb this to belay on small nuts in a recess. A scary pitch.
2 20m. Follow the obvious rake up left to a wall. Traverse back right above the belay and climb the short wall to the top.

Adam's Rib   60 metres   Very Severe   (25.8.73)
A slight route up the prominent right-angled corner with a crack at its apex, to the left of *East Wall Climb*. Start at the foot of the corner.
1 22m. 4b. Climb the corner-crack for 12 metres. Follow its continuation diagonally right to ledges. Move left under the rib to belay in a small grassy bay.
2 15m. Move down right and climb the rib to a grassy ledge. Climb diagonally left up grass to belay at a large boulder.
3 23m. 4a. Move down right and climb the continuation rib. At half height, step round to the right and finish up a crack.

East Wall Climb   28 metres   Very Difficult   (9.05)
The climb is very short, and starts just above the short gully section of the Eastern Terrace to follow an obvious break in the wall. The climbing is really just a way of gaining the hanging gully above.
1 8m. Climb a steep little rib on the left of the main break to a ledge at 8 metres. Turn right into the corner (stance). Alternatively, reach the ledge by a traverse from the left (harder).
2 12m. Climb a short wall to a chimney. Go up this; then quit it behind the chockstone.
3 8m. Step left and climb the easy crack.
The climbing is now over, and the break continues to the top as a rather exciting scree-filled gully.

Illegal Eagle   90 metres   E3   (30.3.74)
A worrying voyage up the undercut wall and prominent crack, just around from *Left Edge*. Start just up from *Left Edge*, 2 metres right of the lower end of a cave, below a prominent jug about 2 metres up the bulging wall.
1 45m. 5b. Climb the bulging wall and continue to a small loose pedestal at 8 metres. Move left to a shallow crack; then head diagonally up rightwards to a ledge at 18 metres (poor protection). Climb up to another ledge, and traverse left to below a crack. Follow this over a bulge and continue up the groove to a grassy platform. Sustained.
2 45m. Climb the easy chimney and continue by loose scrambling to the top.

Flintstone Wall   52 metres   E1   (7.70)
Another scary route, linking the start of *Left Edge* with a finish up the groove left of *Illegal Eagle*. Start immediately left of *Left Edge*.
1 22m. 5a. Follow an ascending traverse line leftwards for 6 metres onto the steep face, until a vague crack is reached. Climb this for 6 metres; then bear back right and climb the wall (crux of *Left Edge*) to a ledge. Peg belay.
2 30m. 5a. Traverse several metres left to a fine groove, and climb it to belay at a loose ledge on the right.
Steep scrambling remains.

★★Left Edge   97 metres   E1   (17.4.54)
A quality, quick-drying route, which should be more popular than it is. It follows the left edge of the main face of The Boulder. The difficulty varies according to the exact line taken, and the climb, like all other routes on this part of the cliff, is poorly protected. Start at an obvious break directly below the edge.
1 12m. 4c. Climb directly to a small stance and peg belay.
2 40m. 5a. Step round the edge on the left and ascend to a ledge at 10 metres. Take the short wall above (crux) to another ledge. Step right onto the front of The Boulder and go up for a metre or two. Move back left into a groove on the edge, or continue straight up the front (harder). Climb the groove to a grassy rake leading easily to good belays.
3 45m. An amalgam of steep grass, rock, and heather gives an anti-climactic finish – unless wet.

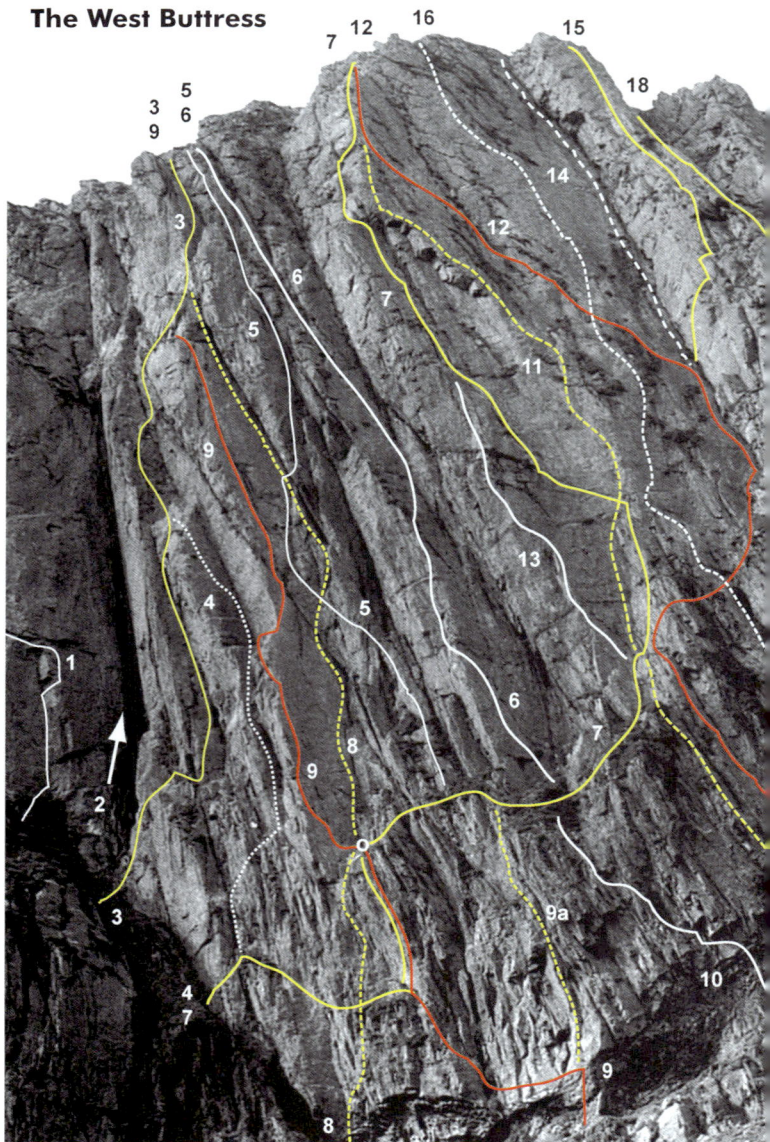

The West Buttress

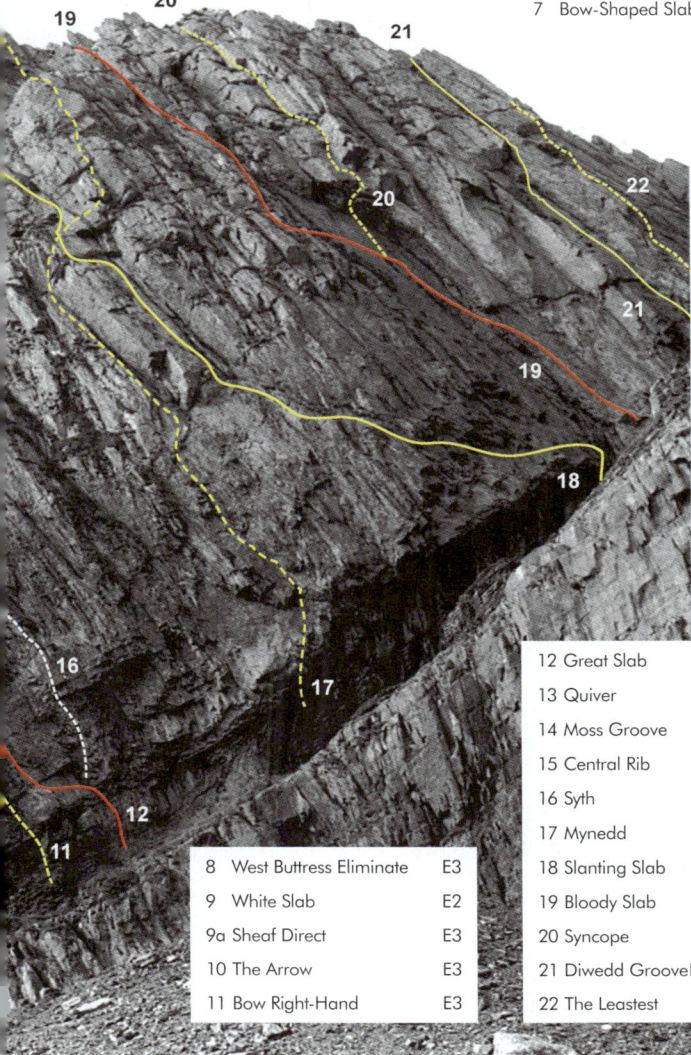

| 1 | The Boldest | E4 | 3 | Longland's Climb | VS |
| 2 | The Black Cleft | E2 | 4 | Gecko Groove | E3 |

5	Sheaf	HVS
6	Narrow Slab	HVS
7	Bow-Shaped Slab	HVS

12	Great Slab	VS
13	Quiver	E5/6
14	Moss Groove	HVS
15	Central Rib	VS
16	Syth	E2
17	Mynedd	E3
18	Slanting Slab	E4
19	Bloody Slab	E3
20	Syncope	E5
21	Diwedd Groove	E2/A2
22	The Leastest	E1

8	West Buttress Eliminate	E3
9	White Slab	E2
9a	Sheaf Direct	E3
10	The Arrow	E3
11	Bow Right-Hand	E3

★★★**The Boulder**   109 metres   E1   (28.10.51)

An excellent route, which breaks out from *Left Edge*, taking the obvious traverse-line across the front face of The Boulder into the upper reaches of *The Black Cleft*. The climbing is serious, but technically quite straightforward and on good rock; another outing where widely-spaced protection is par for the course.

1 12m. 4c. *Left Edge* pitch 1.

2 40m. 5a. A long rising traverse leads away to the right: gain this awkwardly, and then follow it for 10 metres. Mantelshelf onto a slightly higher traverse-line and continue delicately rightwards, crossing a smooth, easy-angled scoop, to reach large holds. These soon lead up to a small stance and flake belay beside *The Black Cleft*.

3 12m. 5a. Move into *The Black Cleft* and climb to the overhang. Swing left to a ledge and muscle round the upper part of the overhang via a shattered crack. Belay immediately.

4 45m. Scramble up the grassy gully to the top.

Variation

The Moscow Variation Finish

3a 15m. 4c. Avoid the shattered crack by traversing across the slab on the left, then ascending direct.

★★**Gemini**   74 metres   E4   (6.70)

A fine twin to *The Boldest*, coming second to it only in its history. Protection is rather spartan. Start 6 metres left of *The Boldest*, below a shallow slender groove.

1 32m. 5c. Climb the groove to a small ledge. Trend left and go up to a shallow groove (peg). Step left and ascend to *The Boulder* traverse. Belay a little higher.

2 42m. 5c. Climb up to a tiny ledge below a small roof. Traverse 6 metres left to a groove (avoiding the upper wall) and take the groove to easy ground.

★★★**The Boldest**   45 metres   E4 5c   (21.9.63)

One of the routes that have marked this cliff out as a forcing-ground for psychologically testing experiences. Difficulties are not excessive but, since the demise of runner placements on the upper wall (resulting in a spectacular 40 metre-fall), a dread air has returned. Start just left of the prominent groove cutting the lower right part of *The Boulder*. Traverse into the groove and climb it to a large flake. Move right onto the arête and go up to the level of the overhang and a tape runner. Traverse left under the overhang to a small ledge. Climb the wall above, trending slightly left to reach a shallow depression. Step right and go up to a dubious small flake (runner). Make a difficult, slightly leftward move up to an incut hold (crux); then move up to follow a line of handholds diagonally left to *The Boulder* traverse. Cross this to belay a few feet higher in a shallow niche. Finish up *The Boulder*, or better:

The Boldest (E4)
The West Buttress
Climber: Karin Magog
Photo: Steve Crowe

★The Direct Finish   38 metres   E3 5c

This very good pitch is by far the best way of finishing the parent route. Climb the wall above the belay, making for the obvious left-facing groove; this proves to be both technical and delicate, but the difficulties soon ease. Scramble up over grass and loose rock for 15 metres to belay. Care should be taken to avoid dislodging rocks onto the second.

★The Boulderer   72 metres   E5   (29.8.79)

A fierce route, which squeezes up the faint line between *The Boldest* and *The Black Cleft*. The scene of another huge fall. Start from the foot of *The Black Cleft*.

1 52m. 5c. Climb easily up, trending leftwards to a horizontal grassy ledge. Step right to the base of an obvious thin crack (belay advisable). Climb the crack and a shallow groove to a small overhang. Surmount this rightwards to gain a vague rib, which is followed to a spike. Step left; then go straight up to join *The Boulder* traverse at a smooth scoop (45 metres of rope from the ground!). Continue easily up to a spike, and belay on *The Boulder.*

2 20m. 5b. Traverse 5 metres left; then climb directly up the steep slab to easy ground.

★★★The Black Cleft   111 metres   E2   (4.5.52)

This is the attractively repulsive, obvious, seeping corner formed where the right edge of The Boulder abuts the vast overhanging wall at the start of The West Buttress proper, and it gives a masochistic outing.

1 12m. At the foot of the corner is a pillar about 12 metres high; scramble up the dry corner on its right-hand side to a stance on top.

2 20m. 5c. Step into the corner proper. A war of attrition now ensues: jam and squirm strenuously up to a small stance and belays. Wet suits are optional for this pitch (and the next)!

3 22m. 5c. The corner above is slightly easier but the vegetation more abundant. Claw up through a mini Matto Grosso jungle to a chimney below the first overhang. Turn this by the crack on its right (strenuous). Take the technical groove above to arrive thankfully at a stance and flake belays on the left; junction with *The Boulder*.

4 12m. 5a. Climb the corner up to the overhang. Swing left to a ledge and turn the upper part of the overhang by a shattered crack (desperate if you are wringing wet from the lower pitches). Belay immediately.

5 45m. Grassy scrambling up the gully leads to the finish.

The Direct Start

1a 12m. 5b. The main crack on the left side of the pillar gives a few extra gruelling feet of ascent, whilst in extremely dry conditions one can climb the slab just left of this pitch at a similar standard.

★★★The Black Cleft   Winter VII   (1963)

Best climbed in a very cold spell, when a thick column of ice forms in the lower corner and the route gives one of Britain's best Grade VIIs. Easier in lean condition.

The Great Slab

The main face of West Buttress to the right of The Boulder comprises an impressive but confusing array of mainly tall, narrow slabs, with *Great Slab* itself at its centre.

Route-finding is made more puzzling by the fact that some climbs start at the base of the slabs, while others traverse across them from the foot of the Eastern Terrace on the left.

Past guides have tended to present the climbs in the order taken by their 'parent' slabs. However, it has been decided here to follow the more normal left-to-right order of starting-points. Thus these are more easily located and, from them, careful adherence to the text descriptions and the diagrams should enable the correct lines then to be followed without problems.

★★★**Longland's Climb**   126 metres   Very Severe   (5.28)

This, the original breach in The West Buttress, gives a very enjoyable and classic outing. It follows the first feature on the main face of the buttress, a slender slab with an overarching right wall, before it breaks out to the right for its final pitch. The climbing is continuously exposed and has an air of seriousness. The first pitch is optional and rather unpleasant. It is usually avoided by scrambling across to the foot of the slab from the Eastern Terrace, at the foot of *The Boulder*. However, purists will want to start below Middle Rock, to the left of a wet grass fall coming from the end of the Eastern Terrace at a greasy groove.

1 22m. 4a. Climb the wet groove to a large flake. Move out and go up to the terrace. Scramble up to the foot of *The Black Cleft*. Climb a short gully in the corner and traverse right past a huge block to the foot of the slab.

2 28m. 4a. Go straight up the slab and corner-chimney past small stances to a larger one in the chimney.

3 12m. 4b. Continue in the chimney until it is possible to move out onto the right wall. Traverse back left – faith and friction – to the main slab and go up the easier groove to a stance on the right. Or avoid the 'faith and friction' slab by continuing straight up instead of moving right.

4 36m. Continue up easily until able to move right onto a large crevassed ledge.

5 28m. 4c. The Overhang. From the right-hand end of the ledge, climb the strenuous overhang on large well-spaced holds. Optional belay a few metres above. Move right and go up a short chimney to easy ground.

4a The Direct Finish 30m. HVS 5a. From the stance, step left onto the continuation slab. Climb this with poor protection and follow the loose chimney to the top. A very good pitch in a superb position.

4b The West Direct Finish 30m. HS. From the stance, traverse right round the edge and go up across the slab, then back left. Steep and exposed. Continue up the short chimney to easy ground.

★★Longland's Climb   Winter VIII (2.86)

A long and superb winter expedition, and probably unrepeated at the time of writing. A winter ascent gives continuous difficulty with the crux on the top pitch.

The next four climbs are all reached from the top of the (avoidable) first pitch of *Longland's Climb*.

Gecko Groove   46 metres   E3 (17.5.59)

An attractive route, though always a little dirty. Nestling between *Longland's Climb* and the prominent hour-glass-shaped *White Slab* is a very narrow slab which widens out at half height. Descend from the first stance of *Longland's Climb* to a small stance directly below the narrow slab.

1 24m. 5b. Make a difficult entry into the groove from the left (bold). Continue up to the overhang, which is turned on the left. Ascend more easily to a small stance. Junction with *White Slab*.

2 22m. 5b. Climb the groove to a runner at 10 metres. Make a difficult traverse left to the arête. Climb this to the stance on *Longland's Climb* (top of pitch 3).

Finish up *Longland's Climb*, The Direct Finish being appropriate.

Variation

2a 22m. 5c. Climb the groove for a few feet to a sloping ledge. Traverse left along the ledge to the arête; then climb straight up to join the original route.

★★★Sheaf   146 metres   Hard Very Severe (17.10.45)

A cracker, one of the best, finding its way between *White* and *Narrow Slabs*. A route-finding masterpiece. Start 10 metres below the stance of *Longland's Climb*, at the foot of Eastern Terrace and just above the wet wall, at a grassy crack.

1 20m. 4c. Climb the crack and its continuation to a small stance under the rib of *White Slab*.

2 15m. 4c. Make a tricky move to gain a sloping ledge on the right and step round onto *White Slab*. Move right for a metre or two; then descend awkwardly to a ledge at the foot of the slab (Linnell's Leap). Good flake belays higher on the right.

3 25m. Descend a little; then move round the edge on the right to reach a more broken slab. Climb this via some grass to a ledge. Stance possible. Continue up to a corner stance above cracked blocks.

4 22m. 4b. Step out left, and climb the steep slab, making for a small ledge on the arête. Move round into a small broken chimney. Traverse left onto *White Slab* and go up to a belay.

5 20m. 4c. Move right and climb a short groove awkwardly to good runners below the overhang. Reach up for a good hold on the right arête. Make a bold swing out right and step into a groove on the right. Go up this to a small ledge, and belay in the groove above.

6 20m. 4c. Make an enormous stride across to a good hold on the right. Pull round the corner onto *Narrow Slab* and climb this to a stance.

7 24m. Grassy scrambling leads to a stance above the overhang on *Longland's Climb*.

Narrow Slab 148 metres Hard Very Severe (18.8.33)
This takes the obvious narrow and uniform slab just to the left of the
central mass of *Bow-Shaped* and *Great Slabs*, and is reached by a
traverse from the left across the foot of *White Slab* (as for *Sheaf*). The main
pitches are hard but short, though Linnell's Leap will probably prove as
tricky as anything above.

1, 2 35m. 4c. *Sheaf* pitches 1 and 2.

3 14m. Descend a little and go round the edge to ledges. Follow these up
and across to the foot of *Narrow Slab* itself. Belay a little higher on the far
side of the slab.

4 15m. 4c. Climb the thin crack in the slab to a slight bulge; then move
diagonally left to the edge. Go up steeply to an awkward stance.

5 12m. 4c. Ascend easily for a short way; then move right to the foot of a
flake. Climb this to a small stance and belay.

6 12m. 4a. Take the shallow groove in the slab, then a wider crack
above to a good stance.

7, 8 60m. Clamber easily up grassy cracks to a stance at 30 metres or
so. Continue to the top of the cliff. An alternative is to move across onto
Bow-Shaped Slab at the top of pitch 6 to minimize the grassy climbing.

★Bow-Shaped Slab 190 metres Hard Very Severe (20.9.41)
The entry is often dirty, unobvious, and unpleasant, making a way
rightwards to join *White Slab* at the start of its second pitch. From the start
of *Sheaf* and *Narrow Slab* at the bottom of Eastern Terrace, scramble up to
an obvious grassy ledge.

1 8m. 4c. Climb across the steep slabby groove on good holds to the
corner on the right. A metre or two of difficult ascent gains large spikes.

2 28m. 4b. Traverse round the rib on the right and go diagonally up into
a long deep crack (junction with *White Slab*). Climb this and broken rocks
to a stance beside *White Slab*.

3 28m. Descend a little and swing right again round the rib to ledges.
Cross these to the foot of Narrow Slab and continue further to the cave
stance on *Great Slab*.

4 24m. 4a. Step round to the right as for *Great Slab* and ascend to a
stance.

5 36m. 5a. The crux traverse can be climbed in either of two ways:
traverse 3 metres left and make a difficult pull up onto the diagonal line;
or traverse across with your feet on the high line (much easier but a little
bolder). Continue up cracks past various ledges to a flake belay in the
middle of the slab. A fine pitch.

6 30m. 4b. Climb a thin crack in the same line to a stance just above the
final skyline edge of the slab.

7 36m. Climb out of the recess on the left; then move back right onto the
rib to finish as for *Great Slab*.

★★★**West Buttress Eliminate**   156 metres   E3   (3.6.62)

A superb route, possibly the best on the West? It takes the red groove directly below *White Slab* before continuing up the corner-grooves immediately right of that route. The main interest centres around Walsh's Groove, an outstanding 'back-and-footing' pitch high on the climb. Start at the foot of the red groove directly under *White Slab*.

1 39m. 5c. Climb the groove for 6 metres; then move steeply out right on large, widely-spaced holds leading up to grassy ledges. Go over these to a large block. Belay possible. Climb the steep slabby groove just to the left; then move slightly left and go up to a short wall. Continue up to the right to spike belays at the foot of *White Slab*. A poorly-protected pitch with some shuddering holds.

2 34m. 5b. Climb the groove above past a hard move at 10 metres; then take the diagonal crack to belay at a flake on the right.

3 45m. 5b. Walsh's Groove. Climb the short groove above (as for *Sheaf*, which then wisely escapes to the right around the rib). Fight up to the top of the main groove using every conceivable jamming, wedging, and back-and-footing technique – not to mention the odd expletive or two. A unique and brilliant pitch, which provides much amusement to spectators on *White Slab*. Belays on the left, as for *White Slab*.

4 10m. 4a. *White Slab* pitch 6.

5 28m. 4c. From the right-hand end of the ledge, climb the overhang to finish as for *Longland's Climb* or, better, take The Direct Finish (5a).

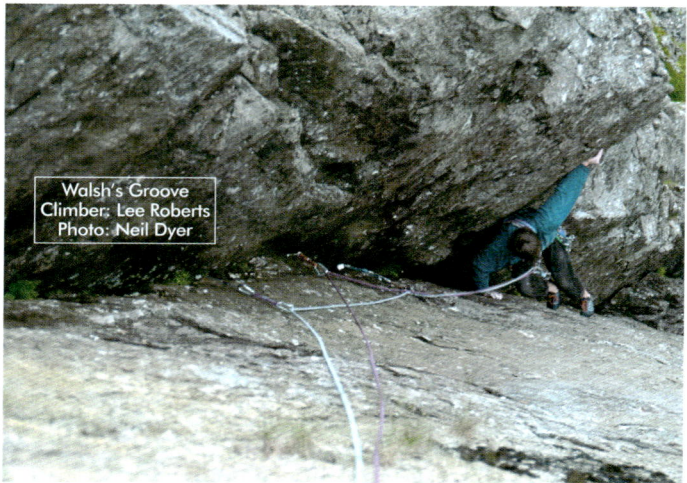

Walsh's Groove
Climber: Lee Roberts
Photo: Neil Dyer

Variations

3a 45m. 5b. Instead of moving left at the top of Walsh's Groove, swing right onto the arête, about 6 metres below the Cannon Hole. Climb the arête and trend left to belay.

★**Lampard's Variation**   70 metres   E2

3b 40m. 5b. Instead of climbing to the large ledge at the top of *White Slab*, climb straight to the crevassed stance of *Longland's Climb*.

4b 30m. 5c. Climb the overhanging crack/groove above. When the angle eases, pull out onto the right arête and continue to the top.

★★★**White Slab**   175 metres   E2   (19.4.56)

The elegant hour-glass-shaped slab right of *Longland's Climb* gives a magnificent expedition of exceptional quality. Though the technical difficulty is not very high (each pitch being E1 only), the combination is long, sustained, and only moderately protected. Lassoing the spike on pitch 4 adds fun to the proceedings but may feel a little unnecessary. About 30 metres right of where the Eastern Terrace runs into the ground, the overhangs are split by a wet grassy groove (this is right of the large red groove where *West Buttress Eliminate* starts). Just to the right of this, a small shattered pinnacle leans against the overhangs.

1 20m. 5b. Step off the pinnacle and make a delicate leftward traverse into a shallow groove (hard and bold). Continue left into the next wet groove. Climb this to a large flake belay. Care should be taken to protect the second man on this pitch, which is very difficult to follow.

2 24m. 4b. Climb the groove and crack (the right-hand one) behind the stance, as for *Bow-Shaped Slab*, to belay just above and right of the foot of the main slab.

3 36m. 5a. From the very bottom of the slab, go up for a few metres, then diagonally left to the arête – Linnell's Leap in reverse. Follow the arête past a peg to a good spike at 20 metres. Move delicately right; then ascend the thin crack to a flake (thin tape). Go left round the edge into *Gecko Groove* and move up a metre or two to belay at a small stance. A sustained pitch.

4 21m. 5c. Traverse back to the arête; then boldly climb rightwards into the groove. (A less bold option is first to lasso the spike and use it for protection.) A more adventurous alternative, and the original way, is to lasso the spike and swing in (5a), and then go up to it. Traverse left for 3 metres and ascend to a belay.

5 36m. 5a. Climb straight up near the edge of the slab to a ledge at 20 metres. Continue up, and finish direct to a stance at the top of the slab. Another sustained pitch.

6 10m. 4a. Traverse easily left and go up to the crevassed stance of *Longland's Climb*.

7 28m. 4c. Finish up *Longland's Climb*, although The Direct Finish (5a), which takes the slab on the left, is more in keeping with the lower pitches.

Variations

2a 24m. Traverse diagonally left and ascend the groove. Harder than the normal way.

White Slab (E2), The West Buttress
Climber: Lee Roberts   Photo Neil Dyer

3a 30m. Climb the obvious diagonal crack to the arête, and then the arête above the spike direct. Harder.

★★**3b Redhead's Direct** 45m. E4 6a. From the spike at 20 metres, step right and climb directly up the centre of the slab (thin, sustained, and poorly protected) to reach the security of the lasso spike – an oft-attempted pitch, mainly by off-route leaders.

4a Austin's Variation 20m. E4 5c. From the edge of the slab, continue up the arête for 6 metres (short and fierce). Trend steeply right across an incipient groove to the stance.

5a 42m. 5b. Traverse right from a little above the ledge at 20 metres into the groove (Walsh's Groove). Climb this to the overhang and continue through the Cannon Hole to the crevassed stance.

Sheaf Direct 126 metres E3

An interesting eliminate, finding a very direct way up through the maze of ribs between *White* and *Narrow Slabs*. The first pitch is the one to get the adrenalin flowing: deceptively steep, sustained, technical, and loose!
1 45m. 5c. Start as for *White Slab*, but go up immediately into a small clean-cut groove (wire runners). Climb the groove; then follow the obvious line direct past creaking hollow flakes for 18 metres to easy ground – spooky. Continue easily to belay below Narrow Slab. An awkward, loose, and exposed pitch, which is poorly protected.
2 15m. Scramble left along grass to the broken slab between *Narrow* and *White Slabs*. Climb up over grassy ledges to a stance and block belay, as for *Sheaf*.
3 42m. 5c. Go up to a large corner stance above cracked blocks at 12 metres. Optional belay. Climb straight up the groove to a good resting-place. Step left and climb a thin crack in the slab until it peters out. Continue up the main groove to a sloping foothold. Use holds on the right arête to gain a large spike. Continue more easily up the last few feet to the final stance of *Sheaf*.
4 Whillans' Direct Finish 24m. 5b. Climb the groove with difficulty for 6 metres; there is one very hard move. Go up a subsidiary groove in the right wall until an escape can be made to finish up *Narrow Slab*.

The Arrow 90 metres E3 (15.8.64)

This rarely ascended climb has a permanently wet second pitch. Start 10 metres left of *Great Slab*, where a narrow rib runs up to the overhang.
1 45m. 5b. Move up and diagonally left from the foot of the rib until a step down can be made into a bottomless groove. A tiny 5mm thread protects a sensational swing left onto the steep wall. Pull up onto footholds and move left to avoid the overhangs and bulges above. Climb a steep slab/groove straight up to grass at 35 metres. Move left to belay at the foot of Narrow Slab.
2 45m. 5a. Climb to the top of the greasy and grassy groove bounding the right side of Narrow Slab. A pleasant scramble over the easy upper section or a finish up *Bow-Shaped Slab* remains.

★Bow Right-Hand   168 metres   E3   (29.4.62)
An exposed and committing route with some superb climbing: sustained and delicate. Start 5 metres left of *Great Slab*.
1 36m. 5c. Pull over the initial overhang (hard and poorly protected). Go up leftwards to a small ledge. Continue more easily up the shallow groove to the cave stance on *Great Slab*.
2 24m. 5b. Climb steeply up the scoop above and step right to the stance at the start of the *Bow-Shaped Slab* traverse. Poor protection.
3 36m. 5c. Continue directly up the blunt arête above to a delicate face move at 20 metres (very bold and in a fine position). Continue more easily to a shallow grassy groove, which leads to a small stance and nut belay.
4 36m. 5a. Go straight up for about 15 metres; then traverse left to the lip of the overhangs. Follow these to the stance on *Bow-Shaped Slab*. A fine pitch.
5 36m. Finish easily up the rib as for *Bow-Shaped Slab*.

★★★Great Slab   180 metres   Very Severe   (15.6.30)
This very fine expedition wanders up and across the largest feature of The West Buttress, giving varied climbing with little technical difficulty except at the start, which is quite tricky and needs some finesse. Probably the best route of its grade on the cliff and a great epitaph to its first ascensionist, this being Kirkus's first new route on the crag. The upper pitches of the main slab are much easier, mainly on good holds, though the widely-spaced protection and considerable exposure give them an air of seriousness. Start at an obvious break about 50 metres up the Western Terrace. A small rock pillar leans against the overhangs, below a short slab capped by an overhang and with a long groove on its left.
1 40m. 4c. Climb up onto the slab and place a good runner. Traverse delicately left into the bottom of the long, reddish-coloured groove, and climb it to a large ledge and cave stance.
2 38m. 4a. Go round the edge on the right and ascend for 12 metres. Traverse rightwards to a shallow corner below a small overhang, pull up to the right, and continue over easy ground to belay at the base of the 12-metre corner[1].
3 12m. 4b. Climb the corner, which is often damp. Where it gets difficult at 6 metres, move left to gain the groove above and continue up to a good stance.
4, 5, 6 90m. The remainder is straightforward. Continue pleasantly up the diagonal line to the left across the main slab, passing some loose spikes and small stances. Finish up the far edge.

Variations
The Top Traverse   44 metres   Hard Very Severe
A fine but poorly-protected diversion, just meriting its grade. The crux is the final move into the 12-metre corner.
2a 24m. 4a. From the cave stance, move right and climb directly up the edge to a stance.

---

1 Hitherto, well known as the '40-foot corner'.

Great Slab (VS)
The West Buttress
Climber: Luke Hunt
(aged 14, first visit)
Photo: Don Sargeant

3a 20m. 5a. Continue up for a metre or so to a quartz ledge. Follow the obvious quartz-flecked traverse, which gets harder near the end, rightwards to the foot of the 12-metre corner.

3b The Original Way 22m. 4a. From the stance at the top of pitch 2a, make a descending traverse rightwards across to the shallow corner below the minor overhang. Pull up right and go up easy ground to the base of the 12-metre corner.

Hydrophobia   E4

Start from the belay at the top of pitch 2 of *Great Slab*.

3c 38m. 6a. Step left into a shallow groove and ascend on diminishing holds to a thin pull right to the break (crux). Pull through flakes above to easier ground and go up to belay.

★★Great Slab   Winter VI   (11.1.64)

A great winter expedition following the summer line. It needs much hoar frost and deep snow.

★★★Great – Bow Combination   166 metres   Hard Very Severe

A superb and very direct way up the cliff. Popular, and deservedly so. Climb pitch 1 of *Great Slab*; then continue with pitches 4 to 7 of *Bow-Shaped Slab*.

★Quiver   32 metres   E5/6 6a   (29.6.74)

A very serious pitch, far harder than originally thought and totally committing. Start at the cave stance of *Great Slab* and climb to a ledge at 3 metres. Go directly up, or layback the flake from the right. Go up to a horizontal fault, and continue a short way right of the left edge of the slab to another fault. Go left to a ledge on the arête, slightly right, then left to the arête again, and climb it to arrive quivering at a grass ledge. Belay by some loose blocks. A nerve-racking pitch that has seen very few ascents.

Moss Groove   78 metres   Hard Very Severe   (14.3.53)

The obvious continuation of the 12-metre corner is always greasy. Start at the stance at the top of pitch 3 of *Great Slab* (the top of the 12-metre corner).

1 10m. Traverse diagonally left as for *Great Slab* to a small terrace.

2 40m. 4c. A slightly rising traverse right leads back into the corner where the crack narrows. Go delicately up and left for a metre or two. Continue straight up; then move back into the corner. Ascend to a stance below the large overhangs. (The corner can be climbed all the way on 50-metre ropes, but this is harder – E2 5b.)

3 28m. 4b. Turn the overhangs on the left by the wide crack and finish direct.

Central Rib   96 metres   Very Severe   (5.46)

An energetic route with a strenuous crack, that wouldn't seem out of place on a gritstone edge, preceding easier climbing up the rib right of *Moss Groove*. Start at the top of pitch 2 of *Great Slab* (the base of the 12-metre corner).

1 12m. 4b. Either climb the corner for 5 metres, step right to a ledge, and go up to the foot of the crack; or ascend to the top of the corner, and then descend rightwards to the foot of the crack.

2 28m. 4c. Go up the crack, battle round the stubborn bulge to gain its continuation, and continue up to an optional stance at 16 metres. Take the groove on the left; then pull out right and go across to a break in the rib. Step round and go up to a stance in the grassy gully beyond.

3 24m. Moderate climbing up the crest of the rib leads to a steepening.

4 32m. Go straight up on broken rocks to finish.

Syth   168 metres   E2   (22.5.71)

The name means 'straight' in Welsh, and straight up the centre of The Great Slab is where it goes. Runners are well spaced, especially on pitch 4. Start as for *Great Slab*.

1 28m. 5c. Climb up to the overhang and turn it on its right-hand side. Continue to below a second overhang and climb it with difficulty – some loose rock. Climb up and left until it is possible to move right onto ledges below a groove. Pinnacle stance and belays.

2 36m. 5a. Above and slightly left of the belay is a groove; climb this to reach the end of the traverse on *Great Slab*. Reverse the traverse and go up to belay as for *Bow-Shaped Slab*.

3 38m. 5a. Climb up 2 metres, as for *The Top Traverse*. Continue rightwards along this for 7 metres. Climb directly up to some grassy patches. Continue to a belay in the middle of the slab on the long diagonal traverse taken by *Great Slab*.

4 38m. 5b. Climb straight up past a peg at 11 metres to a peg belay at some shattered blocks. Bold and poorly protected.

5 28m. 4b. Move slightly right and ascend the middle of the slab until a grass traverse leads leftwards to the top.

★Going Straight   164 metres   E2   (17.7.83)

A good companion to *Syth*, climbing direct to the highest part of The West Buttress. Protection is sparse on the upper pitches.

1 28m. 5c. *Syth* pitch 1.

2 32m. 5b. Move diagonally right to enter the second of two narrow slanting grooves. This gives good climbing with difficult and exposed finishing-moves.

3 36m. 5a. Step left and climb a slim column of rock to a small ledge. Continue up the slab until a ragged crack leads to a large grassy patch. Skirt this on the right to reach the final diagonal traverse of *Great Slab*, which is followed for 5 metres to a niche above the grass patch.

4 40m. 5a. Climb directly up above the stance, following a faint depression which runs parallel to and about 6 metres left of *Moss Groove*. Cross the quartz band and continue for 8 metres to reach peg belays at a good foothold. This is level with the conspicuous cracked overhangs on *Syth*, and 5 metres left of *Moss Groove*.

5 28m. 5a. Take a thin diagonal crack leftwards for 6 metres to the crest of a blunt rib. This leads to the top.

Western Terrace

The Western Terrace was once a popular scramble and descent. However, since the enormous rockfall it has become a dangerous place: it is not recommended as a descent and great care should be taken when accessing routes that start from it.

Western Terrace   Winter II

The Western Terrace can be entered below the *Great Slab* start and climbed, given enough snow to bind the debris on the ledges.

★★**Hidden Treasure**   175 metres   E4 (2 pts aid)   (1.9.83)

A long, demanding, and serious expedition, which follows the central part of The West Buttress, taking an intricate and absorbing line through the initial overhangs, then open slabs and grooves above to join the long groove of *Mynedd*, finishing directly up the central pillar through the overhangs avoided by *Central Rib*. Start 6 metres right of the *Great Slab* pillar.

1 32m. 5c. Climb up past a slender, flat-topped spike; then move diagonally left across the bulge to a good foothold. Traverse right into a corner and climb it until a peg in the arête is used for aid to move up onto the wall on the right. Ascend to the large overhang, traverse strenuously to its right-hand end, and pull up into a crack leading to footholds and a peg belay.

2 24m. 4c. Climb diagonally right for 10 metres to reach a small overhang. Step left to gain a shallow slanting groove. Go up it for 10 metres, and exit onto a small ledge.

3 20m. 4c. Ascend a little; then move right and pull into a groove in the hanging rib. Climb the groove and step right onto a long narrow slab (junction with *Mynedd*). Stance 7 metres higher.

4 40m. 5b. Climb the slab and groove above, as for *Mynedd*. Continue with difficulty past the downward-pointing spike to attain a ledge on the left. Climb on up steep rock, trending right, then back left into the groove-line, which leads to small ledges 6 metres below large overhangs.

5 15m. 5a. Using an *in-situ* wire for aid, swing boldly across the large overhang via the left-hand of two cracks.

6 22m. 4c. Climb over blocks and go along the ridge to belay beside a pedestal abutting the final tower.

7 22m. 5a. Climb delicately up the centre of the front face of the tower for 10 metres until a line of holds leads to the left arête, which provides the finish.

Mynedd   152 metres   E3   (29&30.5.66)

Mynedd is Welsh for 'patience'. The start, at the overhang's widest point, was unique, and on the first ascent involved a somewhat dangerous and spectacular prusik from a poor spike which was rumoured to dwell on the lip of the overhangs, though it would seem that this spike is now missing. The original start was 15 metres right of *Great Slab*, between *Great* and *Slanting Slabs*, at the widest point of the overhangs. Start now by climbing pitches 1 and 2 of *Great Slab*, and taking pitch 12 of *The New Girdle* to an abseil from the stance at its end to the lip of the overhang at 10 metres. The ancient peg is **not** a safe belay.

Alternatively, *Lampard's Entry* provides a harder but shorter route to the same point.

1 36m. 5b. Cross the slab on the right; then take a short wall to the overhangs. Jam out across the overhang to a peg in a short corner. Climb the next overhang to a shallow groove on the arête on the left. Go up the groove to an overlap, which forces you out onto steeper rock on the left (peg). Traverse left into another shallow groove and follow it to an overhang. Step round left, cross a short wall to a grass rake, and climb for 3 metres to belay on a large flake.

2 30m. 5b. Descend the rake for 2 metres and cross the wall on the right to steep slabs. Go straight up these to an overhang at 10 metres. Move left onto a narrow overhung slab protected by a small spike runner (originally aid). Climb the slab for 6 metres to a stance and belays.

3 44m. 5b. Climb up behind the belay until the slab peters out. Continue up the obvious groove (or rib just left of it) to a downward-pointing spike. Swing right to the arête; then traverse right, descending slightly across *Slanting Slab*, to another spike in the corner. Move right round the arête and follow a large crack to a stance and belays.

4 12m. 4a. Take a short slab and crack to a stance.

5 30m. Scramble easily up to finish.

Variation

Lampard's Entry 57 metres E2

The belay on the lip of the overhang of *Mynedd* can be reached from much lower on *Great Slab*:

1 12m. Climb *Great Slab* for 12 metres and take a stance where a small ledge crosses the slab.

2 23m. 4c. Traverse right (foothold round the arête); then make a rightward-rising traverse via two grass lumps to rock ribs. Climb down to a 1-metre spike. Move right into *Hidden Treasure*. (Alternatively, start up *Hidden Treasure*.)

3 22m. 5b. Cross the wall on the right as for *Hidden Treasure*; then descend rightwards to gain a flake and undercuts. Move down and right to the rotting peg at the original belay on *Mynedd*.

Spartacus 122 metres E2 & A3   (30.4.66)

A direct, but unpleasant and serious route between *Gael* and *Slanting Slab*. It comprises shattered, hanging blades of rock and is taken on about five dubious pegs – greatly contributing to the climb's lack of popularity. Start 12 metres left of *Slanting Slab* below a prominent crack.

1 40m. A3 & 5b. Climb up a shattered wall to the roof. Launch out across this on shaky pegs in appalling rock. If you manage to reach it, a crack then leads straight up to a small overhang. Move left onto the arête and climb it for 10 metres to join *Slanting Slab* (in the middle of pitch 1). Follow *Slanting Slab* left for 10 metres and then move right to a grassy ledge and peg belay.

2 22m. 5b. Go straight up to reach and climb a shallow groove; then move right at the top to belay as for *Gael*.

3, 4 60m. 5a. *Gael* pitches 3 and 4.

Slanting Slab   137 metres   E4 6a   (9.7.55)
Impressive and atmospheric, though dirty and broken. The route boldly
follows a curving line of weakness across overlapping slabs to ascend the
large groove right of *Mynedd*. After a very difficult entry (usually aided at
E2, as this is more in keeping with tradition but, if done free, much harder
than what is to follow) the climbing is technically straightforward with only
the occasional hard move. Start about 20 metres left of *Bloody Slab* by a
pinnacle standing under the overhang; there is an obvious rock scar
immediately above the lip of the overhang just to the left.
1 36m. 6a. Either free-climb boldly on loose undercuts at 6a; or use aid
to surmount the overhang and to get established with difficulty on the slab
above at the rock scar (5b). Traverse delicately left across a grassy patch;
then go beneath a bulge to attain a grassy rake running up leftwards.
Follow this to a stance and spike belays in a little corner.
2 12m. 4a. Continue up the rake; then step left round the corner to a
flake crack in a large slab. Move up a little to good nut belays in the crack,
though the stance is poor.
3 44m. 5b. Climb the flake to a large overhang. Move left to climb a
narrow quartz slab to another overhang. Step right and pull over into the
groove above. Climb the groove or the right arête, and continue to a good
stance on the right.
4 45m. Scramble up the gully to the top.

Gael   116 metres   E2 (2 pts aid)   (10.6.62)
An interesting climb, which finds a way up through the overhangs and
slabs above the traverse of *Slanting Slab*. Start by the pillar, as for *Slanting
Slab*.
1 20m. 5b. Surmount the overhang with aid (or free at E4 6a), as for
Slanting Slab. Traverse left for 8 metres to a grassy patch. Peg and nut
belays.
2 36m. 5b. Traverse left a metre or two, until it is possible to pull over the
overhang via a thin crack on the left. Go up the slab above, move right
into a crack, and climb it to a grassy rake (stance possible at the top, but
no belay). Continue up the rib above to the overhangs. Step left and down
into a groove; then traverse diagonally left to grassy ledges on the left of
the overhangs. Peg belay.
3 30m. 5a. Climb the wall above. Step left to a groove and climb it to a
grass ramp.
4 30m. Scramble up to finish.

Fibrin   100 metres   E2 (2 pts aid)   (22.8.66)
A nondescript route linking the start of *Slanting Slab* with the large grass
field below and to the left of *Bloody Slab*.
1 20m. 5b. *Gael* pitch 1.
2 44m. 5b. Climb up to the overhang and move right on undercuts
across the foot of a groove to a peg in a slab. Pass this on its left by a hard
move and climb the slab for 6 metres to a doubtful spike. Swing right to
another groove and follow it to a crack below a short slab and overhang.

Go left for a few feet up the slab; then move across to turn the overhang, using good holds on the right. Move left to grass ledges and a peg belay.
3 36m. Take the rib above to join the easy upper section of *Bloody Slab*.

Bloodlust   116 metres   E2   (2 pts aid)   (7.7.84)
A steep and very direct line up the cliff from the *Slanting Slab* entry.
1 44m. 5b. Cross the overhang on aid (or free at E4 6a); then ascend to the next overhangs. Move right to the foot of a long crackline. Follow this through two bulges, and, where it peters out, continue up, moving slightly right, to belay at the top of a large grassy patch.
2 22m. 5b. Climb directly up the slab behind the stance via a thin crack. Surmount the overhang above by its obvious weakness (this is midway between its left end and the prominent wide crack). Continue up the steep slab above to easy ground and a large chockstone belay.
3 50m. Scramble to the top.

Care should be taken on the next section of the Western Terrace, as much of the rock underfoot is still unstable after the 1986 rockfall.

Thrombin   90 metres   E3   (30.5.66)
A serious pitch, open and delicate with little protection. It takes the thin crack in the slab left of *Bloody Slab*. There is some unstable rock. Start lower down the terrace than for *Bloody Slab*, by a shattered pinnacle below a left-facing groove.
1 45m. 5b. Step left and climb the constricted groove to a large sloping hold. Traverse left to the thin crack and climb it for 15 metres to a good resting-place. Continue up to a shallow scoop. Step right; then traverse horizontally left to reach the large grassy ledges on the second pitch of *Bloody Slab*.
2 45m. Finish up *Bloody Slab*.

★★★**Red Slab**   Winter VII   (2.79)
A fine and rare winter outing is the ice smear that forms just below and left of *Bloody Slab*, rejoining that route for its upper pitches, which in winter are both hard.

★★**Bloody Slab**   90 metres   E3   (10.6.52)
A tremendous route, taking a diagonal line up the right-hand side of the large red slab – the section just right of the subsidiary bow-shaped slab – making for the left end of the line of overhangs and a stance at 30 metres before escaping via a long, bold traverse left. Start just above a rock step and below a prominent boulder; good thread belay.
1 30m. 5b. Climb up; then traverse left and continue up to a runner slot at 12 metres. Climb up to the bulge and turn it with difficulty. Step left and follow the flake crack to the triangular overhang. Turn this on the left to a small sloping stance.
2 28m. 5b. Traverse left and go up to a small ledge. Continue leftwards, descending slightly, to grass, and go up the grassy gully on the left.
3 32m. Climb the rib on the left and continue over broken rocks to finish.

Bloody Slab (E3)
The West Buttress
Climber: Paul Stott
Photo: Keith Davies

Variations

Left-Hand Start   60 metres   E2
This avoids the main difficulty of the climb but is nonetheless a fine pitch with slightly better protection.
1a 32m. 5a. Climb diagonally left to the small flake runner. Step across and down a little to gain the small bow-shaped slab. Go up this to the stance on the parent route.
2a 28m. Follow *Syncope* up to the roof before escaping left under this to belay on the normal line.

Grovel   60 metres   E2   (6.76)
The obvious roof-crack above the second pitch of *Bloody Slab*, just left of *Syncope,* is well-named.
1 30m. 5b. *Bloody Slab* pitch 1.
2 30m. 5c. Move left and up, as for *Bloody Slab*, and climb the thin crack up to the roof. Jam out energetically across the flared roof-crack and continue up easier ground above to a belay. Scrambling remains.

Syncope   94 metres   E5   (17.7.71)
A spectacular and extremely serious direct finish to *Bloody Slab*, taking a line through the enormous capping overhang on some dubious rock.
1 30m. 5b. *Bloody Slab* pitch 1.
2 44m. 6a. Climb left and up to a small ledge, as for *Bloody Slab*. Move left again and climb a crack in the slab to the roof. Work up into a groove in the roof on the right (very poor peg runner missing) and climb it strenuously on poor rock to gain the slab above. Move left and go up to a small ledge; then climb up right to a corner and a ledge above. Peg belays.
3 20m. Move left onto the slab and climb to its top. Scrambling remains.

Haemagoblin   90 metres   E3   (2.5.62)
The lower section of the scarp wall forming a once obvious groove right of *Bloody Slab* collapsed in 1986, although its continuation, starting 24 metres up the crag, has remained intact, and the first pitch now takes the bold open slab immediately left of the rock scar. Start as for *Bloody Slab*, just above the rock step.
1 28m. 5c. Instead of moving left (as for *Bloody Slab*), climb straight up the delicate slab making for a prominent slot at 18 metres. Continue up and pull over the overhang to a rest. Step left; then climb the groove to a sloping ledge and nut belays.
2 28m. 5b. Continue up the groove for 10 metres to a chockstone. Traverse left across the slab into a crack. Ascend this and the overhanging crack to a stance and belay.
3 34m. Continue easily up the grassy slab on the left. Scramble up to finish.

Carpet Slab   (14.10.53)
The lower section of the vegetated slab right of *Bloody Slab* collapsed in the great rockfall of 1986 (see page 144).

Diwedd Groove   89 metres   E2 & A2   (6.10.65)
Meaning 'last groove' in Welsh, *Diwedd Groove* is just this. It is described
with its original start, which uses several nuts for aid (a free alternative
once took the now defunct Carpet Slab). Start immediately right of the
rockfall, below some shattered cracks in the overhangs.
1 24m. A2. Climb the cracks with several nuts for aid. Ascend the slab
above and move left into the groove.
2 45m. 5c. Climb the groove, and move left round the first overhang.
Make a difficult move to reach a crack on the right of the second
overhang, and climb it to a chockstone on the lip of the overhang (tape
runner). Make hard moves out onto the right wall; then traverse round the
corner to a stance and belay below another overhang.
3 20m. Traverse right under the overhang and finish up the edge of the slab.

The Leastest   55 metres   E1   (22.5.61/14.8.83)
Slight and not really worthwhile. After a dangerous start, the climbing
becomes easy and artificial. Start to the right of *Diwedd Groove*, where the
terrace almost meets the overhangs.
1 15m. 5a. Climb up over shattered spikes and make worrying moves
left to gain a shallow scoop on the lip of the slab. Climb up, trending
delicately leftwards over loose flakes to a narrow ledge and groove. Climb
this to a grassy ledge.
2 20m. Traverse left easily to the edge and ascend to a belay beneath the
obvious overhang.
3 20m. Turn the overhang on the right and follow the ridge to the top.

★The West Buttress Girdle   283 metres   Hard Very Severe   (21.5.49)
A long expedition, sustained at a good standard; strenuous and
interesting. It follows almost the whole of *Sheaf* and then links the cruxes of
the old West Buttress routes before finishing by a long diagonal traverse
above *Slanting* and *Bloody Slabs*. Begin at the normal start of *Longland's
Climb*, i.e. at the top of its (avoidable) first pitch (page 85).
1 10m. Descend to the right to a stance in the corner, close under the rib
of *White Slab*.
2 15m. 4c. *Sheaf* pitch 2.
3 25m. *Sheaf* pitch 3.
4 22m. 4b. *Sheaf* pitch 4.
5 20m. 4c. *Sheaf* pitch 5.
6 20m. 4c. Make an enormous stride to the right and go round onto the
upper reaches of *Narrow Slab*. Ascend for a short way to a runner; then
descend easily to a stance and belay in the grassy crack.
7 12m. 4c. Descend a short way and step across onto a subsidiary rib on
the right. Cross the groove and go out to a grassy ledge breaking onto
Bow-Shaped Slab. Climb up to a stance and belay 5 metres higher.
8 26m. 5a. Descend again to a grassy ledge at the end of the
Bow-Shaped Slab traverse. Reverse this, keeping your feet in the obvious
diagonal break, to reach a stance at the far end. Climb up to a small
stance a little higher to bring the second man across.

9 20m. 5a. Traverse horizontally across on the quartz-marked line. This gets more difficult towards the end and leads to the grass field below the 12-metre corner. This is *The Top Traverse* of *Great Slab*.
10 12m. 4b. Climb the slabby corner to a good stance.
11 28m. 4c. Descend to the foot of the *Central Rib* crack on the right and climb it to a break in the rib.
12 15m. Scramble easily along the grassy rake across the shallow gully to an exposed step around the rib. Belay 4 metres further along the continuation traverse-line.
13 20m. Continue in the same line on good holds and grass.
14 18m. 5a. The line becomes more serious again. Away on the right is a quartz break above the overhangs of *Bloody Slab*. Traverse across, making for the quartz break, and make an awkward pull past this into a grassy groove. Continue in the same line past a hand-traverse to belay on a cracked block.
15 20m. Make a delicate toe-traverse across a slab with a step-up at the end to a small bilberry ledge. Step round into the deep grassy chimney on the right, and go easily to the top.

The New Girdle   452 metres   E3 (5 pts aid)   (1966)
A very long, difficult, and demanding expedition.
1 12m. 4c. *The Boulder* (*Left Edge*) pitch 1 (page 82).
2 40m. 5a. *The Boulder* pitch 2.
3 16m. 5a. Follow *The Boulder* until it is possible to move right across the wall and down a groove to *Longland's Climb*.
4 24m. 4b. Descend *Longland's Climb* to *Gecko Groove*.
5 22m. Abseil down *Gecko Groove* to the stance on *White Slab*.
6 21m. 5c. *White Slab* pitch 4.
7 20m. 4c. *Sheaf* (and *The West Buttress Girdle*) pitch 5.
8 20m. 4c. *The West Buttress Girdle* pitch 6.
9 12m. 4c. *The West Buttress Girdle* pitch 7.
10 26m. 5a. *The West Buttress Girdle* pitch 8.
11 20m. 5a. *The West Buttress Girdle* pitch 9.
12 30m. 4b. Descend the grassy ledges; then traverse right across a small slab to a corner. Go down 3 metres to a belay on *Mynedd*.
13 24m. 5b. The Link. Climb down a short way and step onto the steep slab on the right. Climb up towards the overhang until it is possible to traverse to a flake in the middle of the slab. Continue by a difficult ascending traverse to join *Slanting Slab* at a grassy ledge. Descend *Slanting Slab* to a belay.
14 15m. 5a. Continue the descent of *Slanting Slab* and reverse its traverse to a grassy ledge.
15 44m. 5b. *Fibrin* pitch 2.
16 12m. 5a. Move right and reverse the top traverse of *Bloody Slab* to a peg belay in the corner.
17 7m. 5b. Descend slightly and go round the corner on the right to a slab. Go right to a bulge and ascend it on flat holds to the belay on *Haemagoblin*.

18 20m. A1. Move right and climb the overhanging wall with five pegs for aid. Pull onto grassy ledges and follow a grassy crack to a belay on a large spike.

19 22m. Descend the grass for 6 metres; then traverse across a slab into *Diwedd Groove* and descend to a belay.

20 45m. Climb out of *Diwedd Groove* onto the next overlap; then descend grooves until under an overhang and on a weakness leading right. Follow this over a small overhang; then go right again to a groove. Follow the groove to grassy ledges. Continue rightwards to the end of the cliff. A very loose pitch.

Variation

For those with a dislike of aid, grass, and loose rock, or if the pegs are missing: from the belay at the end of pitch 17, go to the top by pitches 2 and 3 of *Haemagoblin*.

The Steep Band

Below the Western Terrace is a steep band of smooth rock: in fact, metamorphosed grit! This is split at three-quarter height by a rock terrace parallel to the Western Terrace and called the Giant's Trod. In the lower part of the band is a steep slab running into a large overhanging amphitheatre with twin grooves on the left and fangs on the right. For climbs finishing on the Giant's Trod it is advisable to escape upwards and descend the Western Terrace – this is tricky and needs care.

Giant's Trod   240 metres   Difficult   (9.21)
This is the scrambly rake that runs up rightwards under the more prominent Western Terrace. Forty metres of scrambly climbing up the ramp leads to belays, and a further 200 metres of scrambling to the finish at the top of the Western Terrace.

★★**West End Icefall**   Winter IV
An excellent icefall forms regularly at the left side of The Steep Band.

Metamorphosis   44 metres   Very Severe 4c   (1974)
Left of the thin cracks of *Beano* is a black-looking crack which is often wet, and hardly worth the struggle under such conditions. Climb the crack to the terrace and continue to the top.

Beano   44 metres   E4 6a   (22.6.75)
A good, hard, and reasonably protected route. Start at the second crack left of *The Steep Band*. Climb up easily for 5 metres to a steepening. Make a couple of desperate moves to enter the crack and continue up to a step left into a shallow chimney/niche. Climb this and move left at the top to a small pinnacle. Continue up to thin cracks and traverse right to climb a

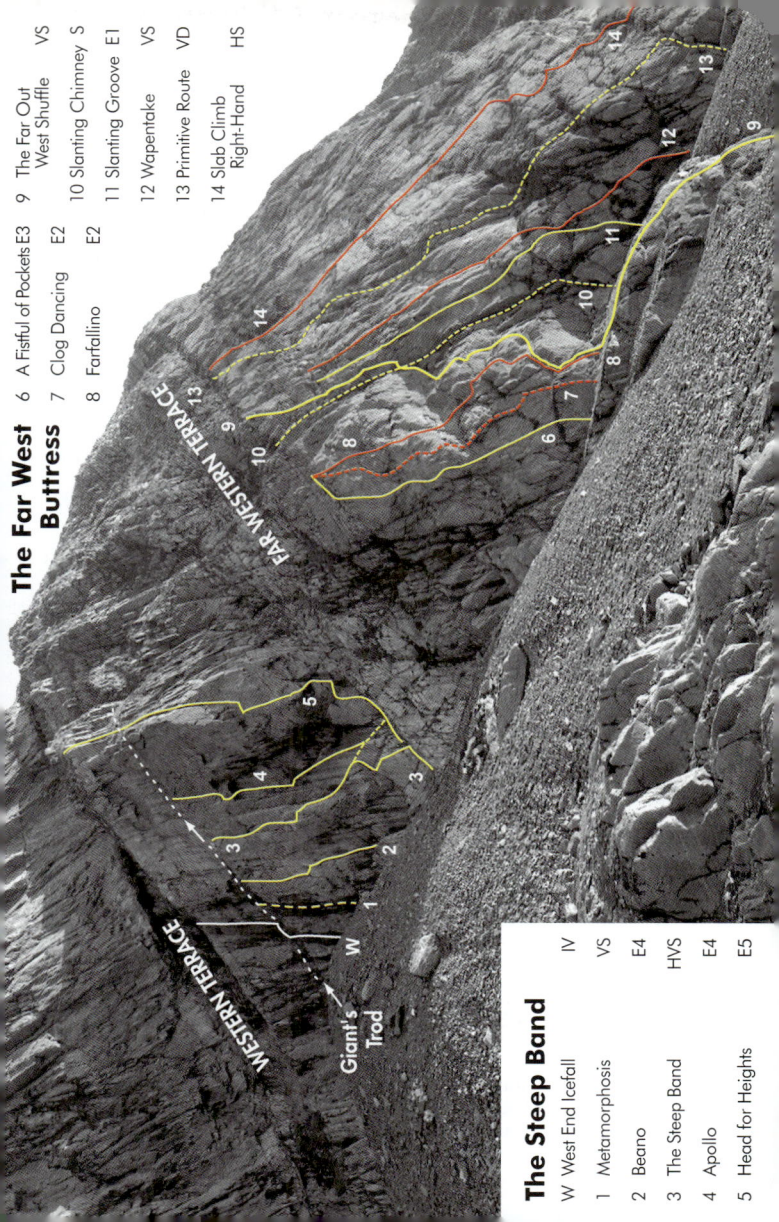

The Far West Buttress

6	A Fistful of Pockets	E3
7	Clog Dancing	E2
8	Farfallino	E2
9	The Far Out West Shuffle	VS
10	Slanting Chimney	S
11	Slanting Groove	E1
12	Wapentake	VS
13	Primitive Route	VD
14	Slab Climb Right-Hand	HS

The Steep Band

W	West End Icefall	IV
1	Metamorphosis	VS
2	Beano	E4
3	The Steep Band	HVS
4	Apollo	E4
5	Head for Heights	E5

FAR WESTERN TERRACE

WESTERN TERRACE

Giant's Trod

thin flake crack and the grooves above to easier ground. Continue to a peg belay on the terrace.

★The Steep Band   44 metres   Hard Very Severe   (10.60)

A traverse across the slab below the overhanging amphitheatre leads to a finish up the two obvious grooves on the left. The difficulty is short-lived and well-protected. Start by scrambling up the right-hand side of the slab until level with the bottom of the right-hand of the two grooves.

1 10m. 4c. Cross the slab awkwardly into a short overhanging corner. Go up this and move left into the bottom of the groove. Good belays. Alternatively, traverse across the slab at a higher level above the corner to the same point (harder).

2 34m. 5a. Climb the steep groove above to a slight bulge at 5 metres. Make difficult moves left around the arête into the other groove. Continue more easily up this and its continuation groove to the Giant's Trod. Scramble off up to the top.

Apollo   48 metres   E4   (23.5.70)

A very steep and strenuous route, accepting the challenge of the overhanging groove on the right of *The Steep Band*. The climb is wet, dirty, and poorly protected. Start at the bottom of the slab, right of *The Steep Band*.

1 16m. 5b. Climb the middle of the slab to a niche under the roofs. Poor belay and no stance.

2 32m. 5c. Make hard moves round the overhang to enter the groove and climb it to the second overhang, which also proves stubborn. Continue up the groove above with some very difficult moves just below the top.

★★Head for Heights   60 metres   E5   (29.6.75)

Very steep, airy, and intimidating; a strenuous and technical route, which breaks through the overhangs to the right of *Apollo*, up the right edge of the amphitheatre. Start right of *Apollo*, at the arête.

1 24m. 6b. From the arête, climb diagonally left up a small slab below the roof. Swing round the edge (this was protected by two poor pegs – now missing); then move left again with difficulty. Exit from the overhangs with even more difficulty and climb a short crack to a stance and belay.

2 36m. 6a. A brilliant pitch. Make very hard moves up and leftwards to leave the stance. Climb up past a loose flake. Traverse right and climb the groove above to the top.

The Far West Buttress

Tucked away down to the right of the main crag lies the Far West, an often forgotten area, but here there are good routes that are more amenable than those on the main crag. If you've enjoyed climbing on the Idwal Slabs and now want something a little more challenging, this could be the place to find it. The buttress gives several climbs of up to Very Severe and should be more popular.

As the whole buttress lacks obvious features between the major lines, route-finding can be interesting, though for the most part this is a less steep area of rock that feels less intimidating. Viewed face-on, it is shaped like a broad diamond, about 150 metres high in the middle. There are three distinct lines on the buttress, *Slanting Chimney* on the left, *Deep Chimney* in the centre, and Forgotten Gully on the right. All three lines slant up from left to right.

Facing more west than north, it comes into the sun much sooner than the main cliff, as early as 2 p.m. in July.

The most obvious way down from the routes is via the Far Western Terrace, parallel to the Western Terrace, but this is **not recommended** as the rock is very poor indeed. Instead, the best method is to scramble up right to the top of the buttress and walk westwards down the ridge scree-slope to a flat grassy area well to the west of the main crag. There, an easy open gully provides a safe and fast descent. At the foot of the gully the path continues down diagonally back to the foot of the crag.

Far Western Terrace   130 metres   Winter III
More appealing in winter, but it needs a good covering of ice in the lower section.

The next two routes take the best of the good rock left of *Farfallino*, although the lines are fairly indistinct. More variations would be possible but rather pointless.

Descent is best made by abseil or via the top of the cliff.

★A Fistful of Pockets   50 metres   E3   5c   (17.5.92)
Start a little to the left of *Clog Dancing*. Climb the slanting grooves up to the roof of *Clog Dancing* (gear). Step back down, then left to the very toe of the small overlap. To get established on the headwall, follow the vague crackline using pockets, and finish boldly in a fine position.

★Clog Dancing   50 metres   E2   (17.5.92)
Start below a large scoop/bay 10 metres left of *Farfallino*.
1 25m. 5b. Climb up into a small scoop, then up a groove to a ledge with spike belays.
2 25m. 5c. A steep pitch climbing directly to the niche in the overlap just left of *Farfallino*. Step left from the belay and climb upwards across a wall to the roof/overlap just left of *Farfallino*. Climb the crack in the roof to another spike belay.
Scramble off.

An excellent (★★) combination is to start up *Clog Dancing* and join *A Fistful of Pockets* at the roof.

3	A Fistful of Pockets	E3
4	Clog Dancing	E2

5	Farfallino	E2
6	The Far Out West Shuffle	VS
7	Slanting Chimney	S

8	Slanting Groove	E2
9	Wapentake	VS
10	Primitive Route	VD
11	Slab Climb Left-Hand	S
12	Slab Climb Right-Hand	HS
13	Deep Chimney	VD

14	Parapet Route	S
15	The Ridler	E5
16	Forgotten Gully	S
17	Sun Dance	VS
18	Trick of the Light	E4

Bwlch Cwm Brwynog

WESTERN TERRACE

FAR WESTERN TERRACE

The Far West Buttress

The Steep Band

1	The Steep Band	HVS
2	Head for Heights	E5

The Far Out West Shuffle 72 metres Very Severe (14.4.88)
Start by a small rib at the toe of a subsidiary buttress, 10 metres left of and below *Slanting Chimney.*
1 24m. 5a. Ascend the crest of the rib for 6 metres; then continue up the bulging wall to a large grassy ledge.
2 24m. 4c. Climb a rib and step right to a good ledge. Take the wall above and continue in the same line to another good ledge. Flake belay up to the right.
3 24m. 5b (one move, which is avoidable). Traverse right over *Slanting Chimney* and climb strenuously up the lower left-hand arête onto a rib. Continue in the same line, with a tricky finish, to a poor belay.

★★Farfallino 68 metres E2 (21.5.88)
The buttress left of *Slanting Chimney.* The route takes the butterfly-shaped (or X-shaped) groove-and-crack-system in the upper wall. Excellent climbing on rough rock. Start as for *The Far Out West Shuffle.*
1 24m. 5a. Climb the rib, move right up a ramp-crack, and take a direct line to the left of the half-way ledge.
2 24m. 5b. Enter the groove from the right (wires) and move up to good holds. Follow these leftwards, and pull through a bulge to easier ground. (This is not the groove *immediately* left of *Slanting Chimney.*) Spike belay.
3 20m. Scrambling remains.

★Slanting Chimney 75 metres Severe (8.9.19)
A good climb, which is difficult in adverse conditions. Start at the foot of the chimney, which is the obvious line on the left-hand side of the Far West.
1 12m. Ascend easily, and follow the crack to a ledge.
2 28m. Climb up into the chimney and follow it strenuously to a large grassy ledge.
3 35m. Continue up the chimney to finish just left of a huge jammed block. Alternatively, climb the clean rib on the left of the chimney.
The Original Finish   50 metres
3a 22m. Climb the chimney for 6 metres and step out right to a ramp leading up right (care should be taken as there is another line leading out right at a lower level). Move up right; then ascend steeply up a rib to a ledge below a small overhang.
4a 28m. Traverse right along the ledge; then follow first a groove, then a rib, making for a deep groove on the right. Climb this to a grassy recess and then finish easily.

★Slanting Groove 78 metres E1 (21.5.88)
Start at the foot of *Slanting Chimney* by a triangular grey slab, aiming for the fine peapod groove left of *Wapentake.* A superb pitch with a lot of scrambling above.
1 20m. 4c. Climb the slab to a bilberry ledge. Step right and take the enjoyable rib to belay as for *Wapentake* at the foot of the groove.

2 22m. 5b. Enter the groove by layback and continue to an easing below the niche. The entry to and escape from the niche give entertaining problems. Belay immediately.
3 36m. Easy climbing up grass and ribs to a shattered zone and dubious spike belays.

Wapentake   109 metres   Very Severe   (25.8.73)
Six metres right of *Slanting Chimney* and parallel to it is a crack which is grassy in its lower section. Start where the grass meets the scree.
1 25m. Follow the crack (on either side) to a grass ledge.
2 15m. 4a. Make a move up the crack; then pull out right onto a ledge. Move 2 metres right, go up a crack, and move back left into the main crack. Go up to a grassy ledge.
3 30m. 4b. Climb easily up to the right for 6 metres to reach a shallow scoop split by a thin crack, which leads to a grass ledge. Move left onto the wall and gain an obvious hold. Go up left to a spike and take the groove above to a large field below a corner. Spike belay.
4 24m. Climb the slab on the left and go up a short rib to a ledge below an overhang. Turn this by an obvious crack on the right. Climb the groove to a small terrace below small overhangs.
5 15m. Easy rock leads to broken ground. Scrambling remains.

★★★Primitive Route   118 metres   Very Difficult   (5.9.19)
A good and varied mountaineering route for its grade. Start at a ledge just left of the foot of the buttress, below a short corner.
1 28m. Climb the corner or make an excursion left up a line of flakes, to a prominent jammed block. Move right a metre or two and climb the leftward-slanting crack, or the fine slabs hereabout near their left edges. Good stance and belay.
2 16m. Climb broken rock to a huge grassy bay below the twin chimneys.
3 24m. Climb the right-hand chimney for 10 metres. Step left and continue up the left-hand chimney. Climb diagonally right to a good stance and peg belay.
4 8m. Go up right to an obvious stance and flake belay.
5 8m. Climb the small corner and the short slab to grass and another belay.
6 24m. Make a rising traverse left across ledges to a short corner. Alternatively, climb the corner above the belay to overhanging rock, and traverse 15 metres left, passing a chimney half-way, to belay on a grassy ledge below the corner (better).
7 10m. Climb the corner to a grassy recess.
The Direct Finish   Very Severe
6a 36m. Climb a small rib on the right of the stance, passing a large grassy ledge on the right. After another 6 metres, gain a smaller ledge below a flake crack. Climb this to where it widens and continue up to small ledges. Go easily up the corner for a short way; then step right and climb the arête.

Primitive Route (VD)
The Far West Buttress
Climber: Chris Naylor
Photo: Nick Dixon

★Slab Climb Left-Hand 166 metres   Severe   (12.9.19)
A pleasant route, though not quite as good as its twin. Start just left of the
toe of the buttress.
1 22m. Climb up leftwards on sloping sills of rock to a small ledge just right
of the starting-ledge of *Primitive Route*. Climb the cracked wall above for 3
metres; then move right onto the slab and climb this diagonally right for 6
metres; then climb straight up to the furrow. Belay below an obvious crack.
2 30m. Climb the crack and continue up grassy ledges to the left end of
a large field.
3 20m. Climb the indefinite crack to a large flake and, from its top, move
right up the slab to a ledge. Then descend the break diagonally left to belay.
4 30m. Go easily back right, rising slightly, along the grassy break to join
Slab Climb Right-Hand and continue to a belay in *Deep Chimney*.
5 42m. *Slab Climb Right-Hand* pitch 4.
6 22m. *Slab Climb Right-Hand* pitch 5.
Forty-five metres of easy scrambling remains.

Parapet Route 81 metres   Severe   (3.8.37)
A very artificial and devious route, which is really an alternative finish to
Slab Climb Left-Hand.
1 45m. *Slab Climb Left-Hand* pitch 1; then traverse diagonally right to
Deep Chimney and step across to a rock recess.
3 36m. Traverse a metre or two right and descend to the lip of the
overhang. Work obliquely up right for 22 metres, keeping to the edge. The
slab finishes in a grassy recess.
Eighty-five metres of scrambling remains.

★★★Slab Climb Right-Hand 166 metres   Hard Severe   (1973)
A really excellent climb on superb slabs after a tricky entry, and one which
should be far more popular. Start just left of the toe of the buttress by the
hexagons.
1 36m. 4b. Traverse right for 6 metres on the sloping 'Giants Causeway'
of rock to a corner. Go up this, and at the top climb diagonally right up the
pleasant slab. Belay on the blunt spike atop the grass furrow. A great pitch.
2 24m. Go easily up grass on the left until it is possible to step up right to
the foot of the large slab. Continue easily to a ledge and peg belay.
3 42m. Move diagonally right to the edge of the slab and follow the edge,
passing ledges at 30 and 36 metres to belay at 42 metres in *Deep Chimney*.
4 42m. Move back left onto the slab and take the most pleasant-looking
line to easier rock.
5 22m. Climb easily up the prominent arête on the right.
Forty-five metres of easy scrambling remains.

★★Deep Chimney 164 metres   Very Difficult   (7.05)
A vintage climb. Start in the corner below the chimney at the foot of the crack.
1 50m. Climb a few metres up the crack, and then traverse left on good
holds to the corner. Go round the corner to a grassy stance. Make a
delicate step up; then, after a few metres, follow broken ledges to a stance
beside the 'deep chimney'.

Slab Climb Right-Hand (HS)
The Far West Buttress
Climber: unknown
Photo: Nick Dixon

2 24m. Climb the chimney to a good belay at an uncomfortable stance.
3, 4, 5 90m. Continue up the bed of the chimney to the top. Stances at
15 and 30 metres.

★Direct Start   28 metres   Severe
Directly below the line of *Deep Chimney* is a right-angled groove. Climb
this to a stance at the foot of the chimney. A pleasant pitch.

★★The Riddler   40 metres   E5 6b   (10.5.00)

Right of the Direct Start to *Deep Chimney* is a bottomless groove in the
impressive steep wall. Start below and right of this at the obvious
weakness. Climb leftwards on compact rock and move up to a bendy flake
below the groove. Move up and left to place good protection in a slanting
crack, and then return to the flake. Now gain the groove (this is the riddle)
and climb it to a final layback crack and belays in a niche. Finish either up
one of the *Slab Climbs* or down *Parapet Route*.

Round past the steep wall is Forgotten Gully, which is taken by the next
couple of climbs. They lie close to each other and the logical line to take is
Sea of Cloud to the peg runner on pitch 2 and continue up *Road of Ghosts*.

Sea of Cloud   140 metres   Very Severe   (25.7.72)

After a start up Forgotten Gully, the route escapes left to reach the upper slabs.
1 22m. 4b. Climb the gully until a move can be made out left to a slab
(just below the pasture). Trend rightwards up the slab and then round an
arête onto grass. Go up the corner to a ledge.
2 28m. 4c. Climb the corner-crack to a peg at 12 metres. Follow the
obvious groove above and left of the peg to a stance.
3, 4, 5 90m. Take easy slabs left of the gully to the top.

Road of Ghosts   156 metres   Very Severe   (29.8.72)

This climb takes the slabs on the right of Forgotten Gully, and then follows
the gully direct to finish. Start just right of Forgotten Gully.
1 30m. 4c. Climb to an obvious flake which slants up right, and follow
this to gain a large grassy ledge. Take a shallow groove on the left for 5
metres and then traverse left to a ledge and peg belay.
2 36m. 4c. Step out right onto the slab and climb into the small corner
above. Climb the crack; then move left and up until a step left can be
made to join *Sea of Cloud*. Climb the corner past the peg runner and
continue directly up the gully.
3, 4 90m. Finish easily up the gully.

Sun Dance   144 metres   Very Severe   (27.7.72)

Start at the foot of the right-hand corner of the huge recessed section of
cliff right of Forgotten Gully.
1 36m. 4a. Traverse left across grassy slabs for 25 metres to the base of
a blunt arête, which is below and to the left of the obvious slanting crack.
Climb diagonally right to the foot of the crack (nut belay).
2 36m. 4b. Climb the leftward-slanting crack in the steep wall until a
short groove leads to a large flake. Belay on top.

3 36m. 4a. Traverse left for 3 metres. Go up a short way until it is possible to move back right above the belay. Take the easiest line up slabs to a large belay.
4 36m. Finish up easy slabs.

★**Trick of the Light**   80 metres   E4   (9.5.00)
Sustained and serious climbing up the obvious crackline in the huge recessed section of cliff right of Forgotten Gully. Start by scrambling up slabby (4a) rock below the line to belay at a steepening.
1 50m. 5c. Climb a groove on the left to reach the crack-system and follow it till beneath an evil-looking block near the top. Traverse left across the slab and move round the left side of the overhang to a slabby groove leading to a grass ledge.
2 30m. Climb diagonally rightwards on slabs to the top.

White Rose Garland   319 metres   Hard Severe   (26.8.73)
A girdle traverse of the Far West. A not-too-serious mountaineering expedition, which requires either a knowledge of the other routes or natural route-finding ability. It is rather vegetated but contains some interesting pitches. Start in a corner about 20 metres below the Far Western Terrace.
1 44m. Follow the obvious traverse which goes across the buttress at half height to belay in *Slanting Chimney*.
2 15m. Go up *Slanting Chimney* a few metres; then climb a ramp on the right to a large grassy ledge. Spike belay as for *Wapentake*.
3 30m. Move down, right, and round the arête. Traverse right for a metre or two and make a step down to a grassy ledge. Climb diagonally right up ledges to belay as for *Primitive Route*.
4 8m. Descend the short slab and corner (pitch 5 of *Primitive Route* in reverse).
5 40m. On the right is an obvious grassy break leading to *Deep Chimney*. The pitch takes the rising traverse-line 8 metres lower on the clean slab. Step right and descend for 3 metres to reach the line, and follow it to *Deep Chimney*. Go up this for 10 metres to a spike belay.
6 32m. Move down for 3 metres and wander rightwards along the terrace until able to descend diagonally right to a corner at the top of a field.
7 50m. Go down the field until able to move rightwards round an arête. Go up right into the corner. Climb up 3 metres to a good spike and continue up slabs for 15 metres; then traverse right into Forgotten Gully. This pitch is supplied with several ledges and can be split.
8 8m. Ascend the gully for 3 metres; then move out right to a flake belay.
9 22m. Move left for 3 metres; then go up a few metres and back right above the belay. Climb slabs to a belay.
10 24m. Go diagonally right down the pasture, making for a huge spike below the skyline rib. Belay at a large flake below.
11 22m. From the flake, climb the rib for 5 metres until able to move right onto easy ledges. Follow the rightward-slanting rake to a belay near a flake.
12 24m. Move easily right and climb a grassy gully to finish.

The Anthology ~ Introductory Note

The inclusion of anecdotal snippets within guidebook First Ascents lists goes back at least to the 1942 Edwards/Barford *Clogwyn Du'r Arddu* guide, but the real possibilities so offered were not realized until the late 1980s. Indeed, the slimline fashions of the 70s and early 80s resulted in the ruthless excision of such luxuries.

However, the pendulum swung back, and for the 1989 *Clogwyn Du'r Arddu* guide the author Paul Williams and editor Geoff Milburn amassed by far the most extensive ever anthology of factual information and commentary about both first and subsequent ascents. True, the crag may well be said to have embodied the spirit and history of British rock-climbing from the early days of the twentieth century at least until the rise in popularity of sport climbing in the late 80s. The reputations of the climbs and the climbers were intertwined, and there was no shortage of documented material in numerous club journals and hut logs (not to mention an ether less tangible than that of our current technology, but nonetheless highly productive). Most especially, 1971 saw the publication of an almost unique volume devoted solely to the history of this one crag, *The Black Cliff*, which provided the 1989 compilers with a substantial basis to work from.

The author of the current guide wishes to acknowledge his debt to both those volumes especially. Inevitably, a few errors in the 1989 anthology have come to light, and every effort has been made to track down and correct them. Unfortunately, a number of the original sources either were not then clearly identified, or have not been able to be consulted now. Sincere apologies are offered, therefore, for any further errors that are reproduced here or any quotations that are not properly attributed: the interest and quality of so many of them seemed to justify the risk.

There is always a danger where guidebooks contain both a Historical and an expanded First Ascents list that the one will tend merely to duplicate the other. Ideally, the former will offer assessment and comment from the standpoint of the contemporary scene, while the latter provides occasional insights with the perspective of the first ascensionists and their peers, though it does not always work out as it should. In view of the material available and the 1989 base to work from, it was decided for this guide to dispense with a formal Historical and to expand the Anthology further, mainly through observations of a variety of climbers with intimate knowledge of the cliff, its routes, and the events surrounding them. These observations (concerning grades, quality, and historical significance or ethical validity) are not necessarily those of the author, and indeed it will be noted that several are at odds with the descriptions in the main section of the guide. The latter are, of course (as in any guide), the considered assessments of the author, having due regard to tradition and consensus; but they can never be the final word, and so various alternative views are given voice.

Some further linking commentary of a general nature is supplied: this is printed in blue, justified text, while the extracts referring to the individual routes are in black and indented under the route headings. Quotations (written or verbal) are printed in italics, while statistical information remains in Roman.

To avoid cluttering the layout too much, attributions are kept to a relevant minimum within the section. The following is a more detailed list of the principal sources, but it is not intended to be a formal bibliograhy.

Geoffry Sutton *Snowdon Biography* (Dent,1957)
Geoffrey Winthrop Young *Snowdon Biography* (Dent, 1957)
The Revd W Bingley *North Wales Including Its Scenery, Antiquities, Customs, etc.* (1804)
G D & A Abraham: *Rock Climbing in North Wales* (1906)
G D Abraham: *British Mountain Climbs* (1909)
R Todhunter: CC Bulletin 1912
H R C Carr: *A Climber's Guide to Snowdon and the Beddgelert District* (CC,1926); *The Mountains of Snowdonia* (with G A Lister,1925); Rucksack Club Journal Vol IV
F S Smythe: *Climbs and Ski Runs* (Blackwood, 1929)
L Henshaw: Rucksack Club Journal Vol VI
A B Hargreaves: CC Journal Vol 17
CC Bulletin No 24
FRCC Journal Vol IX
A S Pigott: Rucksack Club Journal Vol VI
Morley Wood: Rucksack Club Journal Vol VII
1942 Guidebook: *Clogwyn Du'r Arddu* by J M Edwards and J E Q Barford (CC)
P J R Harding: *Llanberis Pass* (CC, 1950)
John Streetly: CUMC Journal 1954
R J Isherwood: CC Journal 1968
The Black Cliff: by Jack Soper, Ken Wilson, and Peter Crew (Kaye and Ward 1971)
Sea Cliff Climbing in Great Britain: by John Cleare and Robin Collomb (Constable, 1973)
Hard Rock: compiled by Ken Wilson (Granada, 1974)
Paul Williams: *Clogwyn Du'r Arddu* (CC, 1989)
Jim Perrin: *Menlove* (Victor Gollancz, 1985)
Steve Dean: *Hands of a Climber* (Ernest Press, 1993)
John Redhead: *One for the Crow* (Serious Clowning Publications, 1996)

And the following (except where otherwise stated) in conversation and correspondence with the author, 1998 to 2003, in preparation for this guide:
Bill Birch, Paul Braithwaite, Joe Brown, Ian Carr, Steve Crowe, Johnny Dawes, Martin Doyle, Ian Dunn, Rowland Edwards, Mick Fowler, Chris Gore, Alan Hinkes, Leo Houlding, Dai Lampard, James McHaffie, Karin Magog, Paul Mitchell, Jerry Moffatt, Tim Neill, Hank Pasquill, Andy Popp, John Redhead, Chris Shorter, Louise Thomas, Dave Towse, Ken Wilson.

A word about nomenclature. For at least the first half of the twentieth century, first ascensionists (and the guidebook writers!) were none-too-consistent about the precise format of the route-names. A prefacing definite article comes and goes freely from one guide to another, and the word 'Route' or 'Climb' often got tacked on to the end. Thus *Curving Crack* might equally be referred to as *The Curving Crack Climb*. Nowadays, we tend to abbreviate and may refer to just *Midsummer's*; and the slab routes in particular lose the word 'Slab'. So what once might have been *The Narrow Slab Route* is now often plain *Narrow*. Likewise, 'Buttress' is frequently dropped from the buttress names. The formats settled upon in 1989 have been regarded as definitive, and these are used in full (in line with CC guidebook house-style) wherever they occur in the main text, but in quotations in this Anthology they come in various disguises. So, on a first visit to the crag, don't be startled by someone announcing they have climbed 'bloody', and 'going to the Far East' is not booking a flight to Hong Kong!

On the matter of aid. The number of points given in the route descriptions is, of course, the number not yet known to have been dispensed with (or, in one or two cases, the number commonly used as the route is described). The numbers given in the Anthology are those believed to have been used on the First Ascent. When pondering the latter, it is important to take full account of the very different circumstances, conditions, and equipment that the earlier climbers had to cope with.

Even until the early 80s it was quite common for 'aid' to mean only a direct pull on a piece of gear or standing in an attached sling. Resting on gear, falling on runners, and rope manoeuvres like lassos, tension traverses, and abseils on girdles were not always recognized or acknowledged as aid points, although all these, as far as it has been possible to ascertain, are included in the totals given here. Thus, for example, Ed Drummond is not being disingenuous in his assertion that he used only two points of 'aid' on *A Midsummer Night's Dream*, as he acknowledged also a number of rest points.

Note: two climbers appear in the first ascent information as A Sharp. First or first free ascents with 70s dates refer to *Alec* Sharp, author of the 1976 guide; those after 1980 are by South Wales climber *Andy* Sharp.

Anthology of Ascents

Clogwyn Du'r Arddu – perhaps all in all the greatest cliff in Britain.
(Geoffrey Sutton)

The First Rock Climb
Two clergymen Peter Williams and William Bingley in 1798 not only made the first recognized rock climb in this region, on the Eastern Terrace of Clogwyn Du'r Arddu, but they described the use of hand and knees (to climb with not to fall upon), the sensation of loosened hob nails in their shoes, and even the use of belt as a belay or handhold. (Geoffrey Winthrop Young)

Was this 'fun in the mountains'? Had the two clergymen any inkling of the extraordinary historical significance of what they had done – that it constituted the first tentative probings of what between one and two hundred years later would develop into a major sport, and upon the crag that would be widely regarded as Britain's premier? Quite probably not, but they obviously delighted in the telling of the tale afterwards at least as much as in the finding of the specimens they sought. So we have not only an ascent way ahead of its time, but also an account of it written (incidentally, in the year that Wordsworth published his *Lyrical Ballads* from 'the other place') with all the panache and relish that a twentieth-century climber would devote to descriptions of such adventurous epics.

1798 **Eastern Terrace** The Revd W Bingley, The Revd P Williams
I wandered to Clogwyn Du'r Arddu, to search the rock for some plants… The Reverend Mr Williams accompanied me, and he started the wild idea of attempting to climb up the precipice… For a little while we got on without much difficulty, but we were soon obliged to have recourse to both our hands and knees, in clambering from one crag to another. Every step now required the utmost caution, and it was necessary to try that every stone was firm in its place before the weight of the body was trusted to it. I had once laid hold of a piece of rock, and was in the act of raising myself upon it, when it loosed from its bed, and I should have been precipitated headlong, had I not in a moment snatched hold of a tuft of rushes and saved myself. When we had ascended somewhat more than halfway, there seemed no chance of our being able to proceed much further, on account of the increasing size of the mass of rock above us… The danger of again descending was much too great for us to think of attempting it. I believe it was the prospect downwards that determined us to brave every difficulty. It happened fortunately that the steep section immediately above us was the only one that presented any material danger. Mr Williams, having a pair of strong shoes with nails in them, which would hold their footing better than mine, requested to make the

first attempt, and after some difficulty he succeeded… When he had fixed himself securely to a part of the rock, he took off his belt and holding it firmly by one end, gave the other to me: I laid hold, and, with a little aid from the stones, fairly pulled myself up by it. After this we got on pretty well, and in about an hour and a quarter from the commencement of our labour, we found ourselves upon the brow of this dreadful precipice, and in possession of all the plants we expected to find.   (The Revd W Bingley)

The first *real* route, on the slabby right extremity of the cliff, was in keeping with the usual climbing of the day in Ogwen or on Lliwedd.

1905 July   Deep Chimney   P S Thompson and party
In July 1905, Mr P S Thompson led a party up a chimney towards the western end of Clogwyn Du'r Arddu. It starts some 200 yards west of the llyn at a height of 2,075 feet, by a vertical eighty-foot crack. This was turned by climbing the buttress on its left side, afterwards traversing into the chimney above it. Two good pitches of about sixty feet in height were climbed, and then for the next 120 feet, the chimney became so shallow as to be practically open face. Above this, easy scrambling led them to the top of the crags. The whole climb inclines to the east as it ascends. It is fairly difficult, and they likened the chimney to the B Chimney on Pike's Crag, Scawfell.   (G D and A Abraham)

Its ascent is a trifle strenuous near the top but it is unusually free of loose stones and vegetation.   (H R C Carr, 1925)

An excursion by the well-known Lakeland Abraham brothers was seen as significant in its day, though now it is of only historical interest.

1905 Sept   East Wall Climb   A P Abraham, G D Abraham
It would be a rash thing to say that the cracks straight up the north face of the Clogwyn will never be ascended. Climbs are accomplished nowadays that would have been deemed incredible forty years ago, and it will be interesting to see what the next generation does on the rocks which at present, by general consent, are considered too steep and dangerous. Should that future generation produce men far in advance of the present rock climbers in the art of scaling steep places, they will find many first ascents awaiting them on Clogwyn Du'r Arddu.
                                    (G D and A Abraham)

It cannot be said that this imposing mass possesses much interest for the rock climber. It has been truly said that the easy places are too easy and the difficult places are impossible. However, a splendid day can be spent here exploring the faces and revelling in probably the finest rock scenery that Snowdon affords.   (G D Abraham)

Although twenty years later there were only six routes on the cliff, information was limited and there was some confusion:

The East Wall Climb of *Clogwyn Du'r Arddu*… On page 347 and in the Index of Rock Climbing in North Wales (1906) this is referred to as above. In the Introductory List of Courses it appears as The West Wall Climb. We propose to adopt the former as the more accurate of the two. Mr A evidently climbed straight up the crack from E Terrace – a very difficult proceeding. It is unfortunate that he should describe the crack as a rib. An alternative is to traverse 30 feet to the right into a deep chimney. This traverse begins 15 feet above the start from the terrace. It is exposed, but there are splendid holds. The chimney is difficult to start and exhausting to finish. From a secure stance above the small chockstone, a short traverse to the left takes one back to the crack used on the original ascent. The waterworn gully is more a cascade of SCREE. This is a steep climb of considerable charm. Classification (by traverse and chimney) D, by crack VD.   (H R C Carr, 1925)

This includes an exhilarating chimney and an exit behind a large wedged stone which we shared with a stream. Roberts enjoyed it – it reminded him of potholing; but personally I thought it a detestable place.
        (F S Smythe)

This ancients' delight, an on-sight ascent, news of which caused a sensation in the Pen y Gwryd just after the turn of the century, is now deemed rather pointless and trivial by modern standards… such is progress.
        (Paul Williams)

1912 May   **East Gully**   G H L Mallory, R Todhunter

After an hour or two spent on more or less unprofitable inspection on the face of Clogwyn Du'r Arddu, its Eastern Gully appeared to offer the best route in the direction of Clogwyn y Ddysgl. The direct finish to the gully was taken as its natural termination in preference to the soft option on the left, from a sense of duty and in ignorance of its evil reputation. The character of the first 20 or 30 feet is certainly indefensible, and owing to the extreme steepness of the angle, the ascent of this section without reliable holds proved a severe test of the leader's skill and the writer's patience. But above this, although much of the rock seemed to be the masonry of a pastry cook, it provided a sufficiency of sound holds. We traversed out of the main gully over a little shoulder to the right, a most exacting performance. Then a good belay afforded a necessary element of security in the struggle with a short but difficult crack, and from the crack access was gained to the gloomy recess of the main chimney, which was followed without serious difficulty to its exit at the summit of the crags…   (R Todhunter on the first ascent)

After lunchtime we went round to examine the East Gully. A long and trying scramble up steep earth and grass took us at last into a cavernous recess beneath impending walls. The pitch above us, a steep open chimney 80 feet high, proved repulsive on close inspection so we descended and traversed to the East by a pinnacle and found a way by grassy ledges to the summit of the crags.

(H R C Carr, after making the first ascent of *Slab Climb* in 1919)

The route may have been climbed earlier by O G Jones:
To the left of the Eastern Cliff there is a wide, open gully which bends to the right and narrows down to the thinnest of cracks at a point 200 feet below the top of the cliff. There is a rumour that O G Jones climbed this fearsome looking and loose section, but the writer has more respect for the memory of his friend and his sound judgment than to agree with this. The view downward into this Eastern Gully from the top of the cliff which overhangs its right wall is one of the most thrilling sights in Snowdonia.

(G D Abraham)

This last quotation gives an insight into the psyche and ethics of these early climbers who did not wish to appear in any way reckless. While it may seem hopelessly conservative now, they were often condemned for their wilful neglect of safety then.

The first foray after the Great War gave one of the best of the easier routes on the cliff.

1919 Sept 5   **Primitive Route**   H R C Carr, G A Lister
The Direct Finish was added on 29 October 1973 by G Milburn, D Gregory.

1919 Sept 8   **Slanting Chimney**   H R C Carr, G A Lister
Variation (Original) Finish by C F Stoehr, W K McMillan, H R C Carr on 18 August 1925.

The finish described was extensively gardened and climbed on 27 October 1973 by D Gregory, G Milburn.

1919 Sept 12   **Slab Climb**   H R C Carr, G A Lister
Carr's third expedition of the week discovered a line that still gives a great day out.

The Far West Buttress slants back at an amenable angle and its expanse of rough slabs affords delightful climbing of a quality comparable to the Idwal Slabs on Glyder Fawr. There are several distinct routes, but given a dry warm day and rubber shoes it is possible to wander almost anywhere. In such wanderings lies the joy of solitary scrambling, and I was soon at the foot of the crags. There was a twenty-foot wall to start with, and a stiff groove; firm slabs followed. Little exertion was required; delicate treading took me up; dry turf ledges prompted an occasional laze; the sun on the summit, a pipe. I finished the day by girdling the buttress.   (F S Smythe, on an ascent in August 1921)

The original *Slab Climb* took the easiest line up the rock now taken by
Left-Hand and *Right-Hand Slab Climbs*. The first complete ascent of *Slab
Climb Right-Hand* was on 27 October 1973 by G Milburn, D Gregory (AL).

Exploration by F S Smythe in 1921 was not recorded in Carr's 1926 guide.
The line of *Non Such* has never been identified, while *Giant's Trod* is
described as a climb for the first time in this guide.

1921 Sept   **Giant's Trod**   F S Smythe, E E Roberts

*The weather was good and we spent three days on Clogwyn Du'r Arddu.
The first was devoted to the Far West Buttress and a curious route up the
rocks between the West and Far West terraces. It lies up a sloping shelf,
and involves some awkward and sensational climbing in its lower
portion, where the shelf is narrow and slopes outwards. It is a worthy
little scramble and we named it the Giant's Trod.*   (F S Smythe)

1921 Sept   **Non Such**   F S Smythe, E E Roberts

*Later we made the first ascent of the Far East Buttress. It is a
disappointing climb, and was rendered unpleasant by a horde of
trippers who collected at the Clogwyn station of the Snowdon mountain
railway and howled at us. The rocks are indeterminate, evil, and
untrustworthy, but there was a crack that we named the Non Such which
contained the only clean rock on the climb. We topped the crags to a
shriek of execration from the assembled tourists.*   (F S Smythe)

1926   *A Climber's Guide to Snowdon and the Beddgelert District,*
by **H R C Carr**

The third North Wales guidebook published by The Climbers' Club,
complementing the Ogwen and Lliwedd volumes of some fifteen years
earlier, it includes comprehensive descriptions of walks and climbs in
this area from Cwm Silyn in the west to the Llanberis Pass.

The First Chockstones and New Ideas

The next climb was a leap forward in terms of both its brutish difficulty (still
considered hard at its VS grade) and the first use of chockstones for both aid
and protection. The climbing of such a route as *Pigott's Climb* was, in the
1920s and early 30s, regarded as both foolhardy and dangerous.

*The East Buttress has never been climbed. The final wall [the Pinnacle] is quite
impossible, but the lower 200 feet below a broad green gallery, may yet be
conquered by a bold and expert party. The sheer walls of this crag offer one
of the most impressive mountain spectacles in Britain.*   (H R C Carr, 1926)

*The modern era of rock climbing in Wales seems to have begun with Fred
Pigott's ascent of the East Buttress in 1927.*   (Geoffrey Sutton)

1927 May 1   **Pigott's Climb** (3 pts aid)   A S Pigott, M Wood,
L Henshaw, J F Burton

Variously known as *The East Buttress Route*, *The Original Route*, and *East Buttress* before Edwards and Barford decided on *Pigott's* for the 1942 guidebook. The first ascent was made in ten pitches; it did not take the top corners direct. The top crack fell to J D Hoyland in 1934. Pitch 2 (with its 10-foot corner) was climbed free by C F Kirkus on 8 June 1930 on the fourth ascent. The original finish was climbed without aid by F E Hicks July 1929.

The Wall Finish (comprising *Wall Variations* pitches 3 and 4) was climbed by R A Hodgkin, A D M Cox, Clare Mallory, Beridge Mallory on 23 June 1937. *Wall Variations* pitch 1 was climbed by H I Banner, H Smith, A T Griffith on 5 May 1957; Pitch 2 by H I Banner, B Ingle on 13 May 1961 with 2 points of aid, which were eliminated by W Lounds, M Martin in 1970.

For the first few feet up it is the merest crack, with hardly finger room; but gradually it widens until at 20 feet from the ground a toe may be inserted; and here the right wall is slightly broken up, affording, so it seemed, a chance of turning the middle section of the crack, which looked pretty well impossible from below. At first all efforts to get up this 20 feet were abortive. Even a human ladder with the heavyweights at the bottom, in boots, and the more lithesome ones daintily shod in rubbers at the top, met with no success. In desperation we tried some sinister shiny slabs round the corner to the right but all in vain.
(L Henshaw, 1926 attempt)

Pigott and Wood in combination are as unscrupulous as they are invincible. Nothing stops them and they stop at nothing, not excluding pitons and fixed ropes. If the threatened onslaught of the West Buttress takes place I shall not be surprised to see either of them turning up with the latest Sassolungo rock-drill and a whole belt full of pitons. Personally for their own sakes I hope they do.
(L Henshaw giving a 'glowing reference' in 1926)

On the second attempt, Wood fixed a chockstone and sling in the crack, and Henshaw stood in this while Wood climbed onto his shoulders. Then the chockstone came out and they landed back on the ledge:

The plain fact is that Morley Wood was alone responsible for the idea of putting chockstones into the crack, the evidence being perfectly clear on this point. It may be said that the other members of the party were accessories after the fact; but Morley Wood was the one who conceived, organized, and eventually put into practice his diabolical plan; and if some of the inserted pebbles did remain in, that can only be put down to Providence and not to any dexterity on his part. In any case it was most unfair that one should be compelled to cut six-foot lengths off a perfectly new Beale in order that the party might be lowered down the precipice to safety. I tremble to think what would have happened if Morley's chockstone had not come out.
(L Henshaw)

*Our leader having arrived exhausted at this point stood up on the ledge
and called for a man with guts. Having none to spare we sent up two
chockstones slung in a handkerchief, one of which he inserted in the
crack above and secured himself by passing his rope through six feet of
Beale. This noose and our blessings enabled him to leave the crack and
climb a steep little wall on the right, then swing onto a shelf, by crawling
along which another steep wall was gained leading to the top of the
pitch.*   (L Henshaw, first ascent)

*1st Ascent Classification: Severe, probably 'Very Severe' at present. Leader
needs 80 feet of rope. Note: All chockstones have been inserted, and as
one came out and another moved, they should be most carefully tested on
each ascent. Pitch 5. Second join leader. This 10-foot corner is without
useful holds and unsuitable for backing up. The leader used the second's
shoulders until he could grasp the ledge below the grass fringe. The
second then gradually rises from his knees giving the leader sufficient
support for him to effect a landing in the Conservatory, a big grass
platform which now has a wooden (broomstick) piton in the wall at the
back. A safe manœuvre only for two steady climbers. The 9th pitch is the
most difficult and easily the longest run-out (about 65 feet). Pigott led it
brilliantly and personally I never want to see a finer bit of rock climbing.*
                                                        (L Henshaw)

*The ten-foot corner was for the first time led without the second on the
ledge below. The grassy landing at the top of this pitch is becoming
increasingly loose and the final movements are decidedly risky. We were
soon reunited in the Conservatory and sniffing suspiciously at the
broomstick piton.*   (A B Hargreaves on the fourth ascent by C F Kirkus
                                          and a later ascent on 6 August 1930)

*We may now see the jammed stone as the thin end of a prodigious
wedge, embodying an alteration not natural to the mountain and
predicating immediately the metal peg, the hammer, and the pulley.*
                                           (Geoffrey Winthrop Young)

*Standard: VI. But the main difficulty, the crack pitch, may be attenuated
to considerably below this level according to the number of inserted
chockstones and rope slings that are found or put in it. At present there
has been a slack tendency both to multiply these and to leave them
behind afterwards… The climber may insert or throw away chocks and
threads according to his taste. Perhaps one chock, at about 18 feet and
the thread round it, may be considered basically allowable.*
                                                    (1942 Guidebook)

And So to the West

The West Buttress of Clogwyn Du'r Arddu was seen as even less hospitable
than the East and, while the actual difficulties encountered on *Longland's
Climb* may not be any harder than those on *Pigott's Climb*, the new era of
British climbing was fully in flow.

No breach seems either possible or desirable along the whole extent of the W. Buttress, though there is the faintest of faint hopes for a human fly rather towards its L. side.   (H R C Carr, 1926)

The exploration of Clogwyn with its singular climbing difficulties set the standard of new climbs, and its opening up by the routes of Pigott and Longland began a new golden age of Welsh Climbing.   (H E Kretschmer)

1928 Whitsun   **Longland's Climb**   J L Longland, A S Pigott,
                                     F S Smythe, W Eversden, M Wood

Variously known as *The West Buttress Route*, *The Original Route*, and *West Buttress* before Edwards and Barford decided on *Longland's* for the 1942 guidebook.

A Direct Start was made straight up to the block on the traverse right by F E Hicks, C J A Cooper, W E Woosnam-Jones on 27 September 1929. The Direct Finish was added by M P Ward, J M Edwards, on 10 July 1949; a party also did this pitch in 1951 thinking it to be new and calling it *The West Direct Finish* – the name now given to the original right-hand finish.

I found myself gazing up the most impressive slab that I have seen in Britain. Two hundred and fifty feet high, it slants up to the left in one great sweep, sloping slightly outwards in the same direction. On the right it is bounded by an overhanging wall; and in the angle thus formed is a narrow cleft of terrific aspect. The left-hand and outer edge of the slab is about twenty feet, and the inclination between seventy and eighty degrees. Up it the eye wandered fascinatedly while the mind speculated half-dreamily, awed to passivity.   (F S Smythe)

We became alive to the fact that rain was falling steadily; malicious trickles were beginning to course down the slab and crack; the holds were becoming slimy, and wet holds have a curious knack of dwindling to half the size they appear when dry. There were murmurs from beneath; the tail of the rope, hitherto patient and stoically silent, began to voice its grievances. Longland and I were sheltered and comparatively dry… Retreat was unanimously decided upon… As last man down I had no intention of climbing the wet and slippery rocks. I cut off a length of rope, looped it round the rock leaf, threaded the rope through, and after the usual contortions managed to get into a double-roping position and slide off my perch down the airy reaches of the great slab. Normally there is a certain pleasure to be derived from descending a double rope over a steep rock face; but on this occasion the rope was possessed of seven harsh devils, and instead of a dignified progression I proceeded in a series of profane jerks. The wet hemp clung to my breeches and cut cruelly into my thighs, and when I arrived eventually at the grassy recess it was with a feeling of thankfulness that I was still homogeneous flesh and bone and not sawn into two portions.   (F S Smythe, on a 1927 attempt)

To Henshaw and me far below, the clink of steel against rock heralded the advent of a crisis. Eversden advanced; paused; and descended. Wood, putting a rasp into his voice, called for the shock-troops, but Henshaw, as averse as ever to artificial aids, kicked out the pitons and demonstrated the fallacy of the security they seemed to offer.

(A S Pigott, a 1927 attempt)

But there's no belay. There came a wicked smile upon the face of Morley Wood, at the sheet anchor end of the rope; this was the moment he had been hoping for, and he unslung his rucksack, which was hauled up, mysteriously heavy. I felt inside and found two chockstones: here all dead members of the Alpine Club turned uneasily in the grave. It was none of your imported chockstones; no pudding stone from the Dauphiné, or millstone grit from the steeps of Laddow, but sound Welsh rock picked from the foot of this very buttress. The first chockstone was a beauty, and fitted like a City man into his bowler hat. I sent down the other with my boots. My final complaint was at once answered by the appearance of a large clasp knife on a bight of the rope; and in pregnant silence I cut off a length, looped it round the chock, and passed my rope through it (the dead Alpine Club members meanwhile keeping up a high rate of coffin revolution).

(J L Longland, on the first ascent)

Commencing with his right leg in the crack, the leader advanced until it became necessary to turn round and get his back onto the slab he was previously facing. The manœuvre is necessary in order to get first one and then the other foot onto a good hold on the right. Suitable handholds are lacking, and before it is possible to stand on the hold, one must press upwards and sideways from the slab until a state of balance is reached. For the next step up you use your own initiative.

(A S Pigott, 1928)

Longland had meanwhile with great difficulty changed into rubber shoes; but even with their aid his lead of the section above was a brilliant piece of climbing. To my mind, it is the hardest bit of the ascent, and consists of an overhanging splayed-out chimney from the top of which it is necessary to step far out to the right. It is a long stride, the balance is critical, the handholds mere finger-scrapes, the exposure and the precipice beneath terrific. Only a man at the top of his form, with nerve and skill working in perfect unison, could safely make it. …Certainly those fifteen feet were overhanging; but more than fifteen feet of overhang were required to stop Longland at this stage. Personally I had half-hoped that the previously considered and old-fashioned manœuvre of 'swinging the leader', from the end of the ledge into the groove up which we had planned to go might be essential. Longland, however, settled the question in arbitrary fashion by clinging up the overhang – the solitary piece of pure gymnastics on the climb – and gaining the platform above. …Why describe the remainder of the great slab in detail? It is a job for the guidebook writers. No doubt every handhold and foothold will be earmarked and catalogued in the future because this route is unique so far as I know in Britain. … In a year or so ladies will climb the West Buttress of Clogwyn Du'r Arddu and marvel at the difficulties we encountered.   (F S Smythe)

The outstanding event in 1928 was the first ascent of the West Buttress of Clogwyn du'r Arddu, when the 'human flies' prophesied by the far-seeing author of the Snowdon Guide, materialized in the form of a very strong party headed by J L Longland and A S Pigott. … A magnificent climb; its uniquely exposed situations, continuously high technical difficulty, absolute non-artificiality, and great length (450 feet) make it almost the finest expedition in Wales'.   (CC Journal 1929)

The route is one of the prettiest on Clogwyn Du'r Arddu. Exposure of a high order, a varying succession of problems, these joined by parts far from easy, with the issue in doubt until the last pitch and an absence of any large lateral avenues, combined with a not too high standard, place it amongst the first quality of Welsh climbs.   (1942 Guidebook)

First winter ascent: February 1986.

The Kirkus Years

Great Slab marked the start of a three-year period of dominance that Colin Kirkus exerted on Clogwyn Du'r Arddu climbing.

A man unthreatened by competition because he climbs for the simple pleasures to be derived from the sport.   (Jim Perrin)

On Snowdon there is a cliff called Clogwyn Du'r Arddu. Its name is enough to frighten away many people. It is over 500 feet in height and mostly vertical, quite the most magnificent precipice in England and Wales.   (C F Kirkus)

1930 June 15   **Great Slab**   C F Kirkus, G G Macphee
A characteristically bold lead over some loose rock and a lot of grass. The Green Caterpillar, once a prominent feature of the first groove, has now disappeared.
The Top Traverse, protected by one piton, was taken by R A Hodgkin, A D M Cox, Miss C Mallory, and Miss B Mallory on 21 June 1937.
The *Hydrophobia* pitch was climbed by D Travers on 12 July 1990.

Kirkus described the ascent in *Let's Go Climbing*:

All the way along the foot of the cliffs the rocks overhung. Nobody had yet succeeded in overcoming this overhang. … There seemed to be a faint chance in the middle, where a pile of blocks formed a kind of natural ladder. … It looked a nasty place, but it seemed to me that, instead of climbing upwards, it might be possible to traverse out to the left, above the overhang. This would lead to a narrow slab, which ran up to the skyline and out of sight. …

The traverse was Very Severe. There was one sloping hold where my rubbers would not grip at all, so at last I took them off and managed to get across in my stockinged feet.

I started up the narrow slab. It was far more difficult than it had looked, and wickedly rotten. I threw down every other hold. A thin ribbon of grass ran all the way up on the right, looking like a long and ragged caterpillar. I thought that even this might be safer than the rock and plunged into it. …

I got a long way across, and then stuck. The next move might be possible, by a kind of jump. It would be dangerous, but – well, a new climb was worth a risk. I looked at it a long time. It seemed to grow more terrifying and I was a long way from my second. I came back.

[Kirkus eventually got across at a slightly lower level but was confronted with a 20-foot corner of almost vertical grass.] *I made a mad rush at it. I had to climb up more quickly than the grass fell down. It was nasty and dangerous, but I dug in my finger-nails and toes (I was still climbing in stockings) and clutched and scrabbled until I reached the top.*

[On the next pitch the turf broke away from the slab.] *It was rather like standing on a roll of carpet – with the carpet going on unrolling. It was very difficult and unpleasant but our reward was to come. We had two wonderful 100-foot pitches, right up and across the Great Slab, to its top left-hand corner. The rock was very warm and rough, and we felt profoundly happy and exhilarated. The climbing was just Severe, but it was easy after what had gone before and we seemed able to glide up without effort.*

Macphee said I deserved a kick in the pants or a potato medal, he didn't know which. I felt I deserved more than that. But it had been a marvellous day. We had done 1,200 feet of of rock-climbing, most of it in the Very Severe class.

The climb was not initially received well by all climbers:
Whether anyone will care to explore the perpendicular grass ledges of this last climb remains to be seen. It sounds a horrid place.
(CC Bulletin, November 1930)

The traverse goes round an awkward corner and it is with a feeling of relief that one reaches a vertical snake of grass in which good holds have been kicked… Mother Sod above could not find room in the next for her ever increasing brood which, year by year, was thrust out until there now hung a turf fringe making but a quivering attempt at contact with the slimy rock below. The problem was how to get up before the grass came down. Linnell showed the gardener's touch and scarcely disturbed a blade, but disintegration was in full blast before the last man arrived.
(A S Pigott, on the third ascent in 1934)

The climb is an excellent mountaineering expedition without any gymnastics, but at a high standard all the way. Ledges are large. The first pitch is of most excellent length and position. The fourth pitch can be

difficult, especially when as often it is wet, but it is short and well protected to the extent that the feeling of exposure is slight.
                                                            (1942 Guidebook)

But when Snowdonia holds her clouds, and the slab is damp or runs with water, the middle pitches will tax the boldest man, and many a good leader has elected in favour of a judicious retreat, confronted with the mass of streaming rock ahead.   (M Hardy, 1970)

I read about this route in Let's Go Climbing *by Kirkus at Northallerton Grammar School. I was glad to find that the grass staircase had gone when I did it.*   (Alan Hinkes)

First winter ascent: 11 January 1964.

Sir,
May I trespass on your valuable space to protest against Mr Kirkus's treatment of Clogwyn Du'r Arddu. Not content with climbing this cliff by a route hitherto deemed impossible, for which he has my respectful admiration, he must needs add insult to injury by giving this imposing precipice a regrettable if affectionate title. I find in the Helyg Log-book: 'June 16th. West Buttress of Cloggy. GGM and CFK.' The handwriting leaves no doubt as to the author… But Sir, Cloggy!   (CC Bulletin, November 1930)

Macphee, in fact, proved to have been the 'culprit'. The name stuck.

Menlove Edwards was, fittingly, introduced to new-routeing on Cloggy by Colin Kirkus as they climbed together one of the most outstanding lines.

1931 July 6   **Chimney Route** (2 pts aid)   C F Kirkus, J M Edwards
At the time, considered to be more difficult than and at least as arduous as *Great Slab*. Large quantities of turf were removed and one piton was used to safeguard the slab stance. On the overhang, the leader used a shoulder and rope slings attached to belays not entirely above suspicion – *The Rickety Innards* finish.

The Continuation Chimney was led by C F Kirkus with G G Macphee on 30 August 1931.
The Crooked Finish was climbed by H E Kretschmer. The alternative start was climbed by M P Ward, J E Q Barford, and B Pierre at Whitsun 1947.

…Crack becomes ornamental. Small piton (don't let it fall out) and sadly depleted sod enable one to rise to a good stance and belay. The whole climb is very severe and exposed with one move based on the aforesaid sod of doubtful stability… There is no 'impurity' except the piton and that will be found quite susceptible of removal by even the weakest purist.
                                            (J M Edwards, first ascent)

The piton was in fact removed in 1933 by the very talented Maurice Linnell, who repeated the route without it.

This route has a jaunty air of desperation and we approached it with due respect.
(A B Hargreaves)

In his obituary for Menlove Edwards in The Climbers' Club Journal, A B Hargreaves has this to say on the coming together of these two greats of pre-war climbing:

I have often wondered what happened when Kirkus and Menlove joined together for… Chimney Route on Clogwyn Du'r Arddu. That must have been a most interesting party – a complete contrast of styles and temperaments, with Kirkus (rather the senior) suffering a most embarrassingly efficient and thrusting second. No wonder that between them they forced the 'rickety innards'.

As with the Pedestal Climb and in a lesser degree the Sunset Crack there is great perfection of place, in a well defined break that traces one single line on an otherwise sheer sweep of cliff. The quality of holds is large and good, except for some less perfect blocks at the top of pitch 4. The climb has the good taste to reserve its hardest pitch to the last.
(1942 Guidebook)

The following entry appears in the 1989 guide, and is presumably a Milburn/Williams hoax:

Today a small part of everyone of us was wrenched out of the heart of Welsh Climbing. After nearly half a century of gentle usage, the right auricle of the Rickety Innards was cruelly severed from the still breathing body of Chimney Route. In order that the old man survives for another 50 years, even more reverential and tender treatment is necessary. In fact the wound will probably require extensive swabbing for quite some time, and there is a big danger that the other vital organs around the Innards will be similarly affected.
(Lancet, 25 August 1972)

In 1988, while showing this author some of his routes in the Nantmor region, Paul Orkney Work recounted:
It was a privilege to climb with both Menlove and Colin. Menlove was very powerful and hauled his way up a climb, whilst Colin was more stylish and seemed to climb effortlessly. Menlove would be secretive about the ways to tackle a problem, but Colin was a teacher and would try to help us to follow.

1931 Aug 30   **Pedestal Crack**   C F Kirkus, G G Macphee
Possibly Kirkus's hardest route at the time, though now that it is in a cleaner state both *Bridge Groove* and *Birthday Crack* are harder.

His first ascents on the East Buttress of Clogwyn Du'r Arddu , of the Chimney Route, of the Curving Crack, of the Birthday Crack, and of the Pedestal Crack – the most strenuous of them all – bear testimony to his versatility and enterprise.
(H E Kretschmer)

Technically, the steep section of the crack on the second pitch was probably the hardest climbing Colin had so far pioneered on the cliff.
(Steve Dean)

Of the first ascent Macphee says:

CFK seemed reluctant for once and needed some encouragement, but ultimately we finished the climb in about 2½ hours (65 mins for the second pitch) and it was Very Severe and quite exposed. Then we did a Direct Finish to Colin's Chimney Climb, *not so severe.*

The climb originally started up the rib on the right. The Direct Start was added on 15 June 1932 by C F Kirkus and M Linnell.

The crack is very steep, but is more deep and the sides much more rough than appears from a distance. … The angle demands muscular fitness. The technique is all on one same theme, but playing a great number of variations on it so that there is not room for boredom. The Direct Start is more open and harder, on a similar general plan. The situation due to the narrowness of the crack is one of the best on the Clogwyn. It is only unfortunate, at least from the point of view of gloriousness, that it gets pretty steadily easier as it rises.   (1942 Guidebook)

1931   Terrace Crack   C F Kirkus and party
Not properly recorded at the time. Edwards was unable to identify it in 1942, and the name first appears in the 1950 guide.

1931 October 25   Bridge Groove   C F Kirkus, A W Bridge
This climb probably represented Kirkus's most technical achievement at Clogwyn Du'r Arddu and is one of the earliest routes now to get the modern E1 grade.

Arête Alternative: P Williams, S Ashton on 27 May 1983.

In 1932, Clogwyn Du'r Arddu saw a peg used for aid for the first time.

1932 June 19   Birthday Crack (1 pt aid)   C F Kirkus, M Linnell, M Pallis
It was the birthday of both Kirkus and Linnell.

Hargreaves and Bridge climbed the East Buttress while Kirkus, Linnell and Pallis made another climb on the Middle Rock – the central groove – which they named Birthday Crack. *They used a six-inch nail for aid. This was the first bit of 'steeple jacking', as Hargreaves called it, in Wales. Pitons had, of course, been used earlier, but only for protection.*
                                        (The Black Cliff)

1932 June 19   Curving Crack   M Linnell, C F Kirkus (VL), A W Bridge,
                                        A B Hargreaves, W S Dyson

The first pitch of this climb, the fierce-looking layback crack, was soloed by the talented Linnell whilst the rest of the party failed on the direct start on the other side of the flake. He then handed over the lead to Kirkus, who wrote:

The credit of this climb is largely due to Linnell, who showed that the rather inaccessible-looking crack at the start would go, by climbing it. Standard: Just Very Severe.

It was a fine day after a rainy night, and the rocks were barely fit for rubbers. Kirkus, E T and I watched Bridge and Pigott start the new Pinnacle Route. It is always fine to see a craftsman on his job, and Bridge's lead up the 40-foot crack will always remain in my mind as a magnificent exhibition of climbing technique. He climbed with perfect certainty, obviously finding and using just the right holds, though telling us all the time how badly he was shaping and how much better Linnell had done it the week before.   (Morley Wood)

The fun began right away. Hodgkin with socks flapping loosely round his feet made the 30-foot layback of the first pitch look simple enough. It even felt quite passable until five-eighths of the way up. Then something queer happened down the inside of my forearms, and my fingers suddenly belonged to some other strong-minded individual who was determined to uncoil them. As we were climbing on an old rope that needed testing and a new line that needed stretching, it was nice to feel that the result was not entirely wasted. Sack-work followed; then a brief pause before Hodgkin disappeared round a nasty looking corner into the crack proper. Luckily the climb is only four pitches. The crack was greasy all the way up, and in places muddy. My hair soon became full of mud, because when one's arm is jammed in a hole above one's head, there is nothing else to wipe one's fingers on. But the crane business was very helpful and I was never given the chance to fall off again...

(A D M Cox, having problems after a nine-month lay-off, 1937)

On the first pitch of Curving Crack on Clogwyn Du'r Arddu more than one climber has been unable to make up his mind and has alternated in the middle between going up and coming down, until the matter was settled by Mother Nature.   (A Birtwistle, 1950)

The following two pitches were a hard struggle; I was jammed so tight that movement seemed impossible and I could well believe tales that I had heard about people fluttering their eyelashes to get up difficult pitches – my eyelashes were the only parts of me which were free to move.   (Denise Shortall, 1950s)

The Direct Start was recorded by N P Piercy and A J Woodruffe on 6 July 1940, but was probably first climbed by J L Longland in 1933.

This variation is a tour de force of no mean order, although, in fact, it was done by mistake for the more usual start.   (CC Journal, 1941)

A very fine piece of climbing were it not that the ordinary start is an even more desirable experience.   (1942 Guidebook)

1932 June 26 **Direct Finish to the East Buttress** C F Kirkus, M Wood,
A S Pigott, A W Bridge

The conclusion of a fine series of ascents by Kirkus.

The first wall is steep, short, and wet; the second is longer and has a very awkward move near the top. It was at this point that Kirkus removed a large black slug from an essential hand-hold and threw it at his futile second – accurately… I personally was very pleased to be with Kirkus when he laid the ghost of the 'impossible final wall' of Clogwyn Du'r Arddu.   (Morley Wood, on the first ascent)

1933 Aug 18   Narrow Slab   M Linnell, A S Pigott, E Holliday, P L Roberts
The first ascent avoided the initial part of the slab by a groove on the left. The slab direct was probably first climbed by Kirkus.

From the crest of the arête the eye of faith discerns a small toe-hold down on the right. It is strange to find that it is possible to get a toe into it and, stranger still, to change feet in it. Two further holds precede an ominous gap. The grass is not far away; I was told to jump. The breaking away of a flake hold at that moment settled any qualms I had about that reprehensible practice… the grass held the drainage which made the rock here very greasy and there was nothing to pull on. It was at this stage that I distinctly saw a pointed tail slip out from a hole in the leader's trousers, poke itself into a crevice and press the owner firmly upwards. Immediately I was reminded of the goblins disporting themselves in the dangerous places on the doorway of the Rylands Library. The tenseness of time and place, you will say: possibly; for when I looked again I could see nothing but good honest Beale: but when it came to my turn, I should have welcomed such an aid.   (A S Pigott)

The hardest part, the first 90 feet of the slab are admirable straight slab work of a most pleasant order, the holds nowhere too large, nowhere vanishing to danger point.
                    (J M Edwards, on his ascent in 1941 of what he
        thought was a new route but was really *Narrow Slab* by a new entry)

He realized his error a few days later:
This wretched cliff has not got a new climb on it after all. The latter two-thirds of the thing I called 'Dark Slab' was really Narrow Slab, *which I thought went up the really narrow slab containing Linnell's first pitch* [probably *Gecko Groove*] *sorry'.*

The 1942 guide comments:
Later, Linnell contributed perhaps the hardest route on the West Buttress, the Narrow Slab.

1933   Brwynog Chimney   M S Taylor, J S Jenkins
Originally called *Terrace Chimney*, but not recorded in the early guides. C T Jones and J B Allen climbed it on 6 July 1958 and gave it its current name.

Another contender for one of Britain's earliest climbs now graded E1.

First winter ascent: 3 February 1979.

In March 1934, Maurice Linnell, one of the most talented of the Cloggy climbers of this period, sadly lost his life while climbing with Kirkus on Ben Nevis. Kirkus survived but climbed little of difficulty thereafter and nothing more new on Cloggy. The incident is described very fully in *Hands of a Climber*.

1935 May 5   **Jubilee Climb**   M S Taylor, J R Jenkins, T U L S O'Connor
The Coronation Variant was added later in the year by Jenkins and O'Connor.
The variation finish was done by P Crew, Miss J Cox, and A M Brodie in August 1960.
First winter ascent: 1979.

In 1937, Arthur Birtwistle climbed the 'Drainpipe Crack' (that was later to become the first pitch of *Vember*) and actually continued some way up the line that, later still, became *November*. He had thought that the crack had been done by Kirkus, but Kirkus's attempt in 1932 had resulted in his having to be assisted by Alf Bridge to regain a position from which he could retreat.

1937 June 24   **Sunset Crack**   A D M Cox, R A Hodgkin,
                                              Miss C Mallory, Miss B Mallory

…the crack eases below the overhang and a pull across to a good ledge on the left can be made. From here it is possible to escape down a grassy rake should the sandwiches have been left at the bottom by some mistake.   (P R J Harding)

The top pitch of Sunset Crack is a complete b—d.   (J E Q Barford, 1946)

1937 Aug 3   **Parapet Route**   P O Work, Miss B W Hoyles

1939: as the Second World War gripped Europe the crag fell quiet.
Longland's: 7 September 1939. Mrs N E Morin and JEQB (1 hour 40 mins). It's an ill wind… Snowdon was deserted and the immortal silence of the hills had returned once more, to resume its long interrupted sway.

However, Menlove Edwards, a conscientious objector, continued to visit.

1941 Sept 20   **Bow-Shaped Slab** (1 pt aid)   J M Edwards, J Cooper
Some of this had been climbed previously by Edwards with various parties, the entry having been done for the first time by him, J E Q Barford, and Mrs N E Morin as part of an attempt on *White Slab*. The higher line for the traverse was discovered by G Dwyer and J B Lawton in May 1948.
Originally, the spikes on the stance at the end of pitch 1 were lassoed and the rope was used for aid. This was climbed free by P Greenwood and F Williams on 14 May 1951.

Party started with high ambitions. Starting on Narrow Slab Route *they overcame the traverse pitch only with the greatest difficulty… the party traversed round right out to the stance at the top of the first pitch of* Great Slab Route… *up this to the top. Had meant to go right but were not able. Whole party was on this climb – utterly rotten: took 8 hours, and that only by hurrying.*   (J M Edwards, 1 June 1941)

This was probably the first ascent of the *Bow-Shaped* traverse with the Narrow entry – perhaps the party was tired at the outset. Entry from Helyg Hut book the previous night: *Blitz. Planes heard 1.30 a.m. passing over NW. 2.00 a.m. engines heard again, followed by whistling of bombs and explosions in hillside between Gallt yr Ogof and Gwern y Gof Farm. 4 craters. Helyg and its custodian were somewhat shaken. N.B. Please pay particular attention to the black-out.*   (E S Chantrell)

Only a short thing, avoiding the first 60 feet of the true slab… pleasantly exposed of course, as ever on Cloggy.
                              (J M Edwards understating a pitch that repulsed
                                                  all comers for several years)

An epic retreat from the crux of *Bow* by one party was effected only by leaving 100 feet of rope and two slings with karabiners, dangling from the crag. Witnessing the proceedings, and commenting on the *in-situ* gear, G F Parkinson on 8 July 1945 made this entry in the Helyg Log: *It is regretted that the end of my leave tomorrow makes it impossible to try and arrange for the removal of this unsightly evidence of bad mountain craft.* How modern values have altered!

Everyone thought that the 'magic hold' used by Menlove on his first ascent had been broken off by successive attempts to repeat it.   (P R J Harding)

Graham Macphee arrived. I had to invite him to join us for 'it was he, the Black M'Phee', who had given it the more famous name of Cloggy. … I had climbed with him on Nevis and on Cyrn Las, but each occasion turned out to be an epic. … When we were assembled on the stance below Bow's crucial traverse I nipped up the blunt arête for some twenty feet to fix a running belay loop. Clipping in the spare rope I descended and tried to explain to Mac how he could use it as backrope protection across the crux. However wondrously exciting my vision had been during our walk up Cwm Glas Bach, of the great Macphee pendulating across Bow to end up in a flying yo-yo onto Narrow, there on the wild fastnesses of Cloggy's West Buttress it became mortally terrifying. … I called for Mac to come. Supported by Fred in the Circle and me in the Gods, with a back rope in the Wings, no epic incident could possibly occur. Or could it? I should have remembered that Macphee was a great competitor; anything J M E might have done, G G M would do better, or at least try to do so. On the hard move he tried to go even further left; then with one hand gripping the cliff he got annoyed with the back rope and tried frantically to flick its runner off with his other hand. He seemed determined either to climb the pitch single-handed or win the Pendulum of the Year award. Fred and I with bated breath could only watch, gripping our ropes and marvelling at his singular strength of arm, even more at his command of language, terrible language. Foul Scottish oaths rent all the quiet of Cloggy's western front. I prayed that neither Mac nor the back rope runner would come off. Fortunately, before either happened, he let go of the rope to concentrate entirely on climbing and swearing, thugging and cursing his way up to the easier, traversing line... I then continued on the thinning crackline which leads to the Bow's topmost edge; a long run-out. Unfortunately, 120 feet of rope was scarcely enough and reaching the finishing ledge I could only pull up to lie half on, half off, chest down, unbelayed. And Fred had given me all the rope. Knowing Fred had a good belay, I shouted for him to bring Mac, then waited, relaxed, listening as occasional words floated from below. No epics now, all was serene and Mac was on an easy bit. Suddenly there was a wild horrendous cry. I had heard it on Nevis and on Cyrn Las! A simultaneous snatch at my waist pulled me backwards off the ledge. Miraculously I stopped just short of take-off point for the Welsh Yo-Yo Record. Balanced on forearms, in a sort of elbowed mantelshelf, at the Amen end of the ledge, I gingerly turned my head down to glance. For King Louis! Fred was completely off his perch, bent double, hanging from the belay; a twangy rope stretched down to a swinging Scotsman; some tiny rattle of distant stones echoed the fate of Macphee's erstwhile holds. Mac's life was hanging by a Fred! Horrific though this scene undoubtedly was, worse still were... those dreadful curses which only a pure bred Scot can deliver so loudly and continuously'.   (P R J Harding, fun and frolics on the fourth ascent)

It is regretted that on 28th October (1950) the lasso pitch of the Bow-Shaped Slab suffered some damage. Our party of three successfully lassoed the nearest spike and roped across the gap. Shortly afterwards the last man knocked it with his elbow while taking in the rope, when to everyone's consternation it broke off and disappeared into the depths. The further spike remains intact and as far as can be judged is secure.   (C J W S, Ynys Hut Book 16 December 1950)

1942   *Clogwyn Du'r Arddu* by **J M Edwards** and **J E Q Barford**

This guide was first published in The Climbers' Club Journal and then reprinted as a pamphlet, which is now something of a rarity. Though compiled hastily and in difficult conditions ('We have left out the Far East and Far West Buttresses, not from forgetfulness but for lack of time'), it is of considerable historical interest, containing advanced ideas on photodiagrams, grading, and ethics that have many times since been advanced as original.

Continental numerical gradings were used, which equated Severe with IV to V, and VS with VI. Bearing in mind that early ascents of routes in existence at this time would usually have been, perhaps significantly, harder than they are now, it is interesting to note the assessments of the following routes, all currently graded VS: *Pedestal Crack* (IV), *Curving*

Crack (V), *Longland's Climb* (V), *Narrow Slab* (VI). These would tie in very accurately with current Alpine grades.

Of the question of vegetation, the guide comments:
Yet the early climbers noted that the Clogwyn was peculiarly fertile of its grass, and that wherever a blade was able to rest its foot it grew and flourished extraordinarily: in most of the early accounts it is put down variously as the situation dictates for admiration or horror; for praise, amusement, or contempt; for cursing or blessing, or a careful silence; for agonized cleaning of it away where it was firm, or equally agonized efforts at its detention where it was already not firm. The disparity arises, however, not in paradox, but because both grass and climbers so far have tackled only the easiest and thus the same places. Viewing the future, the relation of the two is competitive and man's force seems overpoweringly the greater.

And on competition:
The wave of intensification had intensified competitiveness, and the bad as well as the good side results of that: jealousies and so on on one side, an unbalanced concentration on the most obviously and crudely competitive points in development, and so on on another side. Many questions. But these things big and little, stand half submerged perhaps already, like the boulders of the moraine as the fresh washings creep over them, of earth and of goodwill.

1943 September 13: Sergeant Colin Kirkus was shot down and presumed lost whilst taking part in a bombing raid over Bremen, Germany.

Alf Bridge in a letter to Graham Macphee wrote: Colin *'missing' from raid on Bremen, night of September 13/14. We must hope on.*

And later: *I am glad of the privilege that was mine, in being so close in friendship to a man whose qualities of courage, kindness and loyalty were of noble standard.*

Jack Longland had the final word in his moving obituary: *Clogwyn Du'r Arddu is a big enough memorial for any man, and without any sort of doubt or rival claims Du'r Arddu is Colin's cliff.*

1945 Oct 17   Sheaf   J Campbell, A D M Cox
This route was climbed in an attempt to access what later became *White Slab*. A fine piece of route-finding, both committing and bold.
The various pitches of *Sheaf Direct* were climbed as follows: top pitch by D D Whillans in 1959, pitch 3 by P Crew and D J S Cook on 31 May 1966, pitch 1 by A Rouse and J Cardy in June 1971.

Note to future climbers: do not jump across on Linnell's Leap as the grass ledge has been removed.'   (Cromlech Club Log, 1959)

One wag replied: 'For Sale: One Linnell's Leap in good condition, a must for all West Buttress Parties'.

1946 May   **Central Rib**   H A Carsten, G G Macphee

There were no more new routes on Clogwyn Du'r Arddu for another three years, but a new generation of post-war climbers took up the challenge of repeating all the existing ones. Foremost (though not first) was Peter Harding, who by May 1949 had only *Sheaf* and *Bow-Shaped Slab* to complete. He set out to combine ascents of these (with a descent of *Narrow Slab*), but the expedition developed into what was considered at the time to be a major prize.

1949 May 21   **The West Buttress Girdle**   P R J Harding, G Dyke

We had no intention of doing a girdle – it was The Sheaf *and/or* Bow-Shaped. *The mist was right down to the scree above Llyn Du'r Arddu and my intention on taking Linnell's Leap to start* The Sheaf *was to try the Jump! I had climbed across White Slab on two or three previous occasions and noted that the piton I had climbed up to on the first, was now missing, or at least I couldn't see it! Getting myself psyched up to jump across, I shouted to Gordon, belayed back round the edge of White Slab, to give me some rope, then leapt into space. He must have only heard me shout '… rope!' And I dropped vertically, frantically grabbing for the grass as I passed my objective grass ledge. Fortunately, Gordon heard my second yell and didn't take in any more rope and I dug my fingers into the turf and scrambled up onto it. I never did Linnell's Leap again – always climbed across! … The penultimate pitch was magnificent, a delicate traverse across a slab with some nice steps up at the end to reach a bilberry patch. Then a step round into the final upward chimney. It was in that last cleft that Du'r Arddu had a final say. The pitch was easy and we were moving together when a falling stone severed the rope between us as neatly as a knife cut. It had been a grand day – 8 hours climbing, 1100 feet. We rested on the summit for a few moments before moving off. Du'r Arddu had at last yielded her girdle.*
(P R J Harding, on the first ascent)

The climax of Harding's deeds was the Girdle Traverse of the West Buttress, which was an expedition of length and continued difficulty unmatched in Wales with seven or more Very Severe pitches.
(Geoffrey Sutton)

Harding's new outlook on the use of pegs enabled him to raise the standard of climbing above the pre-war level and to lay a foundation for the future.
(Paul Williams)

To borrow a quotation: 'une course presque incomparable par la beaute et la vinete des passages d'escalade.' The subsequent swim in the llyn was much less than might have been expected.
(J Hammond, C Bonington, 11 May 1953)

1950   *Llanberis Pass* by **P R J Harding**
Affectionately known as the Bumper Fun Book, it also covered Clogwyn Du'r Arddu.

The Joe Brown Years Begin

Next year saw the first appearance on the cliff of a climber who was to dominate British rock-climbing throughout the 50s and early 60s. He, Don Whillans, Ron Moseley, and a small group of exceptionally talented young climbers formed The Rock and Ice Climbing Club, which ushered in a new golden era of development on Clogwyn Du'r Arddu matching that of the 30s.

The name of this new star was Joe Brown. Other climbers who had hitherto been considered at the very top of the ladder tried to repeat his climbs (often in good condition when the first ascent had been done in bad) and failed, or perhaps with difficulty they managed one or two of the easiest ones.

(Geoffrey Sutton)

But the activities of Harding and his contemporaries were very much overshadowed by the sudden appearance of Joe Brown onto the climbing scene.   (Paul Williams)

1951 June 24   **Diglyph** (1 pt aid)   J Brown, M T Sorrell
Brown was attempting the grooves in the left side of the Great Wall that eventually became *Daurigol*. However, he noticed this crack and became engrossed in its intricacies – to the point where at one stage he managed to get the spike of his peg hammer jammed between his knee and the rock, threatening to immobilize him completely.

Decidedly awkward, thrutchy and hard.   (Bill Birch)

1951 Oct 13   **Vember**
          J Brown, D D Whillans
A long-standing problem. The first pitch was, and still is known as the 'Drainpipe Crack'. Kirkus got some way up it in 1931, and it was led in 1937 by A Birtwistle. Brown had laid siege to this route and was repulsed from the second pitch as early as 1949.

The Drainpipe Crack
Climber Paul Stott   Photo: Malcolm Eldridge

…but I shall always remember The Move. The shallowest of chimneys with an appalling exit.

(Tony Smythe, in *Hard Rock*)

A memorable climb. My partner (Gerry Gore) climbed the second pitch on sheer bottle, bravery, and arm strength – an impressive effort.

(Alan Hinkes)

1951 Oct 28   The Boulder   J Brown
The rest of the party was unable to follow and the upper part was climbed in one runout by tying three ropes together.

The Moscow Variation Finish was climbed by R James, A Ovchinnikov, and J Walmsley on 29 May 1960.

On the crux he attained a position of hanging from the fingers of one hand in a semi-layback posture. A runner which got in his way had to be disengaged with his free hand. The moves from this position were singularly lacking in security. It seemed like an age as Anatole moved up and down, always straining his fingers. I could feel the tension of the situation and wanted to climb over and help him. It was magnificent to witness a trial of strength and determination – a wonderful sense of striving for security of movement. At last the body position was finally adjusted and the move made to comparative safety. There was immediate relief and satisfaction. I wondered just how I would find the problem of the crux. Then Anatole vanished from sight and I was alone at the end of the rope.   (J Walmsley, on the 1960 Russian Meet)

1952 May 4   The Black Cleft   J Brown, D D Whillans (AL)
The Direct Start was added by E Metcalf and B Fuller in 1959.

After my ascent in 1959 my clothes reeked of rotting vegetation and I had to travel home in a filthy smelly state, much to the irritation of other passengers on the train. The clothes were so badly contaminated that they had to be thrown away. Three weeks later, the bloody route was almost completely dry; and considerably easier!   (H I Banner)

I tried this route in the drought summer of 1976 – it was still wet!

(Chris Gore)

First winter ascent: 1963.

1952 June 6   Pinnacle Flake   J Brown, D D Whillans (AL)
From the top we took the usual way to the summit by the Direct Finish Whillans's Continuation to East Buttress. *After the first pitch I worked out to the left round the corner and on to* The Pinnacle Face. *Moving up I eventually reached the foot of the huge flake, only to return, down again, because of thoughts of rain and Ivan's concern for MacFisher (Mac was one of Ivan's junior test engineers at Rolls-Royce, and strictly, they were out testing an experimental Bentley – any accident like falling*

off Cloggy because of me would have landed Ivan (and Mac) with tricky questions to answer). I made a mental note to return, but I never did.
(P R J Harding)

Spent hours trying to do Pinnacle Flake, one of Mr Joe Brown's easier climbs, and were quite unable to leave the ground. We departed, muttering (after Monsieur Paragot): 'Il est fou, complètement fou, le Monsieur Brown.' (Ynys Hut Book, 1955)

1952 June 7   Spillikin   J Brown, D D Whillans (AL), J R Allen
The line of the route had been spotted the day before. The rock was steep and loose, composed of wobbly spikes and flakes called 'spillikins' – hence the name.

Nothing had so far been climbed on The West Buttress to the right of *Great Slab*, though several climbers had eyed, and a few had tried, a line on the red slab above the guarding overhangs. Its ascent, in both summer and winter conditions, fell to outstanding and bold climbers of their day.

1952 June 10   Bloody Slab (1 pt aid)   J Streetly
Previously known also as *Red Slab*.

The rest of the party were unable to follow, and when the 200 feet of rope was run out Streetly soloed out to the top of the cliff. This was the hardest slab in Wales at the time and only Streetly's second climb on the cliff. One peg runner was inserted after 70 feet of climbing.
The alternative to the first pitch was found by P Walsh in 1959.

This smooth and overhanging portion of the buttress was known on account of both its nature and its reddish colour as Bloody Slab. A name as well as an adequate description of what was to be expected. … The slab was very smooth and, under the overhangs, nearly always damp. Added to this was the fact that most of the climbing would depend on pure friction owing to the apparent lack of any obvious holds. Those holds we could see all sloped the wrong way because of the overlapping structure of the rock. On the whole a rather discouraging picture, but nevertheless still worth a try – I can remember thinking quite happily at the time – 'Never say die till you're dead.' … With the difficult move below and the uncertainty of what was still to come, life at this point seemed to depend more on faith, than friction. … On the upper portion of the slab there was no trace of any real hold so all the movements had to be carefully studied in order to maintain three points of contact with the rock while looking for, or making, the next move. Shifting carefully off the grass, movement could again be made diagonally upward to the left on very tiny rugosities until another large loose flake was reached. This appeared to be resting on a useful little ledge, so, bridged on very small toeholds, it proved quite a surprise when a tentative pull removed the whole issue – all twenty odd pounds of it! This presented an awkward problem, more so in view of the fact that I was holding on to it! One could, of course, hold the flake against the rock, but not for long, and it was too heavy to throw clear without falling off. Throwing would of course remove two very good handholds – and if I dropped it – well, my feet were just below. Ted and Brian down below could not have known what was going on until, with a little push to the left, I half dropped, half threw it just clear of my left foot to slither noisily down the slab and over the overhang to crash, after a moment's silence, to the screes below. Just to complete the picture, the groove from which the flake had come was rounded top and bottom with no trace of the hoped-for hold. Almost desperate examination of the rock, however, revealed a tiny flake, the top of which was craftily knocked off with the hammer to produce a neat little quarter-inch ledge. Using this as a fingerhold, a move could again be made across and up to another grassy strip. Proceeding super-carefully up this (a 90-foot lead out from the shaky flake runner) it again became possible to move onto the more rugose left edge of the slab which led up to a good grassy ledge... At this point, like all good things, the 200 feet of rope came to an end and the trouble really started.   (J Streetly on the first ascent)

In 1977 Dave Hollows led Bloody Slab *in hush puppies; things had come on!*   (Hank Pasquill)

1952 June 14   **Llithrig** (1 pt aid)   J Brown, J R Allen
On the first ascent the upper cracks were running with water – the name means 'slippery'.

The pendulum was eliminated by C J Phillips in 1967.

Geoffrey Sutton put *Llithrig* into perspective alongside the great climbs from earlier periods. (*Avalanche* was, just after the turn of the century, considered to be the most exposed and difficult route of its day):
The difference between two climbs such as Avalanche *on Lliwedd and* Llithrig *on Clogwyn Du'r Arddu is the difference between Mr Owen's horse-drawn carriage (in which, if he did not walk, Archer Thompson perhaps came to the hills that time) and a modern twin-cylinder motor cycle (on which Brown probably arrived). Each is an excellent achievement of the human mind, each fundamentally to the same purpose, but representing a different ideal or stage in the development which now seems inevitable, each one a creature of its time.*

1952 June 15   **Octo**   J Brown, M T Sorrell, D Belshaw
Brown's eighth new route on the cliff, and again an outstanding line. It was graded HVS in previous guides.

This route is way harder than The Hand-Traverse *[graded E3 in this guide].*   (Paul Mitchell)

1952 June 20   The Corner   J Brown, J R Allen, D Belshaw
Also known as *Cloggy Corner*, doubtless to avoid confusion with
Cenotaph, which was also climbed by Brown and Belshaw, just two
months later.

The Direct Start was added later by J Brown and party.

1953 March 14   Moss Groove   R Moseley, L Rogerson

1953 May 9   Gargoyle   J Brown, P G White
The Direct Start was climbed by R Evans and J Pasquill on 17 July 1971.

1953 May 10   The East Buttress Girdle   J Brown, J R Allen,
                                                D D Whillans
The ascent took six and a half hours. The line had been fancied by
several of the earlier Cloggy pioneers.

1953 June 7   East Gully Wall (1 pt aid)   J Brown, D D Whillans
The aid point was eliminated by J Brown after making the peg
un-lasso-able in the late 50s.
Moseley's Variation was climbed by R Moseley, P G White, and
T Waghorn on 16 April 1954.
The Direct Start was climbed with two points of aid by R Edwards and
R Rejous on 9 May 1966, and climbed free by A Sharp and J Harwood
on 20 August 1984.
Norm's Finish was added on 4 May 1995 by N Clacher.

1953 June 14   East Gully Groove   D D Whillans, J R Allen
Long thought impossible.

The Direct Start was climbed by J Smith and J Brown in 1957.

1953 Oct 4   Carpet Slab (1 pt aid)   J Brown, D D Whillans
Probably climbed free by R Edwards in 1965.

Most of the first pitch disappeared in a massive rockfall in February
1986 and has yet to be re-climbed.

1954 April 17   Left Edge   R Moseley
The rest of the party were unable to follow.

The modern way of doing it was found by D D Whillans on the second
ascent in 1955.

1955   *Llanberis Pass* by P R J Harding – reprinted, with a
          ***Supplement of New Climbs* by R Moseley**
The ten-page supplement was the first time that many climbers had
access to even the briefest details of the Rock and Ice routes.

1955 was an exceptionally hot and dry summer in Wales and all of the new routes climbed have very slow-to-dry sections.

1955 June 5   **Camus**   G J Sutton, Miss C A Clarke
Most of this had been done by the Abraham brothers in 1905.

The route is not recommendable, unless to one's enemies.
(First ascent description)

First winter ascent: 4 February 1979. Much better in winter!

1955 July 9   **Slanting Slab** (2 pts aid)   D D Whillans, V Betts.
First free ascent by I Carr on 14 July 1983.

Even as you crouch in slings on the eaves of the slabs, only twenty feet from the second, thermos flasks and solidity, the exposure begins to snap at you. Once over the lip, the snap becomes a snarl, as the sandwich of slab, constricted between the undercut base and the long roof that pushes the line away to the left, merges in the open face.
(Dave Cook, in *Hard Rock*)

1955 Aug 30   **Woubits**   J Brown, D D Whillans (AL)
A typically fierce lead by Whillans (pitch 2) up yet another imposing line.

Soloed on-sight by R McHardy in June 1970 – a remarkable and groundbreaking undertaking.

Woubits? Woubits!!? What the hell's a Woubits?   (Don Whillans)

The name was picked out of the dictionary by chance – it means a scruffy little bloke.   (Joe Brown)

We scrapped plans for The Mostest and went into Woubits the day after Peter Crew's ascent. Dave (Gregory) nearly came off the first moves and I had a gruelling time on the second pitch in spite of Crew's new piton glinting encouragement thirty feet ahead. Peg marks from a previous retreat did not help and I had a mental picture of a square man in his ratting-hat bridged on the same inadequate holds and perhaps also experiencing some difficulty'.
(Jack Soper in *Still More of Arfon*, FRCC Journal)

1956 March   **The Sceptre**   J Brown, D D Whillans
It didn't seem very significant.   (Joe Brown)

1956 April 1   **The Orb**   R Moseley, J Smith

After many years of exploration and probing by leading climbers such as Birtwhistle, Edwards, Harding, and especially Brown, a long-standing problem was finally solved by Moseley in a race with Whillans, and *White Slab* has become one of the favourites of the current generation.

1956 April 19   **White Slab** (1 pt aid)   R Moseley, J Smith
The entry and the slab above Linnell's Leap had been climbed previously
during various attempts by J Brown, D T Roscoe, J R Allen, and
R Moseley, but on the final one Brown had had to retreat to the stance of
pitch 5 after becoming ill as a consequence of eating contaminated
sandwiches, and the team finished up *Sheaf*.
Later, Moseley returned and entered by Linnell's Leap to complete the route.
The whole climb was done next day by D D Whillans and D T Roscoe.
H I Banner climbed the variation third pitch and went through the Cannon
Hole early in 1959.
J A Austin climbed the variation to the lasso pitch in 1959.
J H Deacon found the modern way of finishing pitch 5, also in 1959;
previously the pitch had traversed right into Walsh's Groove.
J Redhead climbed directly up the slab to the lasso spike in 1981. This has
since often been climbed in mistake – with a notable solo ascent from
J Dawes, and a frightening one in 1985 by A Popp carrying a full sack!

*The most conspicuous slab is a rather light-coloured one with a long
crack in its upper part, known in the past variously as the Concrete Slab,
or the Hourglass Slab; in future, it will be known by neither its texture nor
its shape, but by its colour – the White Slab.*   (CC Journal, 1945-46)

*From a previous position on the arête one can just make out a
hand-sized spike. This is lassoed – on the first attempt, by the lucky or
skilled, and never by the doomed.*   (Peter Crew, in *Hard Rock*)

*A tremendously epic day on this route, which took eight hours in all.
While on the stance above pitch 2, a bloke peeled off from* Narrow Slab
*and we had to rescue him. Then a bloke peeled twice off Linnell's Leap
while Al was waiting to start pitch 3. On the way down, a bloke above Al
slipped off and nearly took both of them down the cliff. All this, millions
of falling bricks, and rope burns from the rescue. The route, however, is
magnificent.*   (D Mathews, A Cowburn, 15 June 1968)

A route to be done over and over again.   (Bill Birch)

*I'd recommend the 'trad' way: try lassoing the spike – harder and more
fun than climbing.*   (Alan Hinkes)

1956 July 24   **Taurus**   D D Whillans, J Brown
A typical Whillans shocker that has stood the test of time. It is thought by
many to be worth E4, in which case it would be one of the earliest
climbs of that grade.

*Brown started up the groove and about 20 feet below the roof encountered a
large tottering block. He was off form, in unfamiliar footwear (an experimental
pair of Vibrams) and his defence mechanism did its job. He could see no way
round the block and, scarcely daring to breathe on it, retreated. Whillans was
not satisfied. He was on peak form and did not have much truck with loose
blocks anyway. He climbed up to the offending obstacle, gave it a thump,
wrapped a sling round it and pressed on.*   (The Black Cliff)

The tottering block survived a few years, eventually coming off with Phil Gordon and nearly terminating the life of his second, one Chris Bonington. (ibid)

Taurus leered at me round the corner and he (Mike Kosterlitz) leered at me too. Frying pans and fires. I took all the slings and pegs and, trying to plan some excuses, I ventured out. Getting to the roof was reasonable, in a loose sort of way, and I put a nut in a little hole at the back of the great overhang. This was it – the dreaded Taurus. Unrepeated for years, loose and overhanging, and unprotected and desperate. I felt to be at the centre of all black steep rock in Wales. (R J Isherwood, 1968)

1957 March 30   **Moonshine** (4 pts aid)   H I Banner, Miss D N Morin
The Direct Finish was added by R Edwards and J Costello with one point of aid on 20 August 1966, and climbed free by P Williams and M Barnicott on 21 June 1986.

1957 April 9   **The Mostest** (4 pts aid)   J Brown
The second was unable to follow. The route was thought at the time to be the hardest on the cliff.
First free ascent by E Jones in 1968.

I put a peg in the back of the overhang and got a runner in the roof on a poor chockstone. I moved onto the arête on the left of the overhang and laybacked the arête so that my head and shoulders were right above the overhang, but I couldn't get into position to leave go to get hold of anything above. So I had to layback down under the overhangs to the peg. I did this three times and eventually thought, 'Well, I'm not going to get any better at doing this.' So I stuck a peg in my mouth and laybacked the arête again. I jabbed the peg into a fault and moved back down. I came back up, hit it with the hammer and just got hold of it like a jug, without clipping. Then I looked down at the peg. It wasn't in a crack at all – it was just resting on a hold with the end biting into the texture of the rock. I lifted it off. (J Brown, on the first ascent)

The Mostest particularly sticks in my mind, as a Morrison-inspired early start saw us reaching the top of the cliff at 8 a.m., just as the second party on a very busy day arrived at the crag. (Mick Fowler)

Mostest Direct Start was added by J Brown and J Smith later in 1957 (first winter ascent: 18 February 1979).

1957 May 3   **November** (8 pts aid)   J Brown, J Smith
R Moseley had previously abseiled down and inserted about eight chockstones, which Brown used for aid.
First free ascent: R McHardy and P Braithwaite, June 1970. A particularly important free ascent as the first had used so much aid.

In summing up this impressive bold lead by McHardy, Braithwaite later wrote: *Really not enough has been made of this ascent. Richard was a*

Shrike (E2), The Pinnacle
Climber: Ed February   Photo: Ray Wood

real visionary and this was much harder than the other hard routes of the time like T Rex, Mammoth, and the like which we had climbed. Richard was outstanding; he always climbed on sight and free and he had very pure and ethical views about climbing. When he did November he didn't have any wires, he just set off on sight with long runouts and thundered up it in big style. Brilliant. Several years later much was made of Left Wall and the like as free routes, but this really was the biscuit.

Soloed by R Fawcett in 1977.

1958 May 4   **Beanland's**   C T Jones, B D Wright, A Cowburn

1958 Oct 25   **Shrike** (4 pts aid)   J Brown, H Smith, J Smith
H Smith led over the first overhang using a peg and two slings.
Climbed free by J Perrin on 9 June 1968.
Soloed by P Jewell 1987.

On a subsequent ascent in 1966 by the Birch brothers, Bill remembers setting off on the second pitch with, at best, poor protection in store and feeling that: 'I was just unsure whether I would have the strength to complete the pitch.'

Shrike, Vember, and The Mostest on Clogwyn Du'r Arddu were magnificent routes up stunning, obvious lines that just cried out to be climbed.   (Mick Fowler, 1995)

…goes on for ever, but still stops too soon.   (Alan Hinkes)

I've done White Slab and The Boldest and they're loose shite, but Shrike – that's excellent. Mind you, on reflection I still can't see the point of Cloggy!   (George Smith)

1959 produced the memorable long hot summer that brought the cliff into mainstream climbing and introduced a host of new pioneers. The grip of the Rock and Ice was broken. Leading figures in this new era would include Hugh Banner and Martin Boysen.

1959 March 28   **Coma Grooves**   R McHaffie, J Douglas
Apparently, this took the rock to the right of *Deep Chimney Route*.
Several teams have tried to locate the route without success.

1959 May 17   **Gecko Groove** (1 pt aid)   H I Banner, R Beesley
A sling on a spike was used to enter the first groove. First free ascent by A I Hunt c.1965.
The variation finish was done by Mr and Mrs J A Austin on 2 June 1962.

1959 May 24   **Boomerang** (1 pt aid)   J Brown, G D Verity
First free ascent by D Murphy c.1966.

1959 Sept   **Woubits Left-Hand** (3 pts aid)   J Brown, M A Boysen
The Cloggy debut of Martin Boysen, who was destined to become one of Britain's leading climbers of the 60s and make some very significant ascents on the cliff. Joe Brown, looking for a replacement second (the first having declined to follow), met Martin at the start of the route. He had to agree with Martin after the climb that he could have climbed the pitch without the peg, had he tried.
First free ascent by A Sharp on 30 June 1975.

I moved up into a very smooth-looking corner, put in a peg and climbed up into the V-shaped section. I was only a move away from the top. If I could get myself onto the wall on the left I could get over the top. I kept going up to this position and back down to the peg. I must have done this three times before I got really exasperated. I was certain it could be done without a peg if I only could stay there long enough to work out the moves. But I was bridged across the groove in a really strange position. So I thought 'to hell with it', got out a peg, Ding, Ding, Ding, and it was all over. When Martin came up the first thing he said was 'I'm sure that top peg wasn't necessary'. I thought that if I had offered him the lead he would have got up without the peg, and I was certain that I could have, if I had been more patient.   (Joe Brown, on the first ascent)

Two magnificent routes were down to the keen eye for excellent, technical climbing that Hugh Banner brought to Cloggy.

1959 Oct 4   **The Troach** (1 pt aid)   H I Banner, R G Wilson
First free ascent by R Evans in 1967.
Soloed by A Sharp in August 1976.
A sling was used to start on the first attempt; this failed at the roof. Banner placed a peg and abseiled off. The line was then inspected on abseil – but not cleaned. On the actual ascent, the abseil peg was removed and another peg was placed (on lead) under the roof. A shoulder was used to start.

Joe dashed up to the cliff thinking that 'Masterplan A' was to be an attempt on Great Wall, and hung around on the first 15 feet of that route. There was a huge crowd watching, including many notables including Whillans, who did Pedestal Crack at least twice to get a close look at the proceedings.   (H I Banner, first ascent)

Hugh continued in the lead. For a long time he was spread-eagled high on the wall below a little overhang. Then suddenly the rope jerked, I had a quick glimpse of flying feet and a descending tuft of grass, then came cries of victory. I looked down at the crowd of spectators: they spanned the generations: Dave Thomas, Brown, Whillans and Morty, a youngster then unknown; Peter Crew, with Jack Soper.   (R G Wilson, first ascent)

I witnessed a great piece of climbing here, Eric Jones of Tremadog and the N face of the Eiger had just got back from the N face of the Matterhorn with Eddie my brother, and he had frost-bitten feet so he could only wear a clapped out old pair of big walking boots. With these on his feet he led Troach in fine style with perfect foot technique. When we got down I remember asking him, 'Bloody hell, Eric, how did you stop on?'   (Bill Birch)

1960 May 7   **The Hand-Traverse** (1 pt aid)   H I Banner, C T Jones
A sling was used to rest. The route was done free regularly by 1968. Soloed by A Sharp in 1976.

I inspected The Hand-Traverse. The Hand-Traverse may have inspected me too, but it didn't say anything. It just sat there like a long, straight, permanent grin, just wide enough for your finger-ends but sadly, not continuous, and slanting upwards too.   (R J Isherwood, 1968)

1960 May 28   **The Bauble**   C J Mortlock, T Wiseman

1960 June 26   **Guinevere**   C T Jones, M P Hatton

1960 October   **The Steep Band** (3 pts aid)   C T Jones, L Brown (AL)
The crux groove was streaming with water on the first ascent. Climbed free by B Ingle on the second ascent.

The next period saw another new generation of pioneers such as the Alpha team of Peter Crew, Baz Ingle, Jack Soper, and Martin Boysen, who systematically looked for quality gaps in the crag in which to thread their routes.

1961 April 27   **Scorpio** (2 pts aid)   N J Soper, P Crew
The aid was used in the small blank groove above the ledge. Climbed free by T Herley in 1968.
Soloed by R Fawcett in 1977.

The next little ceiling involved a traverse into a blind crack. This was laybacked to an apparent jug which turned out to be useless. … I had over 100 feet of rope out and good holds were only 10 feet above, but the intervening section appeared quite blank. Thirty minutes later, after the whole flake on which I was hanging had moved out in response to my efforts to place a peg, a rope became desirable. A Sheffield party supplied it gleefully. With its aid I was able to clean mud and lichen from a hold large enough for two fingers and the move could be made. Pete, blue with cold and displeased at my incompetence, came up rapidly and left the nuts in place. Back on the pedestal and thoroughly annoyed, but in sunshine now, I started up again and soon completed the first legitimate ascent. We called it Scorpio, from the sting in the tail.
(Jack Soper, first ascent, in *The Black Cliff*)

After doing Silhouette I did Scorpio. To compare them: Scorpio is terrifying!   (Louise Thomas)

1961 May 22   The Leastest (2 pts aid)   L Noble, C J Mortlock (AL)
First free ascent by A Sharp, J Harwood on 14 August 1983.

1961 Aug 31/Sept 1-2   The Pinnacle Girdle (some aid)
                                                    N J Soper, P Crew (VL)
Months had been spent by various people investigating the line. A
long-standing problem. The original finish went down *East Gully Groove*
and up *East Gully Wall* variation finish. The modern finish was added by
the same party on 29 April 1962. The route is probably the best of the
Cloggy girdles.

1961 Oct 7   Serth (3 pts aid)   B Ingle, P Crew (AL)
First free ascent by C J Phillips in 1968.
Direct Finish by I Carr and J Adams on 7 September 1984.
Soloed by P Jewell in 1987.

*It is very good to run pitches 1 and 2 together; this saves all the messing
about on the belay, and you can avoid the descending bit as you can
climb directly up the right arête of the upper groove on pitch 1 to the
quartz break. I climbed it like this in 1992 but never recorded it. It felt
really natural. It's good to carry lots of ¼-inch tape slings to protect the
upper part of pitch 1.*   (Ian Carr)

1962 April 27   The Shadow (1 pt aid)   P Crew, B Ingle (VL)
Soloed by R Fawcett in 1977.

*I think this is definitely E3 – you really have to work for your protection on
pitch 2.*   (Ian Carr)

1962 April 28   Daurigol (3 pts aid)   B Ingle, M A Boysen (AL)
The aid was used on the second pitch. Climbed free by R Evans,
J Pasquill, J Syrett in August 1971.

1962 April 29   Bow Right-Hand   N J Soper, P Crew
Originally called *Bow Variations* and graded HVS.
The final pitch had been climbed previously by N J Soper and P E Brown.
The Direct Start was climbed by L E Holliwell, B Whybrow on 19 August
1971 with a point of aid, and free by A Pollitt, P Williams on 12 July 1983.

1962 May 2   Haemagoblin (2 pts aid)   B Ingle, P Crew (VL)
Probably climbed free by M Kosterlitz c.1970.
The first 25 metres of the right wall of the initial groove disappeared in
the '*Carpet Slab* collapse' of February 1986. Re-climbed by P Williams,
D Lawson in May 1988.

The huge wall to the right of *Daurigol* had been tried by some of the best climbers of the day. Controversy flared when Crew pipped Brown to the first ascent by using some six points of aid.

1962 May 27   **Great Wall** (6 pts aid)   P Crew

A long and difficult lead taken in one pitch, firmly establishing Crew as a leading figure on the Welsh scene. The route was graded HXS (one of only a few in the UK) for some time, and as such became *the* favourite HXS.
J Brown had previously climbed what is now the first pitch.
The first free ascent was made by J Allen and C Addy on 28 June 1975.
Soloed by J Moffatt on 12 July 1983.

It rained so the second man, B Ingle, didn't follow, but he did a good job holding the rope and abseiling for the gear.
(Peter Crew – from the first ascent description in the Ynys Hut Book)

As Brown's rule at that time was to use no more than two pegs per pitch, he decided to retreat, leaving the abseil peg marking his highest point. Over the years, this peg on the wall became a constant reminder of Brown's superiority over the rest of the field. He tried to climb back up the wall on several occasions but could not get past the difficult lower section. The wall grew in reputation, just as Cenotaph Corner had years before; the final blank section grew from Brown's original estimate to a figure that sometimes reached 40 feet; the wall became known as the 'Master's Wall' – Brown's own territory, on which no-one else dared to trespass, and it was assumed that sooner or later it would fall to the Master... On the Sunday it was still blowing hard, but I persuaded Bas to go up to Cloggy, just to 'have a look' at the wall. I think he realized that it was going to be more than just a look when I carried both our 300-foot ropes up to the crag. ... The first half of the climb went quickly and I arrived at Brown's abseil peg feeling fresh and confident. Neither of us was very keen to belay on the minute stance, so I fixed a couple of runners and carried on. The next 40 feet or so seemed easy and then I came to the final crack. As the chocks were in place I had not brought any up with me. I realized what a mistake this was when the first one dropped out. I moved up again to the next chock, a small pebble, fixed a sling in it and stepped into the sling. The chock split in half. By now I was getting desperate as I could not take much weight off my arms and my last decent runner was about 50 feet below, on the ledge. Just above the split chock the crack almost closed, so I spent the next ten minutes working a sling into this constriction using a peg. By this time I was absolutely shattered – I was half-standing in the sling on the split chock and using a layback hold with one hand. I sat in the sling to have a smoke and the mist cleared a bit. ... Once I had recovered the rest went easily. ... We had a bit of a problem naming the route. Everyone knew it as the Master's Wall, and if Joe had climbed it that would have been the perfect name. But it seemed presumptuous so we opted for the Great Wall.
(Peter Crew, in *The Black Cliff*)

Five years later, Ed Drummond wrote an account for *Hard Rock* of his own ascent (for which Crew held his rope) beginning with the now immortalized phrase: 'Seal cold in my shorts I was feeling a little blue…' and concluding: 'He was still in love with that wall. Lovely boy Crew, arrow climber. Wall without end.'

John Allen (16 yrs) frees Great Wall *but uses chalk.*   (*Mountain*, July 1975)

John Allen (17 years old) climbed Great Wall *on Cloggy completely free on the 28th June – I'm giving up and going to the Alps.* [Actually, Allen was 16 at the time.]   (C Dale, in the Ynys Book)

Some climbers consider this route to be E3, some E4:

I consider it to be E3, especially now the upper crack is better protected, and micro-cams are carried by lots of people. I was miles away from E4 when I did it first time around.   (Ian Carr)

1962 June 2   **Naddyn Ddu** (2 pts aid)   P Crew, B Ingle (VL)
The name is derived from the North Country greeting 'Na then, thee'.

First free ascent by D Murphy in 1968.
The Direct Start was climbed by A Strapcans on 17 May 1975.

Started up Naddyn Ddu, but got bored by the looseness, so traversed off. Probably the worst route in the world. Minus 3 stars.
                                    (A Sharp, Ynys Hut Book, 29 June 1975)

Poxy; frighteningly so.   (Dai Lampard)

1962 June 3   **West Buttress Eliminate**   B Ingle, P Crew (AL)
A very fine discovery.

The final groove was climbed by the short-sighted P Walsh in mistake for *Sheaf*.
Soloed by J Taylor in 1973.
Lampard's Variation Finish was climbed by D Lampard, I MacNeil on 15 June 1994: a better finish for those wanting pitches more in keeping with the rest of the route.

Definitely only two stars – the first pitch is frightening and the third is desperate and escapable.   (Martin Doyle)

1962 June 10   **Gael** (2 pts aid)   B C Webb, B L Griffiths

1962 June 17   **Pinnacle Arête**   (3 pts aid)   M A Boysen, C J Mortlock
First free ascent by J Perrin in 1968.

Over the good spell at Easter Boysen had climbed White, Woubits, Mostest *and* Slanting *in two days and was on brilliant form, but a spell of glandular fever had kept him ill in bed for over a month. Eventually the strain grew too great and, slightly recovered, he staggered to Cloggy with Colin Mortlock. … Mortlock remembers Boysen painfully elevating himself up the 130-foot pitch, pausing to retch violently into the gully. News spread that Boysen had found it very hard and, as nobody realized just how ill he was at the time, the climb gained an inflated reputation.*   (*The Black Cliff*)

1962 July 28   **The Croak** (1 pt aid)   D Yates, R Phillips
First free ascent unknown.

1963   The Black Cleft (Winter)   M Boysen, B Ingle
Climbed during the big freeze of 1962/63 over three days (cutting steps) – an outstanding achievement.

P Braithwaite made an audacious solo of this winter climb in 1982, a year in which he was also climbing E5, and did a winter ascent of the Walker Spur.

After soloing Black Cleft the plan was to go round and solo Central Icefall but my car had spun off the road on the Cloggy track and I'd lost some time, so I cut my losses and headed to the Grochan in Llanberis where I was able to solo Central Gully [a hard V], and then go down to Craig Ddu and solo Crown of Thorns [IV]. Not a bad day!   (Paul Braithwaite)

Not many people know that Tut soloed The Black Cleft in full on winter conditions in the 80s. I can't imagine anything more tenuous. When I did it I underestimated the amount of rack you need for such a hard route. I was totally stretched and run out reaching the stance. As I scraped away at blind rock looking for a belay, a rescue helicopter came in for a closer look. Blind panic set in as the whole upper slope released deluges of powder. I just managed to hold it together. Nick Bond, using borrowed axes and crampons and on his first big winter route, skipped over the top bulge. Looking back you sometimes wonder how you survived those reckless college days.   (Ian Carr)

1963   *Clogwyn Du'r Arddu* by **H I Banner** and **P Crew**
The first comprehensive and definitive guide devoted exclusively to the cliff. The pace of development on both sides of the Snowdon massif had been so extensive that the area covered by Harding's guides of the 50s now merited three separate volumes. Don Roscoe's *Llanberis North* had appeared in 1961, and Peter Crew was also author of *Llanberis South*, which followed in 1966.

1963 May   **Slurp**   C J Mortlock and party

1963 May   **Little Krapper**   C J Mortlock, L Noble (VL)
Colin Mortlock was consistently self-deprecating in the names he gave his routes. These two have proved better than he credited, and *Little Krapper*, originally coming in at HVS, has become a quite popular E3 after a 30-year wait!

The First Bolt on Clogwyn Du'r Arddu

It was something of a paradox that Crew, who was later highly critical of subsequent bolting on Cloggy, was to place a bolt on *The Boldest*. Crew, of course, was leading on sight and found himself well above any other protection and fully committed to the pitch. The ascent was witnessed by several other leading climbers of the day, who were generally agreed that the bolt was justified. Later, using the bolt for protection, Cliff Phillips dug out a crack and protection below, the route was soloed in 1970, and the bolt was finally removed in 1973.

1963 Sept 21   **The Boldest**   P Crew, B Ingle
  An expansion bolt was placed for protection; this was removed by
  E Grindley in 1973.
  Soloed by A Rouse in 1970.
  The Direct Finish was climbed by C J Phillips, P Minks in 1969.
  First complete ascent with the Direct Finish by P Nunn and
  P Braithwaite in June 1970.

The moves across the top of the groove seemed desperate – friction for the feet and undercut handholds, so as soon as I could stand on a small ledge to the left of the overhang, I tried to put another peg in, but this was hopeless and I had to press on. I was surprised at the number of holds on the next section, but they were all fragile flakes. After each move I became progressively more depressed as I realized I couldn't get down. After about 30 feet I could rest again. With the last runner 40 feet below I was getting scared, especially as a party on The Boulder *were having an epic above me. I had visions of the second falling off and taking me with him. I moved across to a flake on the right and tried to fix a peg. But this only went in about half-an-inch, so I moved up onto the flake and found that I could stand in balance. This solved the problem immediately and I put the bolt in. There was a hushed silence and then furtive mumbling from the crowd as the cardinal sin was committed. With the bolt in place I began to feel happier and holds started to materialize on the first section. Eventually I plucked up courage to move off the bolt. There was a long reach for a small ledge covered in grass, but I had to knock a flake off it first. From the gasp that came up from below I gathered that the crowd thought I was off. In a few feet I was on the Boulder traverse and it was all over. The leader of the Boulder party was still patiently waiting, his rescue dependent on my getting up the climb. He seemed more relieved than I when I joined him on the stance.*   (Peter Crew, in *The Black Cliff*)

2nd ascent. Ed Ward-Drummond, Hugh (Hubris McPerfidy) Drummond – attempted over 3 days (12th, 13th, 15th) partly due to not having read a description and losing the line at the top of the groove. Actual ascent took 2 ½ hours. Graded 6a.   (Ynys Hut Book, 1967)

...the bolt... Alan Austin nearly choked on his Yorkshire pudding when he heard the news.   (D Gray, CC Journal 1970)

Hank Pasquill, the strong Lancashire climber (responsible for some hard gritstone routes which would, decades later, be graded E5) made an early ascent: 'I think I did the third or fourth ascent of *The Boldest*. I thought it was easy, found it all right, but I got this massive rope drag which was a problem. It was easy but I had an epic with the drag.'

Grindley chopped the bolt before leading the hard moves on sight. Feeling against the bolt had been growing in recent years, and Grindley's action will probably receive widespread approval.

(*Mountain*, July 1973)

Al Rouse soloed up behind us watched by R McHardy, who then went on to solo Woubits.   (Paul Braithwaite)

I climbed by bold long moves on the big holds of the shallow groove to reach the roof. From here the rest of the route is hidden and I paused in a wide bridge before launching out leftwards on shattered undercuts and sloping footholds. Now I was committed and a wave of real pleasure accompanied precisely executed moves.

(A Rouse, first solo ascent, in *Extreme Rock*)

Really hard and really bold. It might be a three-star history but the rock is only worth two.   (Karin Magog)

1964 Jan 11   **Great Slab (Winter)**   C Davies, A Davies (AL)
A large gannet was observed perched by the lake; a superb winter route.
(Claude Davies, first ascent)

1964 May 30   **Little Eastern**   R G Wilson, E Townsend

1964 Aug 15   **The Arrow** (1 pt aid)   H I Banner, R G Wilson
Climbed free by C Foord, M Wragg in July 1984.

1965 April 3   **The Key** (2 pts aid)   J Brown, D E Alcock
First free ascent by A Sharp, J Harwood on 14 August 1983.

1965 April 30   **The Far East Girdle** (3 pts aid)   J Brown, D E Alcock
The only aid used now is the rope for the 40-foot abseil.

1965 June 2   **Sinistra** (1 pt aid)   J Brown, J Cheesemond
The point of aid was a shoulder, to start pitch 3. First free ascent probably by P Whillance in 1979.
Direct Finish climbed by P Whillance, solo, on 31 August 1979.

1965 July 4   **Aries**   D E Alcock, B A Fuller

Trapeze (3 pts aid)
T Herley, D Blythe
Slings and pegs were used for aid
on the overhang on pitch 2,
which is often wet.
First free ascent by A Sharp and
R Carey in 1976.

*At this time, this pitch was
considered by most to be a
justifiable aid pitch. Trapeze was
really an aid climb, as was one of
my pitches on* The New Girdle of
The West Buttress.
                    (Rowland Edwards)

Trapeze (E5, second free ascent in 1977)
Climbers: Andy Sharp & Pete Lewis
Photo: Sharp col.

The year 1965 saw the emergence of
Rowland Edwards, with new attitudes
to the sport that were to cause the
establishment all sorts of problems
(first at Cloggy and later elsewhere,
most notably in Cornwall). There can
be no denying his forcefulness or the
difficulty and potential quality of
many of his climbs, but his willingness to use
'quarry' tactics on a traditional mountain crag (which he himself justified in
terms expressed in the quotations below) aroused fierce opposition. Initially
he penetrated some of the last gaps on the West Buttress, but he was to
return in the mid 70s to climb some fine routes in good style.

Diwedd Groove (several pts aid)   R Edwards, M A Boysen
An alternative free start up *Carpet Slab* was made, but this disappeared
in the 'great rockfall' of February 1986.

The two points of aid on pitch 2 were dispensed with by A Sharp and
S Clegg in July 1977.

*I had succeeded in climbing the first pitch and had belayed Martin on a
six-by-two-inch foothold covered in soil, the sum total of the area he had
to stand on. I had led the route up to the big roof, a good two-thirds of the
way up the groove. Martin shouted up that I would not have enough rope
to complete the next part of the pitch (we were on a 125-foot rope). I
eventually made it onto a small ledge on the left where there was a large
flake forming a chimney. I could not get through this as the ropes had by
now gone tight and Martin was calling up that there was no more rope. I
shouted down that if he could untie I could make it a little further and get
onto a good belay. I was at this time jammed half-way into the chimney.
Martin untied, but unfortunately his foot slipped off the small foothold, and
he plummeted over the roofs below. For myself, who had been expecting*

*just a load of slack rope, I received an almighty pull on my waist.
Fortunately, I had the presence of mind to immediately wedge my body
across the chimney and, although I was dragged backwards for a few
feet, I managed to hold the fall. By this time Martin was hanging under the
roofs with the awesome prospect of continuing down over the Steep Band to
land on the screes below. With me holding on for dear life, he climbed back
up the rope, hand over hand, to the belay, and I could continue, now having
the slack rope I needed. Martin in his usual calm way, seconded the pitch
immaculately.*   (Rowland Edwards, on the first ascent)

In The Black Cliff *Ken got it all wrong, and just wrote what he thought
was sensational to get good copy. My bolting which went on on the cliff
was nothing like that which was reported. I think that if you consider that
none of my routes have been freed, then there must have been
justification for using the bolts to gain new areas of rock. I knew at the
time that these climbs would never go without aid. Aid climbing was not
and is not a dirty word. It still constitutes one of the main skills in big wall
climbing, and it is good fun. Diwedd Groove has still never been
repeated as I did it. Most climbers come in from the left. This route used
no pegs and no bolts. When Martin seconded me he was gobsmacked
at what he had to climb on. I used small Meccano nuts on tent cord for
protection. Most of the climbing was free.*   (Rowland Edwards)

The reference to 'no pegs' would appear to apply to the first (the main
aid) pitch only, as the 1967 guide describes the first of the aid points on
pitch 2 as a peg. In the view of the author and editor of this guide, this
criticism of *The Black Cliff* cannot be sustained.

1966 April 30   **Spartacus** (5 pts aid)   R Edwards, A Harris
An intimidating route, forced using advanced artificial techniques.
During the ascent, Edwards dropped a huge grass sod filled with rocks,
which temporarily knocked Harris unconscious.

*Spartacus has also never been repeated as we did it, which again says
something about the style in which we did it. If it can be climbed, well,
maybe, but it certainly could not then!*   (Rowland Edwards)

1966 May 29   **The Arête Finish**   A G Cram, P Scott
They graded it HVS – it is now thought to be E3/4.

1966 May 29   **Chicane** (2 pts aid)   P Crew, G Birtles
Climbed free by M Fowler and P Thomas on 14 July 1979.

1966 May 29/30   **Mynedd** (2 pts aid)   R Edwards, R Evans, M Eldridge
A unique solution to an impossible-looking entry.
A second ascent was made by R Isherwood, but the two-foot
double-pointed lasso spike has now disappeared.

Lampard's Entry was climbed by D Lampard on 15 June 1994; finding no alternative belay he was forced to reverse.

Using patience, skill, and the rope – lasso the flake, and prusik up to it. The flake is solid for a downward pull but doubtful if the pull is outwards.
(Rowland Edwards, first ascent description)

1966 May 30   **Thrombin** (1 pt aid)   P Crew, Miss J Baldock
Tension from a peg was used to cross the lower part of the slab.

1966 Aug 22   **Fibrin** (2 pts aid)   R Edwards, J Costello

1966   **The New Girdle** (13 pts aid)   R Edwards, J Costello,
E G Penman

The route was climbed in several stages. On 14 October, Edwards and Costello did *The Boulder* and the bolt pitch across the right wall of *The Black Cleft*; then, working systematically across the cliff, they descended the 12-metre ('40-foot') corner and continued to the top of *Fibrin*. Some weeks later, Edwards returned with 'Spider' Penman: they reversed *Bloody Slab* to *Haemagoblin*; did a short aid pitch; then descended to *Diwedd Groove*, before crossing *The Leastest* to finish on the Western Terrace. Unluckily, Edwards broke his neck after slipping from a door-frame whilst doing pull-ups. Obsessed by the incomplete girdle, he returned alone with his neck still in plaster to complete the remaining section – the abseil down *Gecko Groove*, and the lasso on *White Slab*.

The use of bolts to cross the right wall of *The Black Cleft* triggered an uproar in Welsh climbing circles at the time, and an alternative way – continuing up *The Boulder* and abseiling down White Slab (slightly different from the route as now described) – was quickly found.

The climb was done in a single day by E Ward-Drummond and T Barley on the third ascent in 1971.

If I could have climbed out of the Black Cleft *wall in any other way I'm sure that I would have done anything to avoid the use of the bolts. It still hasn't gone free.*   (Rowland Edwards)

That bolt ladder was ghastly. We ripped into him, saying Cloggy doesn't need that sort of thing. Paradoxically, I suppose, Crewy had put the bolt in The Boldest, *but that was a different matter – protection rather than aid, and placed* in extremis *too when he found himself committed and unprotected.*   (Ken Wilson)

1967   ***Clogwyn Du'r Arddu*** by **H I Banner** and **P Crew**
A revised and updated edition of the 1963 publication by the same authors. Pitch grades were introduced for the first time, but only for a selection of routes, and confined to a list at the back.

1968 June 14   **Route 68**   D S Potts, B Ingle (AL)

1969   **Mordor** (3 pts aid)   C J Phillips, R Kirkwood
First free ascent by A Sharp and S Humphries in 1976.
Brilliant! Possibly three stars when clean.   (Ian Carr)

1970: a great, dry year for Cloggy. There was a new move to clean up some of the remaining aid of the past, such as that on *November*, which was eliminated by McHardy and Braithwaite. The year was also notable for the cutting-edge solos of *Woubits* and *The Boldest* by McHardy and Rouse.

1970 May 23   **Apollo** (5 pts aid)   L Dickinson, B Molyneux
First free ascent by A Sharp, J Lamb, and S Clegg in July 1977. The name *Spacehound* was proposed, but it never caught on – neither, really has the route!

1970 June   **Gemini**   A Rouse, L Dickinson
Only the leader's second visit to the cliff.
Not as scary as The Boldest.   (Karin Magog)

1970 July   **Flintstone Wall**   G J Gilbert, A S Cole

1970   **Easy Rider**   D Yates, D S Potts
A great find.

1971 May 22   **Syth** (1 pt aid)   D E Alcock, M A Boysen, A Hunt, D Jones
A much fancied line.
Climbed free by J Taylor in 1973.
Pitches 4 and 5 were added by D E Alcock and A Hunt on 26 May 1971.

1971 June 4   **Gormod** (4 pts aid)   D E Alcock, A Hunt (VL)
Two pegs and two slings were used on the second pitch. Nevertheless, this gave a challenging excursion up a futuristic line. All the aid has now rotted and a free ascent would be far harder, though with modern equipment safer.
I would guess (from trying moves during abseil on a very wet day during checking for this guide) about E5ish.   (Nick Dixon)
The exact line of this route was probably misunderstood for some time. *Tut and I prepared this as a new route in the early 90s We put in a few pegs in an overhanging groove, below a roof, but we got rained off and never managed to finish it. I assumed it to be the same line – up an overhanging groove to a roof, then a hard exit.*   (Ian Carr)
In fact, this line to the left is still unclimbed.

1971 July 17   **The Leech**   R Evans, J Pasquill (AL)
The Direct Finish was found by A Rouse and R Carrington in 1975.

A great eliminate addition, which has become popular.

*Ray was always at Cloggy and he dragged me up often enough. I
remember* The Leech; *we cleaned it on the way up, which I suppose was
a bit stupid, looking back. Ray had very hard morals.*   (Hank Pasquill)

1971 July 17   **Syncope** (2 pts aid)   R Edwards, K Toms
First free ascent by A Sharp and P Lewis on 21 June 1983 – a fine effort.

Perhaps a route qualifying for the 'bolder than life itself' tag.
(Paul Williams)

The peg has gone, and it is very short-lived and not particularly hard.
(Dai Lampard)

1971 Aug   **Curving Arête**   R Evans, C Rogers
Forced without any of the aid which had been prophesied by Crew in
1966: 'Can't be done, only two jugs. It would need at least four pegs.'

*Never 5b, it was terrifying. Even after Nick Dixon dropped me a top
rope, it still felt harder than 5b.*   (Ian Dunn)

Soloed by many in the 1980s and 90s.

1971 Aug 17   **Soledad Brother** (3 pts aid)   D J S Cook, B Griffiths
*Some aid from slings and one peg used in the upper part of pitch 2 for
gardening… and to avoid a bivouac. These aids should not now be
necessary.*   (First ascent description)

1971 Aug 22   **Land of Hope and Glory** (1 pt aid)   L E Holliwell,
B Whybrow

The flake crack of pitch 3 was climbed later in 1971 by L E Holliwell,
J W Kingston, and R Ford.
First free ascent: Dai Lampard, Paul Jenkinson in 1988.

1971 Aug 22   **Stomach Traverse** (3 pts aid)   R Evans, C Rogers
Possibly unrepeated.

1971 Sept 17   **Jelly Roll**   R Evans, C Rogers
A neo-classic discovery. Named after jazz musician Jelly Roll Morton.

1972 July 25   **Sea of Cloud**   G Milburn, D Gregory (AL)
Milburn realized that there was a great potential for new routes on the
Far West.

*It struck us both that we were experiencing the same problems as the
teams of the 30s would have found on routes such as* Longland's *and*

Great Slab. *Much of the time was spent tearing away huge grass sods with the aid of a peg hammer.*
(G Milburn)

1972 July 27   **Sun Dance**   G Milburn, D Gregory (AL)
From then on sods of earth thumped down continuously in all directions until it seemed as if it was raining soil. Every so often a big block flashed past and bounded off the slabs into the air and finally smashed into the scree far below. The 'CRUMP' of the grass sods was reminiscent of mortar fire, while the big blocks seemed to explode on impact. By far the worst were the rock fragments which screamed and whined incessantly as they ricocheted in all directions on impact. At the height of the blitz I decided that dodging the debris was like trying to avoid raindrops so I stuck my head into a shallow niche, rather like an ostrich with its head in the sand.
(D Gregory)

1972 Aug 23   **The Republican**   J Perrin, D J S Cook (AL)

1972 Aug 29   **Road of Ghosts**   G Milburn, C Griffiths (AL)

1973 July 7   **Prominus**   J Tout, A Strapcans
The leader was committed after the first couple of moves on the first ascent, and subsequent ascensionists have found this to be a very scary pitch.

A Glimpse of Future Potential
In the early 70s many of the leading Welsh climbers of the day became preoccupied with climbing at Gogarth on Anglesey and, like other traditional areas, Cloggy had become less popular.

Anglesey happened notably because the potential for big routes was drying up on Clogwyn Du'r Arddu. This most famous of all post-war British climbing grounds had dominated ambitions of greater and lesser climbers for a long time. Technical achievements on the steep blank walls of Cloggy progressively reached new heights through the fifties and sixties, spurred on by the masterful performances of Joe Brown. Finally, Cloggy became the only cliff in the entire country to have an entire book published about it. Some time before this a lassitude in purpose had descended over elements in the Llanberis movement.
(*Sea Cliff Climbing in Great Britain*)

There had been some tentative attempts on the huge wall to the right of *Great Wall*. Ray Evans had climbed (on sight) what is now *A Midsummer Night's Dream* to a position by the bolt that Drummond placed. He then climbed down and left onto *Great Wall* just above its first overlap, and descended to the ground. The same day, Hank Pasquill (also in the company

of Evans) had climbed up the first part of what was to become *Indian Face /
Master's Wall*. However, he too descended on closer acquaintance.

*We just had a sniff at it, but Ray knew it would go one day. Ray really did have
Cloggy in his heart at one stage and whilst we knew it would go, it was a bit
hard for then.*
(Hank Pasquill)

1973 July 8   **A Midsummer Night's Dream** (5 pts aid)
E Ward-Drummond

Pitch 1 only, and at a slightly lower level than the current line, under the
sickle-shaped flake and up into what is now *Womb Bits*.
The use of a bolt, skyhooks, and several pegs, as well as top-rope
practice, caused an outcry, and the route was omitted from the 1976
guide on ethical grounds.
This pitch was climbed free by P Whillance and D Armstrong on 28 July
1977 and graded E6, 6b. The higher line was taken which has become
the modern route.
The same pair returned to add two more very difficult pitches on 28 May
1978.
The first complete ascent was made by P Davidson and P Jewell in 1982.

*There has been an attempt to put up a new route on Great Wall, via the
left-slanting weakness that starts midway between Great Wall and
Vember. Four pitons and a bolt were placed, and the line was top-roped
first. This event has triggered off widespread disgust in Welsh climbing
circles.*
(*Mountain*, September 1973)

*This is nothing but a pointless, over-pegged and inferior start to Great
Wall. You seem to have lost all sense of reason if you think it is justified to
use 4 pegs, 1 bolt and 2 skyhooks on any route on Cloggy, let alone this
50-foot diagonal filler-in. You also seem to have forgotten to mention the
fact that you abseiled down, cleaned, chipped and top-roped every
move (on the abseil rope) before completing the ascent. I do not doubt
that you are a good climber, but performances like this show that you
have little thought for climbing and its ethics; you only climb to further
your continued ego-trip. Take a hint from the name of your pointless 'bit'
and wake up.*
(Ed Grindley, Mike Mortimer, July 1973)

*Rocks are not women, pitons are not penises: I am not the pain in your
mind. On the contrary - re AMSND – it is not about waking up – it's
about dreaming and living; about the irreducible marriage of dreaming
(imagining) and living-in-the-world; its heart and hand, mind and body;
not just reason. Your accusation about my 'continual ego-trip' is rather
obscene. What you denigrate is what each of us is – a thinking feeling
self. And if you denigrate the self – you have nothing but dishonesty to
die by. Look at the bumptiousness of what you say – the dictatorial
moralize: 'this is nothing but…' (referring to AMSND) – How do you
know? You haven't climbed it. And it isn't pointless. I learned a lot from
trying to climb that as well as I could, it may help me to climb something*

unknown and extremely hard, better. I'm not saying that it couldn't been done better – I intend to do so myself. But even as it stands, there is some extremely edgy climbing involved that is quite savage – and I think new – mentally. Now that it's been done – in some sense – why not go and improve it? Clip the bolt while leading it if you can, and don't rest on the peg. I know – stated boldly – that 3 pegs, one bolt and a RURP sounds a lot but only one of those pegs was for aid (the second) and the RURP is purely protective also. A good man might crack it without the bolt. But don't be so bloody destructive in the spite you spit out. El Cloggy is in fine shape and no whore either. Nor have the engineers appeared. Let the climb speak for itself.   (Ed Drummond, in reply)

In reply to Drummond, and to help fill out the pages of this book, I'm afraid that, however good a route AMSND is, it won't be going into the next Cloggy guide until it's been led without the bolt. In fact, nothing which utilizes bolts in any manner will be described. Incidentally, Ray Evans had previously climbed to the highest point of the free climbing, on sight and carrying no pegs, but was forced to continue down leftwards to join Great Wall just above the roof.   (Alec Sharp, 1973)

…freed by Whillance in 1977 at E6, 6b – fine effort though this was, Drummond's skyhook blast was the wild ride.

(John Redhead, *High Magazine* 1985)

The route (in its final form) was hailed as a classic by the early 80s and saw many repeats during 1982 and 1983.

Bruce Almost Bounces… Visiting Australian Kim Carrigan, while attempting a repeat ascent of AMSND on Cloggy, fell 65 feet and only avoided making a billabong beneath the cliff by a mere 5 feet. His second, Dougie Hall, saved the day by jumping off his belay ledge to take up slack and was pounced upon by John Redhead to stop him shooting back up again.   (Crags, 1981)

Kim Carrigan, belayed by Dougie Hall, hit the ground on the rope stretch after taking a fall trying to go the wrong way past the top peg placement (which was missing at the time). He fell from above the archway and was stopped by the wire bolt thing. How far is that!   (Ian Carr)

I reached the point where Kim had fallen. Above, on the rock, I seemed to see a dotted white line. I knew that if I went above it and fell off I'd hit the ground.

(D Hall, an attempt at the second ascent, just after fielding Carrigan's fall)

I remember having a prolonged discussion/argument with the Tick [Paul Williams] when he was doing the last guide about the top pitch of Midsummer's. I was convinced it's only 6a, he thought 6b.   (A Popp)

Most climbers now think it is 6a.

Around this time P Whillance is also rumoured to have explored the line to the right, which later became *The Indian Face*.

1973 Aug   **Capricorn** (3 pts aid)   R Newcombe, J Whittle
The skittles are set, now let someone knock them down.
          (First ascent description, referring to the aid used in the top crack)
Climbed free on the second ascent by A Sharp and C Dale on 23 June
1975.

In August 1973, Milburn and Gregory resumed their exploration of The Far
West Buttress.

1973 Aug 25   **Wapentake**   G Milburn, D Gregory (VL)

1973 Aug 25   **Adam's Rib**   D Gregory, G Milburn (AL)

1973 Aug 26   **White Rose Garland**   G Milburn, D Gregory (AL)

1974   **Metamorphosis**   C J Phillips, M Barnicott

1974 March 30   **Illegal Eagle**   A Strapcans, M Barnicott
A very underrated climb at the time.

A Silent Breakthrough
1974 June 29   **Quiver**   P Bartlett, A Brazier
One of the boldest routes in the UK at the time, though unrecognized as
such until recently. Most now think it E6 – if so, it would have been one
of the first in Britain.

At least E5 without a shadow of a doubt, much harder than it looks,
totally devoid of protection and probably irreversible once committed on
the route.   (Dai Lampard)

A fine route, for which the first ascensionist, Phil Bartlett, is rightly very
proud.   (Ken Wilson)

1975 May 17   **Rumpelstiltskin**   A Strapcans, C King

1975 May 23   **Silhouette**   R Edwards, N Metcalf
A classic, and possibly Edwards's best. However, it has recently become
widely known that David Howard Jones had previously climbed at least
part of the route whilst trying to make an early repeat of *Scorpio*.

Just a brilliant route. I went to Cloggy and did it; it was great.   (I Dunn)

1975 June 8   **The Spire**   A Strapcans, C King
A very serious first pitch, which was seriously undergraded.

Alec Sharp contributed only three first ascents on Cloggy, but during his work on the forthcoming guide he was responsible for many important aid eliminations.

1975 June 11   Blancmange Sandwich   A Sharp, S Humphries
A bridging test-piece, which unfortunately follows a drainage line. It is much harder than was first thought.

This line had previously repulsed a number of determined leaders, who found it loose and serious. Prior to their ascent, Sharp and Humphries abseiled down the route in order to topple a ten-foot pinnacle and various other impediments. They were then able to climb the route completely free and without protection pitons. Unfortunately, the climb has been given a fatuous title, presumably to match the nearby Jelly Roll, but this hardly detracts from the style of the ascent and wiser counsels may well prevail on the title before the guidebook appears.   (*Mountain*, July 1975)

Pat Littlejohn was prompted to make the second ascent by the New Climbs booklet that listed the route as Mild XS. He fought his way up on-sight in front of an amazed local crowd that watched as this well-known sandbag was tamed.

I don't think it's had many ascents. I had to give it a good clean from above when I did it.   (Ian Carr)

1975 June 22   Beano (1 pt aid)   C J Phillips, M Crook
First free ascent unknown.

1975 June 29   Head for Heights (4 pts aid)   C J Phillips, N J Estcourt
First free ascent by S Haston and M Pretty in 1983.

Subsequent ascensionists, such as Dai Lampard, have reported the route to be quite hard and the second pitch superb.

1975 July 4   The Sweeper   R Edwards, N Metcalf
Edwards found another good line that had been overlooked by many.

Top end E2 if you stick to the line direct.   (Ian Carr)

1975 Aug 29   Medi (1 pt aid)   R Edwards, T Jepson
Medi and the other route I did at that time didn't use any aid; and this wasn't through the pressure of other climbers but because I would never use them unless justified.   (Rowland Edwards)

Nevertheless, Tim Jepson recalls that tension was taken off the peg on the traverse, and that in discussion after the climb they agreed that this was how it should be described (as indeed it was in the 1976 guide).

Climbed free by A Sharp and S Humphries in August 1976.

My first visit to Cloggy was during the August Bank Holiday weekend in 1975, and Edwards was cleaning what was to become Medi, nearly killing the onlooking climbers. It certainly added to the atmosphere. Many years later, in the mid 80s, I climbed the route and it was still loose! (Chris Gore)

1976 June   **Grovel**   A Sharp, S Humphries

1976 *Clogwyn Du'r Arddu* by **Alec Sharp**
The ultimate slimline guide. Text is crisp and clear, but ruthlessly purged of any superfluity, and superlatives are strictly rationed. It came just too early for E grades, but pitch grades are provided here comprehensively (though still confined to a list at the back of the book) – a great effort in assessing all but six of the routes at VS and above.

1977 July 6   **Hazy Days**   A Sharp, J Lamb, S Clegg
A clean, airy route in the modern style and now thought to be much harder than originally claimed.

1978 May 20   **The Rumour**   J Moran, A Evans (AL)
Someone said to Jim: *Hey, there is this rumour going round that you've done a new route on the Pinnacle. Is it true?*

1978 May 30   **Pistolero** (2 pts aid)   E Cleasby, P Burke, K Myhill
First free ascent by J Moffatt and P Williams on 16 July 1983.
A route which, since its second (the first free) ascent, has become popular.

Phil Burke hanging on the peg on pitch 2 – Ed Cleasby exasperated, 'Come back down. Its only 5a.' Forty minutes later – Ed Cleasby hanging on the peg on pitch 2 – Phil Davidson walking along the foot of the crag shouts up, 'Hey, Ed, is it still only 5a?' Ed's reply was unprintable.

1978 Aug 26   **Desperate Straights**   R Fawcett, S Porter, P Livesey
The first of Fawcett's important climbs on Cloggy.

The first two months of 1979 produced some excellent snow and ice conditions, and Mick Fowler, Roger Baxter-Jones, and Paul Braithwaite were responsible for some very hard and significant first winter ascents – *Silver Machine* and *Red Slab* represent a breakthrough in Welsh winter climbing standards. Several ascents were also made of classics such as *Great Slab* and *The Black Cleft*.

1979 Jan 21 **Jubilee Climb** **(Winter)**   M Fowler, M Morrison
More used to travelling all the way from London to Scotland, the pair
found that North Wales was in perfect condition and that there was
some really superb climbing to be had. This was the first of a superb
series of climbs made by Fowler that season.

Really very good mixed kind of stuff. Excellent!   (Mick Fowler)

An excellent winter climb.   (Dai Lampard)

*The best and most enjoyable of all the winter routes I've done are in
Wales, perhaps with the exception of Sticil Face.*   (Steve Long,
      after a very late-in-the-day ascent of *Jubilee Climb* in February 2003)

1979 Feb 3 **Brwynog Chimney** with **The Arête Start** **(Winter)**
                                              M Fowler, M Morrison
*I remember this one being really hard at the bottom, but we gave it IV as
it was less than 500 feet long.*   (Mick Fowler)

Brwynog Chimney is now thought to be a hard VI pitch.

1979 Feb 4 **Camus** **(Winter)**   M Fowler, M Morrison
This route is *much* better in winter.

1979 Feb 18 **Mostest Direct Start** **(Winter)**   M Fowler, M Morrison
It was this route that drew my eye onto Silver Machine just to its left.
                                              (Mick Fowler)

1979 Feb 24 **Silver Machine** **(Winter)**   M Fowler, C Griffiths
This route climbed a true new winter line. The wet slabs to the left of
Rumpelstiltskin ice up and are not climbed in summer.

*I remember this route being very hard, the first pitch in particular being
exceptionally hard.*   (Mick Fowler)

Still unrepeated.

1979 Feb **Red Slab** **(Winter)**   P Braithwaite, R Baxter-Jones
*Paul Nunn, Roger, and I had gone up to Cloggy in deep snow to do The
Black Cleft but a party was already on that route and moving slowly.
Seeing the fine smear to the left of Bloody, we scrambled up to it. A small
moustache of snow from the right allowed me to access the ice smear that
was only two or three inches thick in places. I realized it was not too hard
to climb, and just kept making easy moves up it, but all the time unsure
where it would take me or what would be at its top. Of course, there was
no protection. I found a blob at the top and was able to place a wire
before making the very difficult traverse left, hanging the tips of my picks
on the tiny edges we use in the summer to climb it.*   (Paul Braithwaite)

1979 July 6   The Axe   P Littlejohn, C King
One of Britain's most prolific pioneers made his debut on the cliff with this immaculate find. On the first ascent, the route traversed in above the initial overhang from *The Croak* (a far harder option).
The usual way, direct over the overhang, was done by J Moran on the second ascent in 1979.
Soloed by P Jewell in April 1987.

The photo of Jimmy Jewell in the old guide is nice; but the route is overrated. I've done better routes at Whitestone Cliff! (Steve Crowe)

Next came the first new route on the cliff from John Redhead, who was to make a huge impact on the Welsh scene over the next decade.

1979 July 27   The Orphan Flagellator   J Redhead, C Shorter
Originally climbed in two pitches, the first starting on the Pedestal and finishing on a stance on Pedestal Crack. (Chris Shorter)

Paul Williams, with another agenda, renamed the route Organ Flagellator in the previous guide. (John Redhead)

We did give it this name at the cliff top (Orphan Flagellator), but by the time we had walked back down to the bottom where one of the orphans was sitting, we had decided that, being fairly recently bereaved, they might not be very amused! I don't think either of them realized and it was a private joke between John and myself. (Chris Shorter)

Fully tricky, mega exposed, bold and brilliant. (Tim Neill)

1979 Aug 29   The Boulderer   P Whillance, P Jewell (AL)
Its reputation has grown over the years since its first ascent.

He's a cool bastard. He led the first pitch with a fag nonchalantly hanging from his mouth, just like you imagine Joe doing in the old days.
(P Jewell, first ascent)

Bob Wightman took a 30-metre fall on this after a hold broke off. A sling on a rounded knobble held him. How it held him, I'll never know, but if it hadn't he would not be here today! The climbing is not very hard but it is bold. (Dai Lampard)

1979 Aug 29   The Purr-Spire   P Livesey, J Lawrence
A fine contribution by this prolific pioneer of the 70s.

Purr-Spire Direct was claimed by N Dixon in 1983 after cleaning significant loose holds and preplacing an ugly nut.
The first pitch was claimed (as the Direct Start) as having been climbed by P Davidson and P Jewell in 1982, by Paul Williams in retrospect in the 1989 guide.

1979 Aug 30   **Vanishing Giraffes**   P Whillance, R Berzins, M Berzins
Next day, a dangerous climb from this very bold leader, who also
soloed *Sinistra Direct* that year.

Master's Wall ~ I

The area of rock to the right of *Great Wall* and *A Midsummer Night's Dream*
was again attracting attention from those with an eye to the future.

1979 August 31   **Spreadeagle**   M Fowler, P Thomas
*I spoke to Pete Whillance, who told me that the holds led off right; so I set
off up the groove and headed off right and up and managed to get a
belay in the Drainpipe Crack. I belayed where the angle of the Drainpipe
eases. I was aiming for a vague crack and not really knowing how to get
to it. I moved left onto the wall and up for 15 feet, then made some really
hard moves to get up a crack to belay as for Jelly Roll.*   (Mick Fowler)

The first tentative probings up the right side of The Great Wall.
                                                                (Paul Williams)

Not very dissimilar to Master's Wall.   (Tim Neill)

Fawcett's most significant first ascent on Cloggy was the 'easiest' line up the
Final Judgement Wall of the Pinnacle. *The Final Judgement* was a spoof
route written up in Ynys Ettws Log Book by Pete Crew and credited to M Yates
and P Johnson (the former had just gone to America for three years and the
latter was dead) on 22 July 1967; it started up what has now become *Psycho
Killer*, reversed *Aries* for 20 feet, before climbing direct to *The Hand-Traverse*
peg and moving left to finish up the prominent overhanging arête. All these
sections are now climbed, the upper half being *It Will Be Alright in the Night*.

1980 May 19   **Psycho Killer**   R Fawcett, P Williams, J Moran
Second ascent by the 'flying Kiwi' Roland Foster in 1982, who clocked in
more air miles here taking a 12-metre fall!

Master's Wall ~ II

In 1980, the line to the right of *Great Wall* (that which was to become *Master's
Wall* and *The Indian Face*) became an obsession of John Redhead, who
committed himself fully to the task, the result of which, after many harrowing
attempts, jumps for ropes and lowers from skyhooks, and a 20-metre fall, was
an impasse at 25 metres. In 1982, Redhead placed a bolt with the intention to
return the following year, provocatively grading the pitch E8 7a.

1982   **The Tormented Ejaculation**   J Redhead
*…my own attempts from 1980 have been well wagged about. I call them
The Tormented Ejaculation − not just mere climbing, but an expression of
the flesh and blood of my work, the poetry of rock-movement inextricably
bound up with the network of shape and colour. A last look at the line and*

'The Tormented Ejaculation' (E8)
Climber: John Redhead
Photo: Keith Robertson

a strange impulse took hold of me. I went for it. At 70 feet I woke up. Ghastly! The aggression was dissipated and fear gripped me. I had climbed with virtually no protection and was now eyeballing a tiny shallow crack. I remembered it from the abseil and it had looked pathetic. It was real now. I contemplated jumping on the scree below before the situation got out of control. I fell a million times, my arms unfolding, my breath fading. A No.1 stopper came to a halt, half-way down this crack, half in, rocking – my weight was on it... The mental preparation was becoming harder and harder. The so-called psyching-up, a pain beyond reason. Out of the acquaintance grew more and more fear. Gone the initial naivety which had sparked off this now terrifying enterprise. I knew the score and was unnerved by it... I distinctly felt a tiny slide on a friction move lower down and became very insecure, with my feet in Canyon boots. I got to the little crack another 20 feet up and was dangerously pumped because of the extra strain on my fingers. The resin was wearing off the boots. I managed to place an RP1, clipped in and was about to place a No.2 when my right foot shot off. The strain came on the RP, ripped it through, and I cartwheeled a long way down the wall.   (John Redhead, *High* 1985.)

That *picture* of Tormented Ejaculation *is the most positive image of rock-climbing I have ever seen.*   (Johnny Dawes)

During research for this guide, the author asked John Redhead: 'What would you have done, John, if you had got to the resting-foothold [on *The Indian Face*] at 85 feet? The climbing above there is miles harder than below; and having fallen in the lower groove, you would have definitely fallen on the top wall, and if you had fallen on that top wall you would have probably died.'
John replied: 'The wall above was virgin and beautiful then and you have to be prepared to die for it. An element of doubt – that's what flips my skirt.'

Isn't drilling bolts called rotary chipping?   (Johnny Dawes)

In 1982, John Redhead brought an up-to-date perspective to Cloggy's Great Wall saga with The Tormented Ejaculation *at a mighty E8 7a, with a bolt marking the high-point of his bold explorations on one of the most celebrated lines in the country. Controversy was inevitable.*
(Bill McKee, OTE 113)

1982 April 10   **Death and the Maiden**   C Shorter, Miss J Herbert
Concerning the main pitch, I have always wondered whether Paul Williams mixed up his left and right.   (Chris Shorter)

1983 July 7   **Moonlight Shadow**   I Carr, P Braithwaite (AL)

Master's Wall ~ III

The saga of the wall right of *Great Wall* continued with a very on-form Jerry Moffatt making a route past Redhead's bolt placement on *The Tormented Ejaculation*. The route was provocatively named *Master's Wall*.

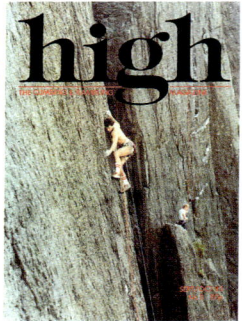

The first ascent of *Master's Wall*
Climber: Jerry Moffatt
Original photo: Roland Foster

1983 July 14   **Master's Wall**   J Moffatt,
                                    P Williams

After close abseil inspection, Moffatt chopped the bolt and climbed the pitch via a difficult escape right to Spreadeagle. Firé rock-boots make a dramatic entry to the UK!
(Paul Williams)

Moffatt was genuinely concerned at the possible creep of bolts into the mountain areas of the UK (bolts had already been placed in the Llanberis Pass and the delineation had not yet been made between sport and traditional climbing). He felt he was climbing better now than Redhead and was in a position to eradicate the bolt from the crag.

I had spent two days belaying John Redhead on the route the previous year and I knew where his line went; he was trying to go right of the bolt, then rightward to a crack, then boldly up the wall. When he placed the bolt I was really offended and thought that it was ethically wrong. I remember at that time there was a risk of bolts going everywhere. Anyway I just went where he was going and I didn't think of going left from the bolt. It was not on sight but also not as well prepared as it could have been. It was really bold and really hard (and I was going really well at the time). It was a total three-star experience.   (Jerry Moffatt)

Ian Carr was climbing above The Drainpipe Crack and moving into *Jelly Roll* as he witnessed Moffatt's ascent:
We'd been on Cloggy every day for a week and had seen Jerry preparing the line started by Redhead. By chance I was seconding the middle pitch of Jelly Roll as Jerry moved past the site of the bolt. The whole crag had stopped to watch. Strung out, Jerry called over, asking advice where the next holds were. About 4 feet above were a chalked set of edges, fingers on layaways, and feet smearing. Jerry went for it, hung the edges and got himself sorted out. I stayed, frightened of putting him off, until he'd moved out left again. At the time it was the most impressive bold and serious bit of climbing I'd ever seen. At the stance, Jerry had no gear to belay with. I gave him a screwgate and moved off up the top pitch of Jelly Roll. Weeks later, in the Cromlech car-park, I got a tap on the shoulder and Jerry returned the krab.

The line was well prepared and top-roped a number of times, and completely chalked. Jerry climbed it in style and it was the boldest at the time. Spaced out way above gear. (Ian Carr)

John Redhead returned to make the second ascent.

Master's slipped by, the greyness in my head a little paler, almost unnoticed – an anti-climax. Sad at the butchered aesthetics, though happily steadied by the purity of movement, I cast my eye at the blinding, deathlike passage that beckons – a little leftwards…
(John Redhead, *High* 1985.)

I slept on the rocks in the sunshine by the lake whilst John abseiled and cleaned the winter from Master's Wall. He awoke me in the evening and I thought it was time to go home. Ten minutes later I was paying out the rope on Master's Wall, which Johnny dispensed with easily in his new Firé boots. My turn saw me without a chalk bag (we only had one between us) but moving quickly, still in that semi state of sleep; Master's Wall flashed past me with slate-like ease. We smiled and spoke little, packed our things, and headed down to Llanberis. At the Halfway House we stopped for lemonade and chocolate. Two climbers sat opposite. 'Wow, that was really something!' The comment came in our direction. I sat back, leaving Johnny to feed his ego in praise. A pause – the follow-up was stunning: 'I've never seen anyone move so quickly, or make something hard look so easy as when you seconded that route.' I nearly choked with laughter; Johnny's face dropped momentarily, and suddenly I was there beside him with a monstrous ego. (Dave Towse)

Moffatt chopped the Bolt – totally justified if it winked cheekily on his route, but it didn't. It shook with fear 10 feet off route on a totally different concept. (John Redhead, 1996)

[In this statement Redhead is referring to the line which moves up left across the headwall and became *The Indian Face*.]

In 1997 at the age of 17, Leo Houlding made a very bold on-sight ascent, finding the route dangerous and the route-finding difficult: *'…the hard bit. The bulk of the route is just wandering, and in the end I did a full-on traverse into* Spreadeagle.'

In 2000, J McHaffie (Caff) attempted an on-sight of this route. However, he probably strayed up onto *The Indian Face*, where he became committed without protection and thoroughly stuck.

I just thought I'd tick the classic historic route Master's Wall. *I got to where the wire should have been and spent twenty minutes trying to find it, but eventually gave up. I moved up after placing a skyhook, and got to a semi-rest where a lot of doubt was creeping into my mind about where to go. I committed to another sequence to get what I thought would lead rightward but it didn't, and I was pumping and my feet were starting to sketch about. It looked really blank above but I managed to get stood on some small crimps. I couldn't move up or right or left; then the sun came onto me. There was no going anywhere so with the sun on me I untied and dropped the ropes.*

Some people by the lake shouted but they got a gobful off me in this state. Adam had a hard time getting to the top (he'd never been to Cloggy before)… Two 9mm ropes tied together so that they would reach eventually sailed across the face above and slid down to me. This is where I kack-handed the knot – I tied a slip-knot. As I fell onto it I started to fall fast and I swung wildly past Vember. The loop I was in was lengthening and slipping. Somehow I ended in Vember and rapped off the same ropes almost before it had happened.

In desperation, I had thrown my rack away and it was scattered all over the bottom of the cliff. To cap it all my ropes got snagged in Vember when Adam dropped them.

I would have given a few pieces of my body, though, to get off that piece of rock. I had gotten onto the climb believing I could climb out of pretty much any situation – that there were no mental boundaries. My arrogant approach on the intricately contrived eliminate showed me that climbing can't replace life.   (James McHaffie, 2000)

The validity of *Master's Wall* as a route remains a subject of contention, and many who haven't climbed it are as eager to pronounce as those who have. It does seem that this great effort by a very on-form and talented Moffatt has left a route that is nevertheless superseded by the much better line of *The Indian Face*. Only time will tell whether it is worthwhile. Undoubtedly, however, this was the best there was until 1986…

1983 July 17   Going Straight   C Foord, M Wragg (AL)
  The second *direttissima* up The Great Slab; it uses the *Syth* entry.

1983 Sept 1   Hidden Treasure (2 pts aid)   C Foord, M Wragg (AL)
  A small amount of aid was used to force a very impressive line.

1984 July 7   Bloodlust (2 pts aid)   M Wragg, C Foord (AL)
  The aid was used to climb the *Slanting Slab* entry.

1984 July 23   Womb Bits   J Redhead, D Towse
  A brilliant eliminate addition to the wall that had been overlooked by the activists of the day.

  …inspected, cleaned and dreamily cruised. Mocking The Black Cliff, *Towse asked, 'Womb Bits, Womb Bits, what the hell's a Womb Bits?'*
                          (John Redhead, *High* 1985)

  [Looking rightwards] *I cast an eye at the death-like passage that remains… a little leftward… can there ever be enough love?*
                          (John Redhead)

  Again, Redhead is referring to what was to become *The Indian Face*.

1984 July 25   **Margins of the Mind**   J Redhead, D Towse
A belay bolt was placed above the roof. This has been removed since and a nut placement excavated beneath.

Clipped into the belay bolt, I watched Johnny as the evening quickly slipped away. He couldn't seem to commit himself to the move above the poor peg, so I shouted up some encouragement. He went for it, snatching the creaking flake above, the crucial stopper 1 in his mouth. In the failing light he couldn't locate the placement. In extremis, he screamed, 'You've let me down, Dave, you bastard, you've let me down.' Like some TV game, macabre in concept, I played with Johnny's life, and talked his hand to the small hole for the runner.   (Dave Towse)

We slept till noon and climbed in the orange of evening. The first line was Margins of the Mind.   (John Redhead)

Redhead had recently made the second ascent of *Master's Wall* and he felt that *Margins* was harder though *Master's* a bigger lead.

After climbing Octo we descended back to our sacks, and I noticed a couple of blokes on the wall to the left. I knew they were well off route, and with the sun setting I thought they could be in for a bit of an epic! So I took a photo and then quickly descended for a pint.
          (Alan Hinkes, on witnessing the first ascent of *Margins of the Mind*)

In July 2003, after inspection and preplacing some wires, Nick Dixon made the second ascent of *Margins of the Mind* over two days and with the ropes re-clipped. He found the route to be very hard and dangerous and considered it probably E8. If that assessment was correct it would have been the first E8 in the UK.

1984 Aug 20   **Human Touch**   A Sharp, J Harwood
Found to be considerably harder than originally thought.

…much harder than it looks.   (Dai Lampard)

1985 July 4   **Dinas in the Oven**   A Popp, N Dixon (AL)
While Dixon made his way down from the top, Popp prepared himself, then led pitch 1 on sight.
The name was coined by Tamsyn Reseigh on the return home.
The central arête was originally climbed via a shallow groove on the right. However, a direct ascent beckoned and Dixon returned for a more fitting middle pitch with D Green on 21 May 1988.
This was the day Dawes climbed *West Indian Face* and the ascent was captured on video by Al Hughes.

More like three hard gritstone pitches: E5, E7, E5   (Nick Dixon, 1988)

I had a clean and a go at what is now pitch one of Dinas in 1982, but it was too unprotected for me. Top-roped it though.   (Ian Carr)

1985 July 15   **Bold Man, Big Willie**   N Dixon, A Popp

Dixon, keen to make the best of a lull in poor weather, climbed the line in cloud and fog and declined to give an accurate grade. Allen Williams, also in the party, wisely declined to follow the route.

Great winter conditions returned to North Wales in early 1986.

1986 Feb   **Longland's Climb (Winter)**   P Braithwaite, I Carr,
                                                       R Baxter-Jones

The ascent of Longland's really was quite something. It was a perfect winter day with deep powder snow right down to our car, and the whole crag was covered. We arrived at the crag and I was bouldering around near the base of Longland's and the turf was really crisp and hard and we just thought we'd go for it. We used no pegs and no aid and it really was hard, much harder than The Black Cleft, and it was a really interesting climb that gave me a real spring in my stride. I remember leaning out on my axes near the top and just giving it whatever was left. It was just one of those days. On the steep crux wall at the top in the dusk I remember someone passing by the base of the crag and shouting 'What are you on ?' Brilliant.   (Paul Braithwaite)

We sat on top of the snow-choked crevasse stance with only an hour or so before daylight ran out. The way forward looked impossible: 'the Overhang'. The rock to the left was even steeper, and escaping the line to the right would involve rope tricks, something we didn't want to consider after such a struggle below.
Tut was in the lead, but before he set off I managed to reach a reasonable wire to the left, saving a fall directly onto the belay. There were two or three flat spiky jugs leading to a fantastic snow arête. With only a sling over a sloping spike and incredible balance, Tut hooked each jug in turn and levitated towards the snow. A one-arm lock-off then allowed a tool to be thumped into the snow above. Amazingly it went in with a reassuring thud, and further placements in névé allowed a long slanting wide crack to be reached.
Belaying and watching the still blue sky darken it seemed like it took Tut an age to do the next 10 metres. Then it was my turn. Three one-arm pull-ups and thud, it stuck and I was locked in the slanting crack. From below I'd assumed it was all over, but the exit up the crack was as sustained and technical as anything below.
At the top, in failing light, Tut pulled out his hip flask to toast our success. Without a benchmark we graded it VI; we know better now!   (Ian Carr)

It seems a grade of VII or VIII is more likely, and at the time of writing this route is still unrepeated.

In February 1986, a massive rockfall, estimated at 10,000 tons, marked the demise of Carpet Slab.

1986   **The Spire Direct**   A Popp, D Crilly

Climbed on sight in mistake for the original route (the party had no guidebook with them) by one of the bolder climbers of his generation.

1986 Sept 24   **Authentic Desire**   J Redhead, D Towse

I climb now not caring, and the beauty in front of me demands and craves my attention, lovingly; I crave authentic desire.   (Dave Towse)

The players and the games. The Black Cliff has lured generations of climbers, attracted, no doubt by its mountainous intimidating presence. Once committed, however, there opens an experience of the simple joy and pain of breathing its spirit. It shocks out of complacency so dramatically, so finally, that the faint hearted scurry to the wings – or worse, back to Halfway House.   (John Redhead)

A remarkable (and the first) on-sight ascent of this route was made by L Houlding in 1998.

The Pinnacle routes are way different from those on Great Wall. Great Wall is a nice place to hang out, but the Pinnacle is in the shadows, and this is a really dangerous route.   (Leo Houlding)

Master's Wall ~ *The Indian Face*

The Indian Face climbs the obvious line on the right side of The Great Wall and is the culmination of the exploration begun with *Spreadeagle*, and continued through *The Tormented Ejaculation* and *Master's Wall*.

To recap: the first part of this route (to an old bolt sleeve at 25 metres) was climbed by John Redhead in 1982 and named *The Tormented Ejaculation*. This represented a high-point in bold climbing. Redhead cleaned the line on abseil but did not indulge in the more thorough practice used today. He had also taken several long falls from the open groove at 20 metres.

In 1983, Jerry Moffatt found a way up and right from the bolt, which he had removed: *Master's Wall*.

Finally, in 1986 Johnny Dawes, having moved to Llanberis to take up the challenge of the best line in the country, climbed the lower groove and then the headwall to mark a major step forward in British climbing standards.

It had been my dream to climb The Indian Face *ever since reading Pete Livesey's 'Shape of Things to Come' article. With this in mind, I moved to Llanberis and dedicated myself to it.*   (Johnny Dawes)

1986 Oct 4   **The Indian Face**   J Dawes, R Drury, S Miles

The history of this route, more than any in the latter part of the twentieth century, marks some of the greatest efforts in British climbing; and the associated passion, heart, and spirit that has been invested here has lead to real risk, real drama, loss, tragedy, success, and euphoria.

Johnny Dawes in 'The Tubes'
Photo: Nick Dixon

This line had come in for attention from some of the leading climbers of their day including, Hank Pasquill, Ray Evans, Pete Livesey, Mick Fowler, and Pete Whillance.   (Johnny Dawes)

We all know where the line goes and this is it.   (Leo Houlding)

Dawes had attempted the line three times on sight, his best effort reaching a high point at around 20 metres.

The Indian Face
An early on-sight attempt by
Johnny Dawes
Photo: Dawes col.

Here, he sets the scene and describes his successful ascent:

Johnny [Redhead], frustrated but proud, placed a bolt like a dog pissing to mark his territory and retreated to recover. An 80-foot cameo, The Tormented Ejaculation graded E8, 7a, a small Matisse sketch, fresh but perhaps unfinished, rests in his portfolio; but the line remained...
Jerry arrived, chopped the bolt, and the Master's Wall remained...
The climbing itself is hard and with eight bolts would rate about E6, 6c; but there is only half a bolt and that stares at you while you laugh at your runners, a tribute to both a man's vision and his short-sightedness. John Redhead's voyages on the wall deserve special praise. Imagine the wall. It is a random woven wire mesh tilted so that it steepens towards the top. At the base of the wall the two thick cables disappear in the turf. The lights in the town flicker as you touch the rock. Each move forms an electric circuit between your hands, you see. As you move, you worry about the outcome of that move. The tension at present resides in a dull 'Dinorwig Power Generator' hum. Then I make a false move and the rock barks out a spark, a whip sizzles down my arm and fades to a sickly warmth in my shoulders; I try another hold – but which one to use? Use the wrong one and retreat may be impossible. The gear is poor and a bad mistake could mean a death jolt full across the heart. So you move taking note of your position and the holds, but as you move higher the voltage grows, and amongst the myriad connections there lie false trails that can kill.
I went up with sticky rubber soles which do not conduct electricity and two friends who knew the score.
Hundred foot up, out above the last gear, I'm faced with the first of the hardest moves, my anxiety has made me enter the moves before reflection and the rock is all in the wrong place. My body feels heavy and lumpy. I slapped out right, a move that should be static, and was committed to the crux; a precarious mantel onto a rounded boss. If I fell off this move the gear would rip as it was off to the left and the gear was only in downward-pulling placements. Once on this you can rest and clip the tied-off RURP, which is most comforting. You stand on your heels, your hands by your side. At this point I noticed a friend I'd met while on holiday in Verdon, on the belay of Great Wall. His face spoke volumes. I went for the crux, the motion startling me like a car unexpectedly in gear in a crowded parking lot. I swarm through the roundness of the bulge to a crank on a brittle spike for a cluster of three crystals on the right; each finger crucial and separate like the keys for a piano chord. I change feet three times to rest my lower legs, each time having to jump my foot out to put my other in. The fingerholds are too poor to hang on should the toes catch on each other. All those foot-changing mistakes on easy moves by runners come into my mind. There is no resting, I must go and climb for the top. I swarm up towards the sunlight, gasping for air. A brittle hold holds under mistreatment and then I really blow it; fearful of a smear on now non-sticky boots I use an edge and move up, a fall now fatal. But the automaton stabs back through, wobbling but giving its all,

and I grasp a large sidepull and tube upward, the ropes dangling uselessly from my waist. Arthur Birtwistle on Diagonal, I grasp incuts and the vectors recede. The Indian Face is climbed and I can rest and feel proud. Longland's, the Drainpipe Crack, Troach, Great Wall, and Midsummer's smile in me again, but like fine antiques in the gallery.

(Johnny Dawes, first ascent)

Probably the most serious route in Britain, and an inspired performance from the leader – who almost 'came to grief' twice during his ascent – despite top-rope inspection!

(Paul Williams)

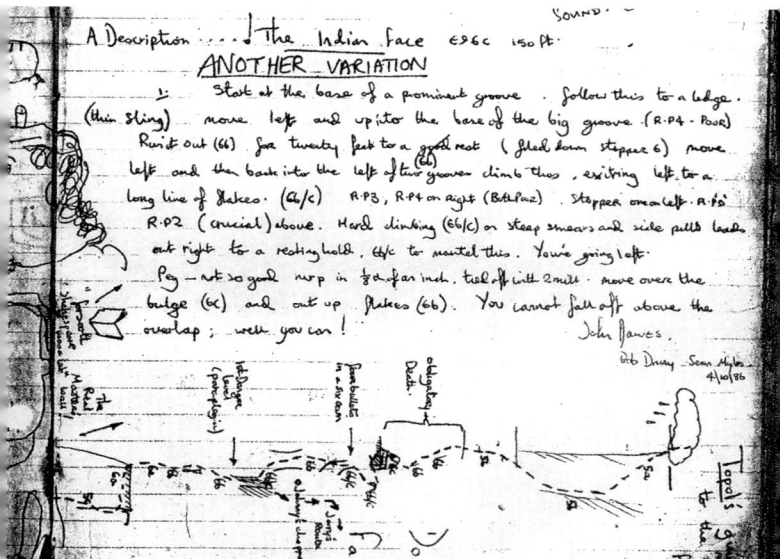

A Description .... the Indian Face E9 6c 150 ft.

ANOTHER VARIATION

1. Start at the base of a prominent groove. Follow this to a ledge. (thin sling) move left and up into the base of the big groove (R.P4 - Poor) Runit out (6b) for twenty feet to a good rest (filled down stopper 6) move left and then back into the left of two grooves climb this, exiting left to a long line of flakes. (6a/c) R.P3, R.P4 on Right (Both Poor). Stopper one on left R.P5 R.P2 (crucial) above. Hard climbing (6b/c) on steep smears and side pulls leads out right to a resting hold. 6b/c to mantel this. You're going left.

Peg - not so good nrp in 3 or far inch. Tied off with 2 mill. move over the bulge (6c) and out up flakes (6b). You cannot fall off above the overlap; well you can !

John Dawes,
Rob Drury - Sean Myles
4/10/86

In 1987, whilst abseiling down *The Indian Face*, John Redhead pulled on the peg on the upper wall and to his horror it came out; then worse – a large segment (30cm by 30cm) of the flake broke off.

Johnny swung across to the flake and carefully put his hand on the rope around the small blade peg. It twanged, and went for the scree. The flake made a twig-like cracking noise. I looked in Johnny's eyes, he in mine. Aware of the consequences, we giggled nervously at one another. I swung over, and then, with appalling ease, we carefully lifted off the flake of Dawes's amazing climb. Behind it, the mark of the peg was visible and, spreading out from it, lines of wetness showing the result of a winter's freeze and thaw.

(Dave Towse.)

Fresh from that den of throbbing climbing gossip, Pete's Eats, emerges yet another snippet of lurid, detail-free information. Innocent John Redhead, once falsely accused of tree-felling in Ogwen, was allegedly abseiling down a direct line on Master's Wall on Cloggy up which he hoped to make a first ascent. Innocently, he swung across to the right, to the peg on Indian Face, Johnny Dawes's pride and joy route. Swings back in amazement: 'The peg just came out in my hand Guv,' said gentleman John. What was more the flake was loose. Being very brave (pun) he returned with Dave Towse, and abseiling together they removed the offending piece of rock, carefully carrying it to the bottom of the crag and all the way back to Llanberis and delivered the flake to Johnny Dawes, which was like waving the proverbial red rag to a sitting bull (groan). It is of course an old custom in Snowdonia to bring down to the valley all loose rock. As the flake's demise has now rendered The Indian Face *unclimbable [Oh, really?] this made Johnny Dawes hopping mad, and while on the warpath, he almost but not quite came to blows. It is now rumoured that he has squawn revenge and might even Sioux.*

(High 1987)

John Redhead and Dave Towse
with 'The Flake'
Photo: Nick Dixon

[The saga continued with *West Indian Face* on 21 May 1988.]

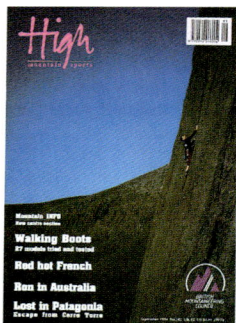

Nick Dixon
on the second ascent of
The Indian Face
Original photo: Gary Smith

In June 1994, after four sessions of practice and the preplacement of most of the protection, Nick Dixon made the second ascent of *The Indian Face* in front of a host of others climbing on the crag. A large team from the DMM factory and Paul Williams gathered at the bottom. Two skyhook runners were used, one of which fell off during the ascent.

Showing the strain after the ascent
Photo: Dixon col.

On the way to the crag I was kissed by a sheep and Clare asked me whether The Indian Face *was an important route. I took this as a positive sign.*

What people don't realize is that the climbing on the upper wall is really hard, the gear now too far away, death real and looming, and that it's too much to remember. You can't head-point it like a grit route; the bubble is going to burst and you'll be there naked, humiliated, and grasping at life. All you'll have is experience, a moment, and regret.

After the ascent, Paul Williams approached me and said: 'That was the second best piece of climbing I have ever seen.' I have always wondered about this.   (Nick Dixon, 1994)

Several days after Dixon's ascent, Neil Gresham made the third ascent. The two of them had spent one day practising the route together on top ropes. Gresham did not use the skyhooks, and placed his protection on lead on a previous attempt. A full account of this ascent is the subject of 'Slaying the Beast' on page 9.

Remember Alain Robert, he's awesome, he's soloed 8b in France; we can do it, it is possible.   (Gresham, talking to Dixon before their ascents)

Johnny Redhead was particularly unhappy, and made his feelings clear in *One for the Crow* about the level of practice used on all these ascents: 'No, top-roping paves the way for a whole host of tactics that weaken the grip on the experience of doubt. Who am I to criticize when I placed the bolt? Who are they to criticize when they top-rope?'

1987 April 17   The Rite of Spring   J Redhead, D Towse
This splendid piece of climbing places Redhead and Towse where they belong, at the centre of The Great Wall's history.

My seconding was a farcical system of backropes and long loops tied into the ab-rope. The backrope runners suddenly pulled out but, fuelled by adrenalin, I managed to reach the line of The Indian Face / Master's Wall; and a wonderful rest – it's amazing how last year's 'killers' are this year's toys.   (Dave Towse)

On-sight second ascent by Nick Dixon (though with knowledge of *The Indian Face*, which is passed *en route*) in 1993.

1987 April 28   Rupert Road   J Dawes, M Raine
A powerful piece of climbing done on sight on a very cold day; the second – who turned into a human icicle – chose to jump off and make huge pendulums, rather than try to climb in his frozen state (bridge-jumping was in vogue at the time). Named after the Sheffield street in which the late Al Rouse used to live.

The second ascent by Dave Green and Dai Lampard was noted for its effervescent and flowery language.

All the pegs were gone, for what they were worth.   (Dai Lampard)

1988 April 14   The Far Out West Shuffle   J Tombs, C J Phillips (AL)

1988 May 21   West Indian Face   J Dawes, N Dixon
Of course, Dawes was very familiar with this piece of the wall, and on making an abseil inspection he found what he considered to be chipped runner placements and enhanced holds, and worst of all an improved runner on The Indian Face. The top placement in The Indian Face certainly looked enhanced to me. There were also wires in the lower placements that Johnny threw over his shoulder in a rage. I was abseiling down Dinas in the Oven Direct [see page 177] at the time, and, at the end of the day, after I had slapped my way up it, Johnny led off up West Indian Face, complaining that the top bit of The Indian Face was no longer dangerous. He thought the upper section now E8. I seconded the route (well, kind of) in the dark and Johnny later returned and filled that placement. Five years later when I returned to do The Indian Face myself, neither I nor Neil Gresham could find where that placement had been.   (Nick Dixon)

It subsequently turned out that *West Indian Face* had indirectly climbed some of another line that John Redhead and Dave Towse were attempting, and this led to a bitter feud between the two Johns. After Dawes did the first ascent of *The Indian Face*, John Redhead thought some holds had been enhanced or broken. In response to this Dave Towse remarked to Redhead: 'In my opinion they look like holds; you can see what you want to see.'

In an overview of the whole affair, Towse comments: 'In my opinion, when Johnny Dawes did the *West Indian Face* he saw what he wanted to see. What is really needed is some recognition of all our shortcomings – we, you, should acknowledge that the perfection is not there, that the on-sight is where it is at.'

West Indian Face *is best forgotten.*   (Johnny Dawes)

1988 May 21   **Farfallino**   J Tombs, H I Banner
A fine addition, opening up a new, less intimidating piece of rock that receives much more sunshine.

1988 May 21   **Slanting Groove**   H I Banner, J Tombs
A typically traditional name from this most experienced of Cloggy climbers!

1988 June 19   **Cathedral Graffiti**   N Dixon, N Harms
Named in reference to the painting of a picture on the rock scar caused by the removal of the flake from *The Indian Face* – painter, John Redhead.

1988 June 20/21   **Opening Bid**   N Foster, R Gregory
Neil Foster's first route on the crag, and a fine one! Allegations of hammering were totally unfounded.

1989 produced another excellent winter when some very fine ascents were made.

I have attempted other routes on Cloggy such as White Slab. *I made a decision not to use aid or place pegs in summer routes, which usually resulted in some scary climbing and equally some very scary retreats!*   (Paul Braithwaite)

It is hoped that these ethics will be maintained should we (ever) again get true winter conditions.   (Nick Dixon)

1989   *Clogwyn Du'r Arddu* by Paul Williams

Buoyed by the success of his 1987 *Llanberis* guide (this had started out as an update of the 1981 book, but the boom in slate had turned it almost overnight into one of the largest rock guides the CC had then published), Williams turned his attention to Cloggy. Swept away were the restraints of 1976, and everything that could possibly be said about the cliff and its climbs *was* said, usually in the most effusive terms imaginable. The style was not to everyone's taste, but for that if nothing else it will certainly become a permanent collector's piece!

In his personally presented copy to Alan Hinkes, Williams wrote: 'There's more fun in this book than all the 8,000-metre peaks.' [Hinkes was by then embarking on his quest to be the first Briton to do all fourteen, and he did not disagree.]

Sadly, Paul lost his life in a climbing accident on Froggatt Edge in 1995.

1989 June   **Face Mecca**   N Dixon, D Crilly

I had spent several evenings during term-time travelling from Shropshire to N Wales to prepare for the ascent. On the day of the ascent, a busy Saturday, I met Darril Crilly at the crag – fortuitous, given Darril had held my ropes on a chance encounter on My Halo earlier in the year. I'd practised the crux on abseil many times, and after leaving the belay with just one krab on my belt, it flowed as in a dream until I was on the upper wall after committing through a 6b sequence (15 feet above the poor lower-only RURPs and 70 feet above the belay). I found moves to finish that I hadn't practised; why?, why? In desperation, now fully here and awake, I slapped and groped with a pylon's span of rope between me and a grinning Darril.   (Nick Dixon, 1989)

The second ascent was made by J Dawes in 1995.

I had ab'ed it and looked at it previously several times but when I tried it I really wasn't fit enough. On the lower section I managed to get the nut part of a Roller in. It lodged poorly between a tiny knob and a flake, so that would give me two runners on the whole route. As I passed this poor runner a tiny part of a flake broke, a mistake, and I fell. I tried to take as much of my weight on the rock as I could as I slumped down. I only fell about three inches but if that pathetic piece had pulled I would have gone 70 feet onto the belay. I just looked at my second, Shane Ohly, and silently intimated for him to lower me back to the stance.

Next time it went well, I passed Nick's poor RURPs at 50 feet and made my way onto the top wall. It's very bold here, 60 feet out. My brain clicked into a dramatic mode where it didn't seem scary. I was really in a blade-runner fall position facing a huge drop; I reached for the ledge but I'd shrunk – it was far too far to reach it. In this strange brain phase I found more dirty little footholds and made it.

Fearsome, technical, snappy, and sustained – scared myself to death. E9, 6c. Good grade, great route, the best experience for years.
                                                    (Johnny Dawes)

It's a shame these routes [The Indian Face and Face Mecca] are out of fashion – they are really hard.   (Johnny Dawes)

1989   The Banyan Tree   N Dixon, C Waddy
   Named with full respect to the enlightenment that had gone on in the area below the Banyan Tree.

1989   Archaeopteryx (1 pt aid)   P Williams and party
   First free ascent by D Lampard and P Williams later in 1989.

I met Paul that night in the pub. 'Dai, you've got to come and do it. There's still an aid point.' I knew I had to work the following day, but that was it, Paul had waved the red rag, there was no escape. I left hurriedly to try to find some justifiable excuse for not going in. It was going to be difficult since I had only just started a locum appointment at Prestatyn vets and was supposed to be in charge of the practice. Finally, in utter desperation, I decided to tell the truth and phoned Jim, one of the other assistants: 'Jim, sorry to phone you so late but something has come up.' I squirmed. 'There's not really any other way of putting this, but I just have to go to Cloggy tomorrow.'

We met at Hafodty, and set off up to the crag at 5 a.m. with all the signs for a brilliant day. As we passed the Halfway House, Paul pointed out the line of the route in the sunrise and it looked stunning. An overhanging wedge of rock placed between the prominent grooves of Woubits and its left-hand twin.

We climbed in glorious heat. Paul's special 'squashed sweetie' nut fitted where he said it would and the aid point fell (as I did twice). Pulling onto the top, we laughed uncontrollably at the name he'd given it – Archaeopteryx – the flying fossil!

The next day I lost my job, but that was a small price to pay for the memories of climbing with a great friend during the long hot July of 1989.

(Dai Lampard)

1991 Sept 9   Virgo   N Clacher, M Tomkins
   Good climbing. The wall below beckons.

1991 Sept 10   Luaka   L McGinley, Z P Leppert
   A fine line and an airy difficult route.

1991   Shaft of a Dead Man   J Redhead, D Towse
   The third of Redhead's brilliant routes on The Pinnacle. Climbed a few days before Dave's Fecundity Ridge, the route is steep, serious, and intimidating.

I had just recovered from a paralysing virus, no doubt self-induced, as most viruses are, which hospitalized me for several days. The births of four paintings (titled The Shaft of a Dead Man) were no doubt the product of this 'alternative' head space.

(John Redhead)

1991 **Fecundity Ridge** D Towse, J Redhead
A marvellous line with the grandest of exposure.

1992 May 17 **Clog Dancing** I L Jones, C Stevenson

1992 May 17 **A Fistful of Pockets** I L Jones, C Stevenson
Two more climbs were added to the pleasant Far West Buttress.

1992 **It Will Be Alright in the Night** M Turner, Ms L Thomas
A route that took three evening attempts before success: the first on sight
and necessitating retreat, the second involving dropped pegs and
abseiling antics, the third after a day's work and finishing in total
darkness. This final successful attempt also involved the whole of the
rope being run out to *The Hand-Traverse* and tied off, with Twid, solo,
escaping in the dark. Louise followed later by Braille!

The Kathmandu air crash in September 1992 claimed two Cloggy devotees,
Mick Hardwick and Dave Harries, both Plas y Brenin instructors who often
visited Cloggy for an evening's adventure after work.
*Later, Mick's ashes were scattered by his family around Cratcliffe Tor, but
Dave's remains were never clearly identified. On a wet winter's day, a group
of us visited Cloggy as homage to Dave and his favourite route Great Wall.
Richard, Dave's brother, carried a flake from the bottom of Great Wall to the
memorial ceremony in Kathmandu, where it was placed amongst the remains
of those who died, and thus close to Dave.
After the grief and anger had subsided, there remain only warm memories,
mine of Mick Hardwick pounding up Mordor bathed in the golden light of an
evening sun. This will last for an eternity.* (Ian Carr)

2000 May 9 **Trick of the Light** P Littlejohn, D Garner
Two fine late discoveries on the Far West.

2000 May 10 **The Riddler** P Littlejohn, D Garner
A fine find up this improbable shield of rock.

2002 July 16 **Feeding Shmae** N Dixon, C Naylor
Time out from guidebook work unearthed this gem, which frightened
the second man somewhat.

Index of Climbs

Index of Winter Climbs

Accident Procedure

First Aid

If spinal or head injuries are suspected, do not move the patient without skilled help, except to maintain breathing or if this is essential for further protection.

If breathing has stopped, clear the airways and start artificial respiration. Do not stop until the patient recovers or expert opinion has diagnosed death.

Summon help as quickly as is compatible with safety. Do not hesitate or delay.

Rescue

In the event of an accident where further assistance is required, dial 999 and ask for the Police. The Police are responsible for co-ordinating all rescues and will contact other services as necessary.
- State that you require cliff rescue and report the exact location (six-figure grid reference if possible) and details of the accident.
- Be prepared to give your own name and home address if asked.
- Follow any further instructions or requests issued.

Helicopter

In the event of a helicopter evacuation, all climbers on or off the cliff should take heed. A helicopter flying close to the cliff will make verbal communication very difficult, and small stones will be dislodged by the rotor downdraught. All loose equipment should be secured and climbers in precarious positions should try to make themselves safe.

The people with the injured person should try to identify their location. **No** attempt should be made to throw a rope at the helicopter, but assistance should be given to the helicopter crew if requested. Do not approach until directions are given by the crew. In particular, keep well clear of the main rotor, the tail rotor, and the engine exhaust.

Follow-up

After an accident, a report has to be compiled. Normally the details will be collated at the scene by the Police or rescue team, who will then pass the information to the Mountain Rescue Council Statistics Officer.

If unreasonable equipment failure is suspected then the British Mountaineering Council's technical committee may wish to investigate; contact the BMC at 177-179 Burton Road, West Didsbury, Manchester, M20 2BB. In the event of a serious accident, any equipment used by the casualty may be impounded.

Local Hospitals

The nearest Accident and Emergency unit is Ysbyty Gwynedd, Bangor.

7 Lliwedd

8 Tremadog

9 Lleyn

10 Meirionnydd

11 Pembroke

12 Gower and South-East Wales

13 Wye Valley

14 Symonds Yat

STRUMBLE HEAD

ST DAVIDS HEAD

GOWER

Swansea

Chepstow

R. USK

R. WYE

11

12

13

14

Guidebook distributor:

www.cordee.co.uk